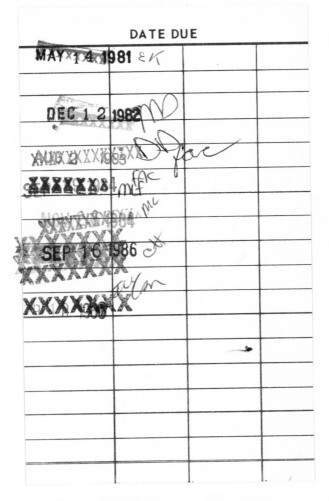

Access to Power: Cross-National Studies
of Women and Elites

Access to Power: Cross-National Studies of Women and Elites

Edited by

CYNTHIA FUCHS EPSTEIN

Queen's College and Graduate Center, City University of New York,
Co-Director, Program in Sex Roles and Social Change,
Center for the Social Sciences, Columbia University

and

ROSE LAUB COSER

State University of New York at Stony Brook
and Center for the Social Sciences, Columbia University

London
GEORGE ALLEN & UNWIN

Boston   Sydney

First published in 1981

GEORGE ALLEN & UNWIN LTD
40 Museum Street, London WC1A 1LU

© George Allen & Unwin (Publishers) Ltd, 1981

British Library Cataloguing in Publication Data

Access to power.
1. Elite (Social sciences)
2. Women in politics
3. Women – Social conditions
I. Epstein, Cynthia Fuchs   II. Coser, Rose Laub
301.44'92   HM141   80-40676

ISBN 0-04-301118-7

Set in 10 on 11 point Plantin by Red Lion Setters, London
and printed in Great Britain
by W. & J. Mackay Ltd, Chatham

Contents

Preface   *page* ix

INTRODUCTION

1   Women and Elites: A Cross National Perspective
    Cynthia Fuchs Epstein   3
2   Where Have All the Women Gone? Like the Sediment of
    a Good Wine, They Have Sunk to the Bottom
    Rose Laub Coser   16

PART ONE POLITICAL ELITES: PARTICIPATION AND BEHAVIOUR

3   Women in Politics: A Study of Political Leadership in the
    United Kingdom, France and the Federal Republic of
    Germany   *Donna S. Sanzone*   37
4   Women in the Economic, Political, and Cultural Elites in
    Finland   *Elina Haavio-Mannila*   53
5   Progress for Women: Increased Female Representation in
    Political Elites in Norway   *Torild Skard*, with the
    assistance of *Helga Hernes*   76
6   Women in Decision-Making Elites: The Case of
    Poland   *Magdalena Sokolowska*   90
7   Women and Political Power in a Revolutionary Society:
    The Yugoslav Case   *Bogdan Denitch*   115
8   Women and Power: The Roles of Women in Politics in
    the United States   *Cynthia Fuchs Epstein*   124
9   Women in Public Life in Austria   *Helga Nowotny*   147
10 Political Attitudes of Women in High Status Occupations
    in West Germany   *Sylvia Streeck, Erika Bock-Rosenthal,*
    and *Christa Haase*   157
11 Women in International Organizations: Room at the Top:
    The Situation in Some United Nations Organizations
    Betsy Thom   169

PART TWO WOMEN AND ECONOMIC ELITES: BUSINESS AND THE PROFESSIONS

12 Women, Business Schools and the Social Reproduction of
    Business Elites: Britain and France   *Richard Whitley*   185
13 Women Managers: Career Patterns and Changes in the
    United States   *Carol Ann Finkelstein*   193

14   Women in Management in West Germany   *page* 211
       Helge Pross
15   Public Bureaucracy and Private Enterprise in the USA
       and France: Contexts for the Attainment of Executive
       Positions by Women   *Catherine Bodard Silver*   219
16   Women and Occupational Elites: The Case of Newspaper
       Journalism in England   *Roger Smith*   237
Biographical Notes on the Contributors   249
Index   252

Preface

This book is composed of papers that describe and analyze women's careers in government, business, and the professions. It examines women's access to and participation in elite careers in the United States, and in selected countries of western and eastern Europe – Britain, France, West Germany, Austria, Norway, Finland, Poland, and Yugoslavia – as well as in international organizations.

This book is an outgrowth of a conference on 'Women in decision-making elites in cross-national perspective,' held at King's College, Cambridge University, in July 1976 under the auspices of the Ford Foundation and organized by Cynthia Fuchs Epstein. Not all the papers given at that conference could be included in this work because of the diversity of material presented, and other papers have been included, invited by the editors to add to the comparative picture.*

The countries represented were chosen because, although they are at similar stages of economic development (with the possible exception of Yugoslavia and Poland, which have been included because of their value for ideological comparison), they exhibit differences in political structure, ideology, and tradition. The contributors have done original research in these countries and have assembled materials from other sources. They often have had to struggle with the paucity of data that are available on women's roles in elites, because of the fact that their small numbers have often led social scientists entirely to omit reporting their behavior.

A number of people and institutions must be given special notice because of their assistance and importance in the production of this book. First, of course, is the Ford Foundation, which supported not only the conference but also subsequent research on elites that has contributed to follow-up work in that area. Peter Ruof of the Ford Foundation was generous with his expertise, both practically and intellectually, in seeing the conference through to completion. Marion Bieber in Europe and Mariam Chamberlain of the Ford Foundation were also helpful and became active workshop participants as well. Currently, the Ford Foundation supports the Program in Sex Roles and Social Change, Center for the Social Sciences at Columbia University, of which Epstein is co-director, engaging in research on women and elites – continuities of work reported in this book.

Both the John Simon Guggenheim Memorial Foundation and the Center for Advanced Study in the Behavioral Sciences granted Epstein fellowships for the years 1976-7 and 1977-8, which provided time and money to continue work on the book and to do subsequent research in settings where the work could be accomplished. Support from the National Institute of Mental Health, the Spencer Foundation, and the Rockefeller Foundation, which made the year at the Center possible, is acknowledged with thanks. In addition, the Research Foundation of the City University of New York is acknowledged for a small grant that allowed Epstein to initiate work on a

*The papers of Skard (Chapter 5) and Sanzone (Chapter 3).

study of women decision makers in 1975. Final touches were accomplished in the tranquil environment provided by the MacDowell Colony, for which special appreciation must be expressed.

Special acknowledgement must be made to Howard M. Epstein, who freely gave of his editorial gifts and knowledge of political affairs in creating the book.

Other persons whom we wish to single out as having contributed in significant measure are Mary O'Neill Berry, Lesley Bower, Allan Grafman, and Susan Ogulnick and Simonetti Samuels – able and diligent research assistants over a period of time – and Anna Tower and Ruth Saccomanno, who typed endless drafts with patience and care.

Introduction

1

Women and Elites:

A Cross-national Perspective

CYNTHIA FUCHS EPSTEIN

Few women hold or have held positions of authority in most societies. The recruitment of women to powerful and decision-making positions is a topic about which little has been written, although it is a topic about which many profess knowledge. Because of the near universality of women's subordination to men this pattern has been regarded as inevitable. Like other persistent social forms, especially when they exist in most societies and in nearly every historical period, scientists, philosophers, and other social observers have attributed these patterns to the biological heritage of human beings or to the functional necessities of social systems. There is a certain attractiveness about these kinds of theories, and they are held with the greatest commitment by the unsophisticated. Explaining some forms of hierarchy as inevitable, for example, serves the interests of those at the top and persuades those at the bottom that there is indeed a reason for the order of things.

But as there have been challenges to ideological systems that support caste distinctions, so also there are social theories today that question the inevitability of women's subordination. Research supporting these theories has drawn on evidence from a variety of cultures to establish that differences exist and that, therefore, so do possibilities for change. Unfortunately, few comparative studies have been done, and generalizations have been made about all of humanity on the basis of a few cases or particular types of societies.

It may be useful to identify some of the theories and explanations of why women appear so infrequently in the ranks of elites. Some are embodied in the reasoning of the papers included in this book. They include the following views:

(1) Women have an inherent incapacity to be assertive and dominant.
(2) Social factors and conditions direct women away from the public sphere toward family-centered priorities.
(3) Impediments to participation in public life are created by time and role strains that flow from women's sex-role-associated duties.
(4) Women's early socialization is an impediment to their assumption of demanding and rewarding careers.
(5) A women's 'culture' exists, which is separate and apart from that of men. This perspective suggests that the women's culture excludes the economic, political, and professional worlds that form the focus of the male culture.

(6) Opportunity structures account for some women's acquisition of decision-making roles.

(7) Prejudice and discrimination limit women's participation in elites.

Some of these approaches complement each other, and others are contradictory. I believe that the most powerful analysis can be made by studying the impact of women's differential location in the social structure – e.g. their access to education, opportunity, and financial resources, all of which are important to the attainment of 'social capital' – a concept used productively in this book to explain women's position in business elites (Whitley, Chapter 12) and international organizations (Thom, Chapter 11).

Cross-national comparison may serve to alert us to ubiquity of patterns, but it also serves to point out differences in those patterns. Male dominance in political systems, for example, appears to be universal, but these studies show that the degree of dominance varies. Cross-cultural comparisons can make clear the factors that make for differences and similarities and indicate those which can lead to greater access for women and for other excluded groups. Such studies can also show why some societies are more flexible than others and which of them are most amenable to change.

But there is a problem that should be kept in mind when analyzing the impact of societies on each other. Societies affect one another, and powerful societies may induce change in weaker ones, creating a similarity of patterns independently of each country's individual history. Ester Boserup's (1970) important book on women in underdeveloped nations points out how the colonizing countries of Europe were instrumental in undermining women's market and political power in eastern Asia and Africa by making access to technology and modern education available only to men. This enabled men to participate and progress in the modernization process, leaving women behind and more disadvantaged than they had been earlier. Thus, men became more dominant in certain societies, because powerful countries created conditions that made them so. If women in these preindustrial countries had been given the same opportunities and resources, it is likely that the profile of power would have been less polarized than the one created by the West's influence.

Impact of particular types may also have more effect than others. For example, the development of a factory system in which work is separated from the home is important in its effect not only on family life but also on the political power of family groups. Shifts from a barter economy to a money economy are also of serious importance. The accumulation of individual wealth in a society in which wealth had been collective and held by the family would make for a different mobility structure and the possibility of differential recruitment to elites. Presumably such changes could help women and other disadvantaged groups.

We are living in a time when rapid change is characteristic of most societies. The world is no longer a place where discrete societies live out their separate destinies. What happens in one country is bound to have effects on another, although change may seem different in different places.

Rapid social change challenges age-old ideas about the characteristics of human nature and its relationship to social causation. Not only are we seeing how much societies may change, but in addition there is a growing body of evidence that individuals can change too, throughout the life cycle. Men and women are not molded at birth or in early childhood; change is possible both in people and in communities.

This book reports on the situation of women in various elites in the United States and selected European countries over the past decade.

The contributors to this book vary in their theoretical emphasis and differ in their evaluation of whether or not there has been progress toward women's attainment of equal rights. Some think that progress has been slow, although others believe that there has been considerable movement in the past decade. Most agree that after the women's suffrage movement in the first part of the twentieth century there was relative inactivity until the appearance of the current women's movements in the late 1960s. Some raise the question of whether women are continuing to gain equity or whether they will actually lose the gains that they have achieved. Current research cannot provide answers to these questions, but it can provide hints about what patterns seem to be forming and what their course may be.

Let us consider some of the important general themes that appear and reappear in these studies. All elite structures possess mechanisms that provide channels of mobility for members of ingroups and close them to members of outgroups. It appears that women are only tolerated as members of ingroups to the extent that their participation is not immediately threatening as a source of competition to those in power and to those who define themselves as within the pool of eligibles who may achieve power. This is true on both a micro level and a macro level, as Coser (Chapter 2) points out.

WOMEN CLUSTER AT THE BOTTOM

Coser also traces the general process by which women cluster at the bottom of social strata. Whatever the sphere in which they appear, women are lower level participants. Thus, even in the Soviet Union, where women constitute a high proportion of physicians, it is men who hold the decision-making posts, who are the professors of medicine, and who are members of the Academy. The same pattern prevails in the United States; although women predominate among American school teachers, men are the principals of primary schools and hold the leading positions in higher education. This theme appears in many of the papers in this book.

WOMEN CLUSTER IN SEX-ROLE-APPROPRIATE ACTIVITIES

Even when they become members of elite groups, women are assigned to specialties considered to be 'appropriate' to women's concerns. Thus, in most countries as well as in international bodies, as Thom (Chapter 11) points out, women are assigned to the ministries of culture, to departments of health and welfare, and to committees on humanitarian issues. These assignments usually carry less power than positions dealing with foreign policy, budget, and defense.

STEREOTYPES REGARDING WOMEN'S INTERESTS

It is commonly believed that women are more oriented to social concerns, more altruistic than men, and less practical in regard to political and fiscal matters. Evidence provided by a number of contributors to this book indicates that women's attitudes are similar to those of men in similar structural positions. This shows up particularly in Streeck *et al.*'s study of West German elites (Chapter 10).

THE POWER OF INTERVENTION

Intervention through quotas, socialization, and social controls has in the past kept women out of elites. The studies in this book show that intervention can bring them in. Positive intervention and the implementation of the ideology of equality (e.g. through law) can create access for women. Some groups object to programs that guarantee women and other minorities a chance for better access to elite positions. Yet, in the past, elite gatekeepers were effective in maintaining existing hierarchies – in sifting and sorting out unwanted groups. These were seen as 'natural' processes rather than as programs. Perhaps this is because the *maintenance* of systems, which require attention and input to keep them going, does not attract as much notice as the *alteration* of systems. Thus, because men have been successful in maintaining their domination of women, little notice has been taken of the methods used to maintain that dominance.

The studies in this book clearly specify how effective intervention can prevent women from being tracked to the bottom of hierarchies. In the United States changes in the laws and the creation of affirmative action programs have required businesses and educational institutions to open their ranks to women. This intervention has confronted the less noticed prior intervention rules, which were created and enforced to keep women out of those same institutions. There are many examples in this book that show how effective intervention can be in changing entrenched practices. We shall see that women form a higher proportion of parliamentary elites where ideology supports their participation and when legislation enacted by the established elites forces gatekeepers to facilitate their entry. In Yugoslavia, for example, Denitch (Chapter 7) reports that women have greater political representation at the top than at the grass roots, for a number of reasons, but most importantly because revolutionary ideology specifies that they should have representation. In Norway and Finland as well, as shown respectively by Skard (Chapter 5) and Haavio-Mannila (Chapter 4), women have been nominated on party lists where there has been insistence that this is the proper thing to do. Where they do appear on the lists, they can win elections. In the United States as well the effort on behalf of equal representation of women and other disadvantaged groups as delegates to the major party conventions, beginning in 1974, resulted in women's greater participation as political actors and placed them in political contexts where they might gather expertise and power.

Women also do better in most countries in liberal and leftist parties. In the United States women Congress members are overwhelmingly from the

Democratic party and seem to do best when they are reform candidates. In the United Kingdom they are preponderantly in the Labour Party, and in Yugoslavia they have progressed as members of the League of Communists. These political groups seem more receptive to women because they are ideologically receptive to the claims of the disadvantaged and less committed to ongoing hierarchies.

To the extent that women come into politics by way of the more liberal elements in their societies it follows that they tend to act politically more liberal. This is not because women in general tend to be more liberal – it appears that their political biases and voting behavior are distributed approximately as are men's (or perhaps men's biases and political behavior are distributed the same as women's) – but because those women who become politically visible and effective attain political status as liberals.[1]

Their greater liberality in politics may also come from their marginal position among the ranks of the elites. Less tied to party organizations, because they are relative newcomers or because they are not usually members of, or privy to the workings of, inner councils, women can be more outspoken when they choose. This occurs not only in political life but also, as we shall see, in journalism.

Smith (Chapter 16) points out that some women columnists for the top British newspapers are permitted to write unhampered by editorial limitations; he suggests that this is because editors may consider their view to be less serious than men's and their responsibility to be limited by their sex.

Ideology has created more opportunity for women who aspire to high places in politics than in the economic sphere. Across the world women have more representation in government than in economic elites. (Yet, government intervention is now forcing economic institutions to include women.) Governments use ideology to legitimate their claim to power, and an important component of contemporary legitimation is the appeal of representativeness. Pressured by feminist movements, parties are pressed to make concessions to women. Thus, women often do better as appointees to political office than as elected representatives, where other impediments slow their path. This is particularly true in countries where there is open competition for both political position and economic status, and it is perhaps less true in planned societies. Appointment to government is an important springboard to elected office.[2]

In West Germany and Scandinavia the political parties have placed women on their electoral lists and made sure that they are visible. In West Germany, as Pross (Chapter 14) reports, there is one woman on the executive committee of each major political party. A lively sex-roles debate in Norway and Finland has also caused women to be placed on party lists. Even in West Germany, as we shall see, women have made more progress in the trade unions, which must appear to be ideologically 'correct', than in the managerial elite. Where the economic sphere is part of the political, women also have greater chances for advancement, as in Yugoslavia, where women have respectable representation on worker's councils. (Yet, in Chapter 6 Sokołowska shows that in Poland management is the 'last fortress' of resistance to women's equality.) It is obvious that participation in the economic sphere is closely connected with the way in which the society's economic structures are related to other social institutions.

ACCESS TO RESOURCES

The implementation of egalitarian ideology is inevitably linked to women's access to, and ability to manipulate, resources. Women fare better where economic resources are not clustered in the hands of private male entrepreneurs. Thus, in capitalist societies, where candidates need money to run for office, women do less well than in Poland or Yugoslavia, where funding is not the critical resource for mounting a political campaign. This access to resources is also important to women's success in attaining professional status. They have had the poorest representation in the professions in which the recruit had to pay privately for an expensive education and equipment and then to engage in professional activity as an entrepreneur. This explains why women could not be dentists and doctors in meaningful numbers in the United States before families learned to support daughters' as well as sons' educations but could be in countries where medical care and education were socialized.

THE TRACKING SYSTEM

Women are generally blocked in the tracking process to the top. Robert K. Merton (1957) pointed out in *Social Theory and Social Structure* that people in high level occupations typically move in a patterned way from one status to another, gaining in rank, training, and acceptability as they go. Introducing the concept of *status sequence* he has shown how the movement is institutionalized, as in the case of medical careers, in which recruits move from undergraduate work to medical school to internships to residencies in specialties and finally to practice. The profession 'reviews' and approves the recruit at each of these steps, permitting the assumption of a new status (e.g. medical student to intern) and the recruit internalizes not only the skills and attitudes required for the level at which he or she is for the moment but also those needed for the next step. Knowing where he or she is heading is important to the processes of becoming an insider or member of a profession.[3]

The status sequences of some elite careers are not always as neatly articulated as they are for medical students, and they are certainly not as commonly understood. Often, potential recruits do not know what the status sequence is. Usually, candidates desired by the ingroup are given the necessary information, whereas outsiders are often frozen out, the process being aided by such popular myths about access as 'The worthy and gifted will succeed.'

Women have suffered in political and economic careers for all these reasons. As lay people they have not known 'what to do.' They have not been sought as candidates nor given access to the information required; and if in spite of these obstacles they found themselves on the ladder to the top, those in power who choose successors and recruits for the elites – Merton has called them *status judges* – have blocked them from reaching the next step.

There is evidence that today it is more possible for women to travel the traditional opportunity routes used by men, as well as successful alternate routes; but the routes, whatever they may be, are by no means obstacle free.

EDUCATION

Different kinds of educational institutions and sequences play key roles in channeling aspirants to high positions, and these have been highly sex linked.

University Education

Higher education has been of the utmost importance for entrance to elites, and women have traditionally had less access to it than have men. Women have been more seriously disadvantaged in some countries than in others, but university enrollments of women are growing all over the world. (See Sanzone's figures on this in Chapter 3.) A university education in and of itself, although important, has a variable impact, however; prestige of institution and other factors have also counted substantially. This is true not only in countries where there is a large distinction between private and public universities but also where certain educational institutions feed graduates directly into professional, political or business elites.

The ancient 'Oxbridge' colleges of England, the elite *grandes écoles* of France, and the Ivy League colleges of the United States all have traditionally furnished a large share of the recruits to their respective national elites. As Robert Putnam (1976) has pointed out in his work on comparative elites, graduation from one of these schools increases so substantially a young person's chances of 'making it' politically that the educational and political recruitment systems are virtually merged (p. 50).

In the United States the men's Ivy League schools have become coeducational, and in Britain a number of the colleges at Oxford and Cambridge are now also enrolling women. We should note that attending one of the 'sister' institutions of the prestigious male colleges has not constituted an alternative route into the elites. Although the prestigious women's colleges and schools in the United States and other countries have prepared some of the few women who have gone on to elite careers, they have not done so in the systematic structured ways in which the male educational institutions have. Rather, they have educated wives for the male members of the elites.

The Business Schools

There is some indication that in Europe, as in the United States, business schools may become alternatives to the traditional upper-class schools as training grounds for economic elites. Should this come about, women, like those men who have not had access to such tracks in the past, may be able to develop technical competence and network contacts. There are problems in evaluating the input of business schools, as we learn from Whitley (Chapter 12). It is not yet certain whether the business schools will develop the prestige that is necessary to become an alternative track. On the one hand, schools like the Institut Européen d'Administration des Affaires in France still have not replaced the *grandes écoles* in the status sequences to the top. On the other hand, some men of elite backgrounds are going on to graduate business training.[4] This has had the effect of conferring prestige on the business schools and reinforcing their roles as alternative routes.

LAW

In almost all countries top decision-makers tend to come disproportionately from the ranks of the law profession. Putnam (1976) has shown that they comprise roughly 15–25 per cent of most national legislatures, and in many countries their share rises to one-third or more. He has further pointed out that lawyers also have traditionally supplied the lion's share of the bureaucratic elite in many countries; more than half of the senior civil servants of West Germany, Italy, and Japan and approximately a quarter of their Swedish and American counterparts have had legal training. Lawyers are less prominent in communist elites and in the other Scandinavian legislatures. It is in the United States that the proportion of lawyers in national politics is the highest.[5] Thus, women's differential access to legal careers has been an important sifting element in keeping them from the political arena.

There has not been much research on the role of women lawyers in various societies. Only in the United States has their participation in the legal profession so dramatically altered in the past few years as to suggest that they will be better placed structurally for access to political office and other decision-making statuses. Holding the status of lawyer not only provides women with credentials to establish their competence but also legitimates their participation where women without such credentials are not usually considered serious participants.

ALTERNATIVE OPPORTUNITY STRUCTURES

Although alternative opportunity structures for women have often resulted in opportunities that are different and less than those for men, there are alternative structures that have opened the gates to women in special circumstances.

Personal Ties to Men of Power
Women entering business or politics by the route of widow's succession are the most numerous and best example of this phenomenon. Personal relationships with powerful men, and widowhood in particular, have presented the most important opportunity channel for women not only in politics but also in business. This pattern is true in the countries of both East and West. Family relationships have even provided the route to top work in journalism, as Smith (Chapter 16) observes, where one might expect that meritocratic criteria would prevail.

Women's Spheres
The sexual division of labor within social systems relegated women to work worlds that were separate from those of men. This often meant that they had no chance to shift to 'men's work.' However, with the recent pressure to open men's work to women their separate activities have often created a pool of eligibility.

In the newspaper world, for example, Smith (Chapter 16) reports that the creation of 'women's pages' by many dailies gave women a chance to obtain news experience, which made it possible for them to shift to 'hard news' assignments. Also, women gained political experience even when they were named to such 'feminine' branches of government as social welfare.

Structural Changes within Organizations

Silver (Chapter 15) points out that there have also been structural changes in business organizations that have favored women (e.g. the shift from family-run businesses to bureaucratic modes of organization). Larger size, as Whitley (Chapter 12) suggests, also causes change in the way in which traditional elites appropriate positions of privilege and control. The greater use of technology has also made room for the 'expert' whose objective knowledge is recognized. Thus, women as technocrats can achieve authority deriving from their expert status. Silver and Finkelstein (Chapter 13) both point out that women are making inroads into middle management.

Crisis

Jean Lipman-Blumen (1973) has pointed out that role change is facilitated by crisis situations. Certainly, women have had opportunities to enter elites during, or as a result of, crises in their societies. Because crisis upsets traditions and offers new routes to power, establishments are often challenged. As Denitch (Chapter 7) points out, war created opportunity for women in Yugoslavia, who had been partisans and had established reputations as leaders and fighters. Further, because a large proportion of male partisans perished, women occupied empty places in the new government established after the revolution. When men went off to war in other countries, women were often given opportunities that they had not had before. Women went into the professions in many societies and were given many jobs formerly barred to them (e.g. in newspapers, armaments factories, and transportation).

PROBLEMS OF INFORMAL STRUCTURE

All over the world women experience difficulties in entering elites because in addition to their lack of formal status prerequisites they lack access to the proper informal networks. Informal networks play important roles in the establishment of opportunity channels, because, as one ascends in any hierarchy, the likelihood grows that recommendations and evaluations will be made informally and that their impact will be greater. There is a direct relationship between acquisition of formal statuses and participation in informal networks. Informal 'old boy' networks tend to arise among men sharing statuses as former schoolmates and as members of the same organizations. When women were excluded from educational institutions and from professional organizations, they were unable to form working associations with men and share in their networks.

Even when women become members of elites, they may find it difficult to develop the informal associations that usually go along with elite membership. American women find it difficult to 'hang out' in political clubhouses, where friendships are established and there is talk of whom the party will support in the next election. Women on Fleet Street, as Smith (Chapter 16) points out, are isolated from the pub culture – a problem that besets women where it is common for men to drink together and decide the issues of their world, away from the visibility of the office, chamber of deputies, or other institutions. Women often have to form alternative women's informal settings (the Women's Room of the British House of Parliament is one place where women Members of Parliament and members of the House of Lords can relax and talk about affairs of state among themselves). When more women are members of an elite, they can share information among themselves, but they are still not privy to the information shared by more strategically placed men. Some of this is inevitable, so long as men and women are provided with different settings in which to relax; but whether segregated settings are kept minimal or remain *de facto* settings for informal decision-making in the elites has important consequences for women's participation.

HOME AND FAMILY

Skard (Chapter 5) makes the point that, whatever work women do elsewhere in their societies, the work at home is theirs. This is a recurrent finding in many reports on research on women in all activities and in socialist societies, as Sokołowska (Chapter 6) points out, as well as capitalist ones. The fact that women are expected to hold primarily home-centered roles is often used to explain their low rates of participation in the public sector, as Nowotny (Chapter 9) discusses in her paper on Austria.

Women's roles as wives, and particularly as mothers, is related to their ability to engage in work demanding a high degree of commitment. Yet, women vary. Some are single; some are childless. Those who are married and mothers vary in their access to paid assistance in the home. Those of high socio-economic class – those most likely to enter elites – have more resources for delegating home responsibilities than others. This suggests that emphasis on women's limitations because of their sex-role-associated statuses is an exclusionary mechanism – an ideological ploy to keep women out of the running for high-ranking activity. Thus, women as a class are regarded as unavailable, rather than women as individuals, who may be available or not.

However, where there is no effective assistance for work in the home (e.g. child care) there is a considerable reduction in numbers in the pools of eligible women who may rise to nationally important work. More assistance would mean more eligible women. Numbers are important, since the more women compete for jobs or run for office, the better chance they have of success.

Curiously, the most successful women tend to have husbands and families. This suggests that the notion that it is only single or childless women who devote themselves to climbing the ladder is a myth. Perhaps women with families are not necessarily defeated by a large number of role demands, and male gatekeepers regard married women with children as less deviant and 'unnatural' than single women and therefore as more acceptable as members of their institutions.

Yet, it would be foolish to minimize the constraints on women that come from the family responsibilities placed on them and the low priority that most societies assign to assisting them. Coser (1975), in a work on role acquisition and geographical placement, has argued that, when societies do not provide day care facilities, they perpetuate motherhood as the central role in women's lives and make difficult any effort to expand their role relationships and make linkage with institutions. Not only must women bear the physical responsibilities for child care and home management, but in addition the psychic burden of the problems is theirs alone.

It seems that there is change in the attitudes of younger men toward the sharing of home responsibilities, but there is considerable variation in different societies. Ironically, in the Eastern socialist countries there seems to be more male resistance to such change than in the West. Historical background has a lot to do with the establishment and continuation of traditional attitudes, but change is possible, and intervention by government is often useful in setting the tone for women's equality.

CHANGES IN THE POWER STRUCTURE

Elites rise and fall. Their relative importance may change; a military elite may give way to a political one, or political parties may replace each other in office. Some of these changes may be good for women and some not, although, as mentioned before, women seem to do better when liberals rather than conservatives hold power.

Ironically, women tend to make progress when social institutions lose power. For example, when professional organizations or political parties are unthreatened centers of power, women are usually excluded. Women have often fought to be admitted to these institutions and have sometimes won; on the other hand, their entrance has been facilitated in cases in which these institutions have lost prestige and economic power. Thus, when private clubs decline as bastions of the male elite and need women as members to augment their income, women are welcomed. When political parties lose power and need new members to bolster their resources and do the work (or need work done cheaply, e.g. as volunteers), women are welcomed. When elite schools find that they must compete with other institutions for students, they also tend more readily to admit women. There is no doubt that women benefit in such cases, but the institutions to which they are thus admitted are no longer the same, and it is often questionable whether the prize has the value originally attributed to it.

However, many papers in this book show that the young have more liberal beliefs with regard to equality than the old and that education, which is becoming more available to women and the economically disadvantaged, creates greater support for women's access to decision-making roles.

CONCLUSION

The numbers and percentages of women coming into public life may not yet seem impressive to those committed to change in the statuses of women, but it is important to stress that these are times of transition and that small changes may have a large impact. We have noted that women have not only faced discrimination but also felt the accumulating disadvantages[6] of poorer educations, less access to professional and business circles, and limited control of money. All over the world these conditions are changing at different rates; but even where they are changing at a snail's pace, the direction of change is constant. Everywhere there is discussion of women's equality. This has made for the greater visibility of inequities in society and helped to create places for highly qualified, motivated, and well-situated women who can be most easily absorbed.

More and more women who once were forced to find alternative routes to occupational and political success now travel the same routes as men. Many are doing so by attending university in greater numbers, by becoming more active political party members at lower levels, and by moving into the ranks of middle management. Because they are traveling these routes, today's women have a better chance to get to the top, not only because they are building up the same backgrounds as men but also because they are younger and have time on their side.

The statistics that indicate a modest increase of women in elite structures may not impress the observer of social change, but a look at social trends and directions should offer a more optimistic view of the path ahead for women.

NOTES

(1) Kent Jennings (personal communication) has reported that evidence from political studies indicates that the gap between men and women with regard to political beliefs and behavior is narrowing considerably, as women tend to receive similar education and increasingly join the workforce.

(2) C. Wright Mills (1956) in *The Power Elite* has shown that 62 per cent of higher politicians in the federal executive in the United States were appointed to all or most of their political jobs before reaching top positions between 1933 and 1953. Prewitt and McAllister (1976), who have cited this study, have shown that more members of the American executive elite in the Administrations from Hoover through Nixon came from backgroiunds of appointed office rather than from elected office or other backgrounds.

(3) Merton (1957) has identified this process as 'anticipatory socialization.'

(4) I am grateful to Maurice Sias of the Institut de Droit, d'Economie, et des Sciences d'Aix-Marseilles for this insight.

(5) Although the proportion of lawyers in the top echelons of government has been going down in the United States, the proportion of persons with Ph.D.s has gone up (Prewitt and McAllister, 1976, p. 118). In 1930 there were seven times as many lawyers as Ph.D.s in presidential Administrations. By 1970 there were less than two lawyers for every Ph.D. The proportion of women with Ph.D.s has also gone up; from 1950 to 1972 the increase of women getting Ph.D.s was 756·0, as opposed to a percentage increase of 384·0 for men (US Department of Commerce, Bureau of the Census, 1976). (Witness the number of women economists with Ph.D.s in the 1979 government.)

(6) Notions of 'accumulation of advantage' and of disadvantage in systems of social stratification have been developed by Robert K. Merton in a number of papers including 'The Matthew effect in science' (1968). Other references to the phenomena can be found in Zuckerman and Cole (1975), footnote 89, p. 100.

BIBLIOGRAPHY

Boserup, Ester (1970) *Women's Role in Economic Development* (New York: St Martin's Press).

Coser, Rose Laub (1975) 'Stay home little Sheba: on placement, displacement, and social change,' *Social Problems*, vol. 22, no. 4, pp. 470–80.

Lipman-Blumen, Jean (1973) 'Role de-differentiations as a system response to crisis: occupational and political roles of women,' *Sociological Inquiry*, vol. 43, no. 2, pp. 105–29.

Merton, Robert K. (1957) *Social Theory and Social Structure* (New York: Free Press.

Merton, Robert K. (1968, 1973), repr. 'The Matthew effect in science,' *Science*, vol. 159, pp. 56–63. Reprinted in Norman Storer (ed.), *Sociology of Science* (Chicago: University of Chicago Press).

Mills, C. Wright (1956) *The Power Elite* (New York: Oxford University Press), pp. 226–31.

Prewitt, Kenneth and McAllister, William (1976) 'Changes in the American executive elite, 1930–1970,' in Heinz Eulau and Moshe M. Czudnowski (eds), *Elite Recruitment in Democratic Politics: Comparative Studies across Nations* (New York: Sage & Wiley), pp. 105– 132;

Putnam, Robert D. (1976) *The Comparative Study of Political Elites* (Englewood Cliffs, NJ: Prentice-Hall).

US Department of Commerce, Bureau of the Census (1976) *A Statistical Report of Women in the US*, Current Population Reports, Special Studies Series P-23, No. 58 (Washington, DC: US Government Printing Office, April).

2

Where Have All the Women Gone?

Like the Sediment of a Good Wine, They have Sunk to the Bottom[1]

ROSE LAUB COSER

The collective mental image in Western societies that associates women with home obscures the fact that the proportion of women in the labor force is just over 50 per cent in the United States, and this differs but little in other Western industrialized countries. In the Soviet Union women constitute 57 per cent of the population and almost 50 per cent of the labor force. The idea that associates women with home and family helps to maintain the conviction that men must 'make a living' and women must take care of their families; it helps to maintain the notion that, for women, work outside the home is secondary – that they ought not to strive for a career or claim the same monetary or other rewards, because they are cared for by men.

It is noteworthy that the mental image of 'women at home' in the countries of the West does not accord with anybody's daily experience, for, wherever we go, we see women at work: as salesclerks and cashiers in stores and supermarkets, as tellers in banks, and recently also as postal clerks. Although they are visible physically in everyday services, they are not visible socially as workers. We think of women as being at home; the culture is geared to it, so that repair people and delivery people expect a woman to be at home at any time at which they come and do not feel that they have to plan their day to accommodate the schedule of working women. Although this seems trivial, it is symptomatic and symbolic. It keeps women in their place, at least in our mental image.

Women are typically in jobs in which there is no advancement. They are the secretaries, the nurses, the receptionists, and the sales*girls*. True, in most Western countries they are not at the *very* bottom of the work hierarchy; they are not the errand *boys* or sewage workers, because these jobs go to the men of the underclass – often ethnic minorities – or to others considered inferior. This is not so in the Soviet Union, by the way, where women shine shoes, work on the road, or are seen paperhanging or sweeping the streets.

For Soviet women equalization takes place at the bottom, in a form of negative democratization, as Karl Mannheim (1940) has called it. But negative democratization takes place in the West as well, albeit on another level. For example, the wife of the lawyer and the daughter of the automobile worker can be seen working side by side in the secretarial pool of a hospital or business office; the nurse whose husband is a physician may well work under the authority of a head nurse who is the daughter of an

Italian shoemaker or a Polish plumber. Women are the in-betweens in a class society, serving as an integrating force and making possible some marginal communication between social classes. Women from different social origins may be equals in their work positions, and yet the similarity of their positions does not lead to class action. Negative democratization helps to keep the class system going. By being allied to men through marriage, or hoping to be so allied, women do not constitute a class in itself, let alone, to use Marx's distinction, a class for itself. This helps to minimize the dangers of class conflict.

Yet, recently the new consciousness of women has helped to challenge the class system. It has helped to raise awareness to the fact that power tends to be monopolized not only by the mighty but also by upper classes of *men*, whose interest is to maintain their social and patriarchal privileges.

In all industrial societies, whether they call themselves capitalist or socialist, privileges are maintained by husbands, fathers, and grandfathers. It is mainly after marriage, and especially after the birth of a child, and increasingly as the life cycle proceeds that inequality between men and women, which is more subtle during childhood, becomes striking. For example, although women constitute 49 per cent of the American student body, they constitute only slightly over 10 per cent of the college professors who teach them. It is not in the formative years so much as in the later years that inequality is taken for granted. Men, especially in the middle and upper middle class, work for careers through which they realize their social identity and aspire to positions of power. Women support them in these endeavors, raising their sons to emulate fathers or surpass them and their daughters to be of service to men, whether in the family or in such sex-typed occupations as nursing or secretarial work. Not only are women held back in the development of their skills, but also they tend to be segregated into occupations that typically, as George Devereux and Florence Winter (1950) pointed out many years ago, come under the title of 'exploited.' In occupations in which men are autonomous – in medicine in the United States, in academia everywhere, and in other high-prestige professions – women are outnumbered by men tenfold, and they usually remain at the bottom of the hierarchy.

I shall address myself to two issues. First, by the phenomenon that Alice Rossi (1970) has called the diminishing flow, the presence of women is inversely related to rewards within a given occupation; that is, the higher the rank, prestige, or power within an occupation or profession, the smaller is the proportion of women, with the exception of such almost uniquely female professions as nursing. Second, the presence of women is directly related to the deficit in rewards; that is, in comparing different fields or occupations we find that, where the proportion of women is higher, the deficit in rewards, as compared with those of men, increases.

Suzanne Keller (personal communication) has warned that in studying elites we must be careful to consider the size of the available pool. For example, it would make little sense methodologically to stress the fact that there were few women professors of mathematics or of the natural sciences if we did not ask how many women engaged in these studies; nor would it make sense to point to the relatively small number of Ph.D.s generally if women hardly engaged in graduate studies.

Let us take this more general point first. In the United States in 1968 women obtained only 5 per cent of doctoral or first professional degrees in the physical sciences. Following Suzanne Keller's advice we must ask whether there were few female graduate students in those fields. It turns out that there were not quite so few. Women obtained not 5 per cent but 11·5 per cent of the relevant master's degrees. Could we expect that there should have been more master's degrees? There could have, because they obtained 14 per cent of the bachelor's degrees.

How about the social sciences, where women participate more readily? There, they obtained 12 per cent of doctoral or first professional degrees; but this percentage does not reflect the available pool, because they earned 32 per cent and 37 per cent respectively of the bachelor's and master's degrees (Coser and Rokoff, 1971).

How about mathematics? At twenty leading universities in 1974 under 7 per cent of the full-time mathematics scientists were women. Of course, it will be argued, women do not go into mathematics. Yet, they earned 32 per cent of the master's degrees and 10 per cent of the doctorates in 1973.

In the biological sciences in the same year 12 per cent of employed Ph.D.s were women. Yet, women formed a pool of 21·5 per cent of the doctorates that year, and the women's pool for the doctorate was about 30 per cent of the bachelor's and master's degrees awarded (Vetter, 1975).

In sociology, in the United States during 1968–9, women comprised 12 per cent of the full time faculty in 180 graduate departments, and they comprised 15 per cent of all appointments. Yet, the available pool was much larger; women comprised 33 per cent of the graduate student body. Everywhere, the higher the rank, the smaller is the proportion of women. Women represent one in four of the instructors and lecturers in graduate sociology departments in the United States but only one in twenty-five of the full professors (Rossi, 1970).

Academia is a masculine realm everywhere, whether in the United States, Britain, the Soviet Union, or elsewhere. Some fields attract more women than others (e.g. psychology or foreign languages in the United States). In medicine in the United States, where the proportion of women is increasing faster than in most other fields of science, women comprised 11·1 per cent of the 1974 graduating class but 18 per cent of the total enrollment and 22·2 per cent of the first-year enrollment. However, only 7 per cent of practicing physicians are women, and they are concentrated in the less prestigious and less well-paid specialties (Vetter, 1975).

The United States differs markedly from Soviet Russia in the participation of women in medicine. There, 72 per cent of the physicians are women. This fact is often cited as evidence of the equal rights of women and their equal access to the professions in the USSR. Yet, we must remember that physicians in the Soviet Union do not have to obtain a doctoral degree. There also we observe a downward flow; in contrast to the large proportion of women practicing medicine, only 25 per cent of doctoral degrees are held by women (Lane, 1976, ch. 7).

In Poland the percentage of women physicians has been rising steadily from 12 per cent in 1921 and 20 per cent in 1931 to 38·5 per cent in 1960 and 50·2 per cent in 1973. Yet, the inclusion of women in higher positions

Table 2.1   *Women as a percentage of all academia compared with percentage of physicians who are women: Poland.*

Year	Professors	Docents	Doctors	Physicians
1968	13·8	20·8	32·7	—
1973	12·0	25·7	36·9	50·3

Sources: (1) For professors, docents, and doctors: Census of Personnel, 1968 and 1973. (2) For physicians: *Statistical Yearbooks.*

in medicine has not kept pace with this growth (Table 2.1). Between 1968 and 1973 the proportion of women among those physicians who obtained doctorates grew from 33 to 37 per cent; yet, the proportion of women among professors of medicine declined from 14 to 12 per cent (Magdalena Sokołowska, personal communication).

Let us turn our attention back to the Soviet Union. First, it is to be noted that women have made enormous strides in that country, with an ever increasing number of participants in science and education. Today, more than 49 per cent of students and 28 per cent of postgraduate students are women. They constitute 59 per cent of those who have secondary specialized education. The number of female 'scientific workers' has increased at a faster rate than the number of males, so that the proportion of women among them rose from 36·3 per cent in 1950 to 39 per cent in 1973 (Gvishiani, Mikulinsky, and Kubel, 1976, p. 172).

Yet, what positions do women occupy in the Soviet Union, whether in politics, the universities, or in industry?

More than one-half of the members of the Komsomol – the youth organization of the Communist Party – are women, but only one-quarter of the party's members are women. Further, 4 per cent of the members of the Central Committee are women, and there is not a single woman member of the Politbureau – the body that makes the important political decisions. This is not much different from the United States, where, ever since Frances Perkins served as Secretary of Labor under Franklin Roosevelt, there have been no women in the Cabinet until recently, although there have been some women among representatives and senators.

In general, in the Soviet Union, as Sacks (1976) has shown, women are over-represented in those occupations which require the least skill (p. 90). 'In industry, construction and teaching, and among scientific workers the percentage female declines very rapidly the higher the prestige and responsibility of the position. Census data show that this is also true in medicine' (p. 88). In contrast to the United States, where women comprise only 1·5 per cent of the engineering profession, in the Soviet Union 30 per cent of engineers are women. Yet, they comprise only 20 per cent of engineering foremen, 16 per cent of chief engineers, and 6 per cent of factory directors.

In education more than 80 per cent of the heads of primary schools are women, but women constitute less than one-third of the heads of eight-year schools and 28 per cent of the heads of secondary or middle schools.[2]

In the Academy of Science women form the majority among the junior scientific employees. In contrast, they constitute less than one-third of the senior scientific employees, and there is an even lower proportion of them among the scientific management personnel (following Vvishiani, Mikulinsky, and Kubel, 1976, p. 173). In academia generally, women constitute one-quarter of the associate professors but only one-tenth of the professors (Table 2.2) (Field, 1964, p. 51).[3] It seems that academia is a masculine stronghold in socialist countries as well.

Table 2.2   *Women scientific workers as a percentage of all higher education workers: Soviet Union.*

Position	Oct 1, 1950	Oct 1, 1955	Oct 1, 1960
Directors and deputy directors for training and social work	4·8	5·1	5·3
Deans	6·6	8·5	8·9
Heads of departments	11·3	12·9	12·3
Professors	8·5	8·7	10·6
Associate professors	21·3	22·9	24·4
Other	42·9	41·3	41·4
All women scientists	32·7	33·1	33·6

Source: Dodge (1966), p. 207.

Everywhere, the same pattern exists; the higher the prestige of a position, the smaller is the proportion of women. As a corollary, the higher the prestige of an occupation or profession, the more its rewards are denied to women. Alice Rossi (1970) has also shown that in sociology – and this is true in other fields as well – 'an inverse relation exists between prestige standing of the university and the proportion of women on the full-time faculty at each of the top three ranks in the academic hierarchy.' It is the case not only that the few women who do advance to higher positions are less well rewarded than men but also that the deficit in rewards increases with rank. The report of the Scientific Manpower Commission (1973) has shown that as late as 1971–2 not only did the proportion of women decrease with increase in rank, and not only did women in all ranks in academia receive a lower salary than men of the same rank in all eight regions of the United States, but also in seven out of the eight regions the difference at the full professor level was greater than in the other ranks. Another way of saying this is that, in the professorial rank, over 62 per cent of the men but less than 31 per cent of the women made $20,000 a year or over. At the other extreme, among lecturers and instructors, over 37 per cent of the men but almost 52 per cent of the women made less than $10,000 (pp. 89–90).

I am limiting this discussion to academia, because it is well known, at least for the Western countries, that the diminishing flow of women applies to industry and business throughout. But academia is not only used here as a convenient example; it also serves an important – probably the most important – gatekeeper and traffic director function for the distribution of occupations and positions according to the needs of the market, as these needs are defined in the society. Academia is the gateway to positions of power and influence; to a large extent it controls mobility into these spots. Throughout, the picture is the same; the higher the position, the larger is the difference in rewards between women and men. This leads to my second point, which seems paradoxical at first but is a corollary of what has so far been shown. This is that the larger the proportion of women in a field, the more they are discriminated against. Sacks (1976) has shown that this is so for the Soviet Union, but it applies to the United States as well, where male occupations are highly remunerated even at lower educational levels. Truck drivers, auto mechanics, and delivery men (who had not even finished high school) had median earnings in 1970 of $9,640, $9,070, and $9,060 respectively; in contrast, retail sales clerks, bookkeepers, and typists, who on average had graduated from high school or had even had additional schooling, had median earnings of $6,470, $6,540, and $7,070 respectively (Women Employed, 1977, p. 9).

With an increase in the participation of women the market value of a field seems to decrease. If the salaries of deans of school in the United States can be taken as an index of the market value of the field, it turns out that the more 'feminine' the field, the lower is the market value. Deans of nursing in 1971–2 received an average salary of less than $22,500 whereas deans of pharmacy made an average of almost $26,500. Social welfare deans commanded almost $28,000, but dentistry deans received $35,000. When the proportion of women doctorates decreased from a high 80 per cent in home economics to a medium 53 per cent in the arts, the dean's salary rose from $24,000 to $26,500; and when the proportion of women doctorates reached only 38 per cent in social welfare, the average dean's salary reached almost $28,000. In the United States the deans' salaries of $29,000 and over were all in male professions: engineering, veterinary medicine, law, dentistry, and medicine (Table 2.3).

The inverse correlation between proportion of women and rewards holds true for geographic areas as well. If there are more women academics in a region, it is likely that the difference between the female full professors' salaries and the male full professors' salaries will be larger (Table 2.4). In three of the four regions of the United States in 1971–2 where women constituted 17 per cent or less of the faculty, the salaries of women professors averaged to over 90 per cent of those of males; but in three of the four regions in which women constituted 18 per cent or more of the faculty, women full professors' salaries were under 90 per cent of those of males (Scientific Manpower Commission, 1973, pp. 89-90).

In an empirical study at one university, Tanur and Coser (1978) have concluded from a regression analysis that women's material disadvantages were indeed related to their numbers: 'Regardless of rank or time at [The State University of New York at] Stony Brook, women in fields with a relatively high proportion of women are more likely to have lower-than-predicted salaries than do women in fields where there is a lower proportion of women.'

Table 2.3 *Salaries of faculty deans compared with percentage of women doctorates in each faculty: United States, 1971–2.*

Faculty	Deans' salaries ($)	% of women doctorates	
Nursing	22,417	95.0[a]	
Home economics	24,333	79.0	
Fine arts	26,429	53.0	
Pharmacy	26,400	30.0	(1975–6)
Social welfare	27,875	30.0	(1969–75)[b]
Engineering	29,000	1.6	(of MA)
Veterinary medicine	30,750	9.4	
Law	31,071	7.2	(of LLB)
Dentistry	35,000	1.2	
Medicine	39,000	9.0	

a Estimate.

b Percentage of doctorates and expected doctorates 1969–75 in universities that are members of the Association of American Universities; in 1975 these have awarded 75 per cent of all doctorates awarded to date in the United States and were currently awarding 60 per cent of the yearly total.

Sources: (1) For deans' salaries: Scientific Manpower Commission (1973). (2) For percentage of women doctorates:

    (a) social welfare: McCarthy and Wolfe (1975);

    (b) pharmacy, engineering, veterinary medicine, law, dentistry, and medicine: *Chronicle of Higher Education* (October 23, 1978), p. 11, reproducing from *Degrees Awarded to Women* (National Center for Education Statistics).

Table 2.4 *Percentage of women in faculty compared with female salary as a percentage of male salary, by region: United States, 1971–2*

% of women in faculty	No. of regions in which women's salary is:	
	over 90% of male salary	under 90% of male salary
17 or less	3	1
18 or more	1	3

Source: Computed and summarized from Scientific Manpower Commission (1973), tables 98 and 99, pp. 89–90.

In their comparative study of academia in Britain and the USA, Tessa Blackstone and Oliver Fulton (1974) have provided data from which this inverse correlation between participation and rewards can be deduced. Column 3 of tables 2.5 and 2.6 shows the number of women that would be on the staff of various fields if their proportion in these fields were similar to their proportion in pure science. It turns out that both in Britain and the United States, as the proportion of women graduate students becomes

Table 2.5 *Percentage of graduate students and of academic staff who are women: United States, 1969*

Field	Women as % of graduate students	Women as % of staff	Expected women as % of staff[a]	Difference between observed and expected (%)	Rank of women as % of graduate students	Rank of difference observed and expected
Applied science	2	1	0·8	0·2	1	3
Pure science	17	7	7	0	3·5	2
Medicine	7	10	3	7	2	5
Social science	17	9	7	2	3·5	4
Humanities	46	16	19	−3	5	1

$r_S = -0.62$

a Pure science was taken as the base for comparison.

Source: Blackstone and Fulton (1974), table 2.

Table 2.6 *Percentage of graduate students and of academic staff who are women: United Kingdom, 1969*

Field	Women as % of graduate students	Women as % of staff	Expected women as % of staff[a]	Difference between observed and expected (%)	Rank of women as % of graduate students	Rank of difference observed and expected
Applied science	5	2	3	−1	1	3·5
Pure science	12	8	8	0	2	5
Medicine	24	8	16	−8	5	1
Social science	19	10	13	−3	3	2
Humanities	22	14	15	−1	4	3·5

$r_S = -0.67$

a Pure science was taken as the base for comparison.
b For the United Kingdom the figures for academic social science, education, and social work have not been separated by Blackstone and Fulton.

Source: Blackstone and Fulton (1974), table 2.

Table 2.7 *Women as a percentage of all academic staff compared to women professors as a percentage of all women teachers: United States, 1969.*

Field	Women as % of all academic staff	Women professors as % of all women academic staff	Rank of women as % of all academic staff	Rank of women professors as % of all women teachers
Applied science	1	18	1	1
Pure science	7	16	2	2
Medicine	10	4	4	4
Social science	9	15	3	3
Humanities	16	11	5	5
Education	26	15	6	6
Social work	47	14	7	7

$r_s = -0.63$

Sources: (1) For women as a percentage of all academic staff: Blackstone and Fulton (1974) table 2.
(2) For women professors as a percentage of all women teachers: Blackstone and Fulton (1975), table 3.

Table 2.8 *Women as a percentage of all academic staff compared to women professors, readers, and senior lecturers as a percentage of all women teachers: United Kingdom, 1969.*

Field	Women as % of all academic staff	Women professors, readers, and senior lecturers as % of all women academic staff	Rank of women as % of all academic staff	Rank of women professors as % of all
Applied science	2	18	1	1
Pure science	8	15	2	3
Medicine	9	24	3	4
Social science	10	25	4	5
Humanities	14	4	5	2

$r_S = 0.40$

a Blackstone and Fulton have calculated that the ranks of professor, reader, and senior lecturer in the United Kingdom correspond to the rank of professor in the United States.

Sources: (1) For women as a percentage of all academic staff: Blackstone and Fulton (1974) table 2.
(2) For women professors as a percentage of all women teachers: Blackstone and Fulton (1975), table 3.

larger, the proportion of women on the staff becomes relatively smaller. Further, when data from this study are combined with those of another of their papers on the same subject (Blackstone and Fulton, 1975), it turns out that there is an inverse correlation in the United States (but not in the United Kingdom) between the percentage of women on the staff as a whole and the percentage of women who have attained professorial rank.

In the Soviet Union 'from at least 1940 until the present, the evidence available indicates that it is in those areas where women predominate that wages have been relatively low' (Sacks, 1976, p. 91). Both economic sectors and the professions in which women predominate – light industry, trade, communications, health and culture, communal services and housing, clerical work, medicine, and teaching – are among the most poorly paid. Wage increases in these areas lag behind the national average (Lapidus, 1978, p. 190). Table 2.9 shows the high inverse correlation between female participation and wage levels.

Table 2.10 is a summary of Table 2.9. It shows clearly that, in the sectors or professions in which there is an above average proportion of women, their monthly earnings are below average; in contrast, in the sectors or professions in which the participation of women is below average, their earnings are above average two times out of three. Michael Swafford (1978) has found an inverse correlation of −0·73 between mean wages and the proportion of women in the economic sectors. Data for the Russian Republic show that since 1960 the growth in the proportion of females, particularly in science, government, and administration, has been accompanied by slow increases in wages relative to other sectors (Sacks, 1976, p. 92). The trend in industry is similar. Decreases in the proportion of women in transportation, construction, and industry since 1945 have gone together with faster increases in wages (Sacks, 1976, pp. 91−2).

Figures for a sample of industry in Leningrad (Zdravomyslov and Iadov, 1965, p. 79), showing characteristics of different types of work, reveal a 100 per cent inverse association between the proportion of women in a category and the average wage. A category in which there were only 2·3 per cent women – metalwork fitters on automatic and other equipment – was paid 113·3 rubles. In contrast, where the work was 92·5 per cent performed by women – semi−automated benches in the tobacco industry – the average wage was only 71·4 rubles. Between these two extremes the trends followed the same rank order (Table 2.11)

Interestingly, the Leningrad sample shows no correlation between wages and educational levels in the Leningrad industries. With the exception of the second-highest wage category – labour on control panels of automated equipment – which has a higher educational level than all of the rest, wages seem to have no relation to education. For example, the category of 'manual unskilled labor requiring heavy physical work,' which is at the lowest educational level, is yet relatively high on the wage scale. This contradiction becomes resolved once it is realized that this highly paid category has a low proportion of women. Similarly, the surprise in learning that workers on 'semi−automated benches, e.g. in the tobacco industry,' whose years of schooling are by no means the lowest, receive, however, the lowest

Table 2.9   *Distribution of women workers and employees and average monthly earnings, by economic sector: Soviet Union, 1975.*

Economic sector	No. of women workers and employees	Women as % of labor force	Average monthly earnings (rubles)
Construction	3,002,000	28	176·8
Transport	2,211,000	24	173·5
Industry (production personnel)	1,662,000	49	162·0
Science and scientific services	2,015,000	50	155·4
Nationwide average	*52,539,000*	*51*	*145·8*
Credit and state insurance	423,000	82	133·8
Apparatus of government and economic administration	1,457,000	65	130·6
Education	5,904,000	73	126·9
Agriculture	4,530,000	44	126·8
Communications	1,042,000	68	123·6
Housing and municipal economy, everyday services	2,010,000	53	109·0
Trade, public catering, equipment, supply and sales	6,763,000	76	108·7
Arts	207,000	47	103·1
Public health, physical culture, social welfare	4,851,000	84	102·3
Culture	747,000	73	92·2

Source: Calculated from figures given in Tsentral'noe statisticheskoe upravlenie, *Narodnoe knoziaistro SSSR v 1975 g.* (Moscow, 1976), pp. 542–3 and 546–7.

Table 2.10   *Summary of Table 2.9: participation of women in economic sectors, by monthly earnings: Soviet Union, 1975.*

Women's monthly earnings	No. of sectors in which women constitute a percentage that is:	
	Above average	Below average
Above average	0	4
Below average	8	2

Source: As Table 2.9.

Table 2.11 *Different types of work in Leningrad: sample by proportions of women and wage, 1965.*

Occupation	% of women	Average wage (rubles)	Average years of education
Metalwork fitters on automatic and other equipment	2·3	113·5	8·3
Labor on control panels of automated equipment	8·7	110·1	9·0
Manual unskilled requiring heavy physical work, e.g. dockers	11·0	107·4	6·8
Manual work using instruments and demanding high level of training, e.g. electric fitters	16·5	96·6	8·4
Work on machines and mechanisms, requiring vocational training, e.g. joiners	20·0	89·8	8·1
Work on automated machines, e.g. in tool construction industry	44·2	78·1	8·0
Conveyer belt work on sewing machines needing high level of training, e.g. in shoe industry	86·3	87·3	7·9
Work on semi automated benches, e.g. in tobacco industry	97·5	71·4	8·0

Source: Zdravomyslov and Iadov (1965), p. 79.

wage becomes dissipated when it is noted that three-quarters of these workers are women.

In summary, and briefly: women do not only stay at, or sink to, the bottom. Related to this is the fact that the more women there are in an occupation, the worse is the discrimination in the form of lower wages or denial of promotion or other rewards.

It seems that something more is going on than discrimination pure and simple. Let me mention only three factors, although there are many more at play.

One important factor is women's cultural mandate, which has remained the same in Soviet Russia as in America, Britain, and the West generally, if not in the whole world. It is women's cultural mandate to care for the family. This means: first, that they do two jobs instead of one, so that they simply do not have the time or energy to do the extra work required for advancement and promotion; and second, that where women have to make a choice between career and family, it must be the career that suffers.

But perhaps more important is the fact that this leads employers or agents of promotion to use the women's cultural mandate as a basis for blocking promotions and withholding rewards. This leads to the third factor, namely, that employers and university teachers see women as prospective disturbers of the system (Coser and Rokoff, 1971). Although in fact many women work harder than men – if only to show that they deserve their status, which always seems somewhat illegitimate to others and to themselves – there is a fear that they don't produce their money's worth. I asked the President of the Sociological Association of the USSR why there were so few women professors. His answer was immediate; he said with a smirk: 'Women have babies.' If it will be objected that single women, or married women without children, are equally discriminated against, it must be added that they are considered a 'bad risk;' they may get married or they may have children.

We must ask: what has happened in Soviet Russia, where ideology has strongly called for the equality of women for almost six decades? Also, to take another example, what has happened in the kibbutz in Israel? Why do women there remain confined to the kitchen, the laundry, and the children's house? Why don't they take part in the political decisions and in the directorship of factories or other economic units? Kibbutz women were freed of child care and housework; unlike the women of the Soviet Union, the United States, and Britain, they did not have two jobs. The answer is so simple that it sounds trivial, and yet I think it is crucial; it is that the basic stereotypes about women were not questioned on the kibbutz any more than in the outside world, a point stressed by Suzanne Keller (1973). Let me tell of a personal experience on a recent visit to two kibbutzim in Israel.

At the first kibbutz my husband and I met a couple now close to retirement. In the late 1920s they had been doctoral students, he in Vienna, she in Prague; they both had given up their studies to devote themselves to the Zionist movement. They had been equals at the time. At the time of our visit *he* was lecturing at a nearby school and doing statistical work; *she* was working in the laundry. What had happened to her? She had been 'left behind,' but not because she had had to spend many years raising children and cooking for the family. Her children had been raised in the children's house; the family's meals had been taken in the communal dining room. Perhaps my second story can provide the answer, for it shows that basic stereotypes about women have continued to exist even in a society ideologically based on equalitarianism.

In the second kibbutz we met a man who also had been a member for many years. We did not meet his wife, for she was in school being retrained to become a social worker. Our host prepared to be back home at 5 p.m. when his little daughter would come in from the children's house. He seemed ready enough to share in the after hours care of the child. Yet, when he saw me take the wheel of our car on our ride with him to the nearby regional high school, he said to my husband in surprise: 'How come *you* don't drive?' We explained that we both liked it better this way. When we arrived at the school, he said: 'There aren't many classes going on right now, but,' turning to me, 'you may be interested in watching a cooking class.' I suddenly understood what had happened in the kibbutz in spite of all the good intentions to the contrary.

As long as the basic stereotype is not questioned, things revert to where they were in the past after the first stage of ideological revolution. Equality is not something that can be legislated and then forgotten. It has to be watched over continuously. Rivka Bar-Yosef from the Hebrew University has called my attention to the fact that, if one is committed to bringing about equality, one had to repeatedly examine what is happening and introduce correctives into the body politic and the body social. Not having questioned the old stereotypes, people in the kibbutz were busy solving their economic problems and also trying to avoid as much as possible the development of hierarchical inequality in which expertise or other assets would lead to privileges. They forgot that a system of privileges is inherent in the traditional division of labor between the sexes.

This division of labor has a value-laden component, namely, that what women do is being valued less than what men do. As a consequence it is feared that the prestige of an occupation is being degraded with an influx of women and that male prerogatives will hence be threatened.

Hodge and Hodge (1965) have shown in a statistical study that, to the extent that women receive wages below those demanded by white males, the incomes of men will be adjusted downward by the competitive process. They suggest that discriminatory policies are due not solely to prejudice but also to attempts by white males to avoid competition.

Another consequence bears upon the attitudes of the few women who have 'made it.' As part of the elite they enjoy their minority status. If it is true, as I hope I have demonstrated, that increasing participation of women threatens to decrease their rewards in comparison to those of men, the exceptional woman in a male occupation must be interested in keeping women out. Her own interests would be threatened by an influx of more women, since the rewards that she now enjoys would be reduced. This explains what has been called the 'queen bee syndrome' – the fact that, unless there is a strong feminist movement, many women among the happy few who 'make it' refuse to stress the rights of women and, just like the men, are likely to have little interest in encouraging women to enter their field or to aspire to higher achievements within it.

It follows that it is not enough to call for increased participation of women in such elite occupations as medicine or law. If existing trends were permitted to exert themselves, women in these professions would tend to drift into lower positions – into the routine work of general practitioners, as they do in the Soviet Union, or of law firms. This would once more reaffirm male dominance. By simply swelling the ranks women would not weaken the patriarchal system. Instead, it is by making a claim to equal admission to top positions that women, or other excluded minorities, challenge the closed ranks of the system – that they challenge its institutions of exclusiveness, which are not based only on achievement, as claimed, but on monopolization of privilege. For as long as an exploited stratum is satisfied with being exploited, the elitist system is likely to be maintained. It is by giving up (to paraphrase August Bebel) the damned wantlessness of women that the elitist system can be challenged.

Equality of mobility of women can be achieved only with a complete relinquishment of existing sex stereotypes; but this means a change in the family structure. Full equality of opportunity for women is as important as it will be difficult to achieve, for it implies a change in authority structure in all of society.

NOTES

(1) The phrase was coined by Cynthia Fuchs Epstein (1970). This paper appeared in an earlier version in West Germany (Coser, 1976).
(2) The figures for the Soviet Union that are not referenced were communicated to me, and translated where needed, by David Lane and Felicity O'Dell of Cambridge University.
(3) In another breakdown Michael Swafford (1978) has shown that in 1970 women constituted 9 per cent of the academicians, 20 per cent of docents, 29 per cent of senior research associates, and 48 per cent of junior research associates – figures that don't differ much from the earlier figures of 1950.

REFERENCES

Blackstone, Tessa and Fulton, Oliver (1974) 'Sex differences, subject fields and research activity among academics in Britain and the US,' *Higher Education* (April).

Blackstone, Tessa and Fulton, Oliver (1975) 'Sex discrimination among university teachers: a British–American comparison,' *British Journal of Sociology*, vol. 26, no. 3 (September), pp. 267–75.

Coser, Rose Laub (1976) 'Das Männereich Universität: Diskriminierungen in den USA und in der Sowjetunion,' *Geissener Universitätsblätter*, vol. 9 (December), pp. 38–49.

Coser, Rose Laub and Rokoff, Gerald (1971) 'Women in the occupational world: social disruption and conflict,' *Social Problems*, vol. 18, no. 4, pp. 535–54.

Devereaux, George and Winter, Florence R. (1950) 'Occupational status of nurses,' *American Sociological Review*, vol. 15, no. 5, pp. 628–34.

Dodge, Norton D. (1966) *Women in the Soviet Economy* (Baltimore: Johns Hopkins Press).

Epstein, Cynthia Fuchs (1970) *Woman's Place: Options and Limits in Professional Careers* (Los Angeles: University of California Press).

Field, Mark (1964) 'Workers and mothers: Soviet women today' unpublished manuscript (Cambridge, Mass.: Russian Research Center, Harvard University).

Gvishiani, D. M., Mikulinsky, S. R., and Kubel, S. A. (eds), (1976) *The Scientific Intelligentsia in the USSR* (Moscow: Progress Publishers).

Hodge, Robert W. and Hodge, Patricia (1965) 'Occupational assimilation as a competitive process,' *American Journal of Sociology*, vol. 71, no. 3 (November), pp. 249–89.

Keller, Suzanne (1973) 'The family in the kibbutz: what lessons for us?,' Michael Curtis and Mordecai S. Chertoff (eds), in *Israel: Social Structure and Change* (New Brunswick, NJ: Transaction Books, pp. 115–44.

Lane, David (1976) *The Socialist Industrial State* (New York: Praeger).

Lapidus, Gail Warshofsky (1978) *Women in Soviet Society: Equality, Development, and Social Change* (Berkeley: University of California Press).

McCarthy, Joseph L. and Wolfe, Dael (1975) 'Doctorates granted to women and minority group members,' *Science*, vol. 189 (September), pp. 856–9.

Mannheim, Karl (1940) *Man and Society in an Age of Reconstruction* (London: Routledge & Kegan Paul).

Rossi, Alice S. (1970) 'Status of women in graduate departments of sociology, 1968–1969,' *American Sociologist*, vol. 5, no. 1, pp. 1–12.

Sacks, Michael Paul (1976) *Women's Work in Soviet Russia: Continuity in the Midst of Change (New York: Praeger).*

Scientific Manpower Commission (1973) Summary of Salary Surveys: Salaries of Scientists, Engineers, and Technicians (Washington, DC, August).

Swafford, Michael (1978) 'Sex differences in Soviet earnings,' *American Sociological Review*, vol. 43, no. 5, pp. 657–73.

Tanur, Judith M. and Coser, Rose Laub (1978) 'Pockets of "poverty" in the salaries of academic women,' *American Association of University Professors Bulletin*, vol. 64, no. 1, pp. 26–30.

Vetter, Betty M. (1975) 'Women and minority scientists,' *Science*, vol. 189, no. 4205, pp. 751. The source of data is Scientific Manpower Commission, *Professional Women and Minorities. A Manpower Data Resource Service* (Washington, DC, 1975).

Women Employed (1977) 'Women in the economy: preferential mistreatment,' unpublished report to the Working Women's Conference, Chicago.

Zdravomyslov A. G. and Iadov, V. A. (1965) Personal communication, translated from Russian by Felicity O'Dell of Cambridge University.

Part One

Political Elites:
Participation and Behaviour

3

Women in Politics:

A Study of Political Leadership in the United Kingdom, France and the Federal Republic of Germany

DONNA S. SANZONE

Women have traditionally been excluded from high-ranking positions in both government and politics. In recent years, however, more women have achieved positions of political influence, and several women have been appointed or elected to high executive positions in the governments of France, the United Kingdom, and the Federal Republic of Germany. Their total numbers are still extremely small, and the dearth of women in executive level positions is a symptom of a broader malady, namely, their inferior status in society. The exclusion of women from positions of power relates intimately to traditional attitudes and stereotypes and is compounded by a lack of candidates with appropriate educational and professional experience. Social pressures, legal restrictions, and the labor market all have limited professional and educational options for women. The professions – law, medicine, engineering, the natural sciences – have been

Table 3.1 *Percentage of women in higher education.*

Field	United Kingdom	West Germany	France
Humanities	61	47	66
Education	—	60	—
Medicine	33	26	40
Law	—	15	42
Natural sciences	24	20	34
Engineering	0·03	0·02	—

Notes: (1) Statistics are for 1972 (United Kingdom), 1971 (West Germany), and 1973 (France). These are the most recent years for which complete comparable statistics are available.

(2) 'Higher education' includes all types of post-secondary institutions: universities, teacher-training institutes, technical colleges, and other non-university institutions. Figures for France, however, include universities only.

(3) Figures are for both full and part time students, except UK figures, which represent full time students only.

Source: UNESCO (1976).

Table 3.2   *Percentage of women in sample fields of study.*

England and Wales	40·0%
Federal Republic of Germany	28·4%
France	76·7%

Source: As Table 3.1.

relatively closed to women, who have tended to concentrate in a few areas of specialization – literature, languages, and education.

The percentage of women in institutions of higher education and in various fields of study in Britain, France, and West Germany in 1971–3 are given in Tables 3.1 and 3.2. The data illustrate that women comprised less than half of the total university enrollment in the three countries and overwhelmingly concentrated in such areas as the humanities and education.[1] Since the mid-1960s, however, there has been a substantial increase in the number of women enrolled in European universities. In France the percentage of women among university students increased from 42 per cent in 1965 to 47 per cent in 1973. In West Germany the percentage went from 24 per cent in 1965 to 28 per cent in 1971 and in the United Kingdom from 37 per cent in 1965 to 40 per cent in 1972 (UNESCO, 1976). It is probable that education will have a great impact on the status of women. Differences in legislative history and national attitudes in the three countries have affected the status of women in each of them.

In France, women did not receive the right to vote until 1944, and it was not until 1966 that women won the right to enter the professions, open checking accounts, and own their own businesses. Moreover, abortion and birth control were legally restricted until 1974.

In Britain, on the other hand, women won substantial rights at an earlier date. Britain had the first regular women's suffrage committee in 1855, and enfranchizement came in 1918. Two Acts were passed in 1918: one that gave women over 30 the right to vote, and one that gave women the right to be elected as members of the House of Commons. The right of entry into most professions was formally granted to women by the Sex Discrimination (Removal) Act, 1919. In 1928 the minimum voting age was lowered to 21. Additionally, questions concerning the right to abortion and birth control were legally resolved as early as 1967.

In West Germany women received the vote in 1918, and under the Weimar republic they possessed the same civic rights and obligations as men. The Nationalist Socialist regime, however, denied women equal rights and relegated them to their 'natural' place: 'kitchen, children and church.' The Basic Law, 1949, which established the Bonn government, stated that men and women should have equal rights. This statement of principle was followed by the passage of the Equality of Status Act, 1957, which eliminated some legal discrimination against women, particularly in the area of family rights. However, although West German law has accorded women many basic legal rights, attitudinal and psychological prejudices in West Germany are stronger and more deeply rooted than in France or Britain.

FRANCE

Although there is an underlying tradition of egalitarianism in France, stemming from the French revolution, women have suffered from inferior status written into the Napoleonic Code of the early nineteenth century. Progress for women has been slow and difficult, as evidenced by their failure to win basic political and legal rights until the end of the Second World War. Interestingly, two women served as ministers of state in the Popular Front government of 1936, even before women won the right to vote. The first full woman minister – Germaine Poinso-Chapuis – was appointed to the Ministry of Health in 1947 under the Fourth Republic government of Robert Schuman. However, there were no women ministers in the government of the Fifth Republic until the election of President Valéry Giscard d'Estaing in May 1974.

There were no women ministers in President Charles de Gaulle's Cabinet; nor were there women state secretaries until his last year in office, when he appointed one woman to share a state secretarial position with a man. President Georges Pompidou retained most of de Gaulle's ministers and kept the only woman state secretary – Marie-Madeleine Diensch – in the Ministry of Health.

At the time of his inauguration on May 24, 1974 Giscard appointed a woman – Dr Simone Veil – as Minister of Health and two women to state secretarial positions: Dr Hélène Dorhlac as Secretary of State to the Minister of Justice for Prison Conditions, and Dr Annie Lesur as Secretary of State to the Minister of Education for Preschool Children. Additionally, in July 1974 Giscard created a new ministerial office concerned with the status of women and appointed the coeditor of the newsweekly *L'Express* – Françoise Giroud – as Secretary of State for the Status of Women (Secretaire d'Etat à la Condition Feminine).

Although Giscard was convinced of the need to include women in his government, Premier Jacques Chirac was reluctant to concede any real power to them. The premier confided during a private meeting that it was 'undoubtedly not the President's best idea, but there was nothing to worry about' (*L'Express*, December 30, 1974–January 5, 1975, p. 52). Women were given impressive titles, but they were in fact excluded from the government's inner circle of power. For example, the rich and powerful social security system was removed from Dr Veil's ministry and placed under the Ministry of Labor. Hélène Dorhlac was relegated to an office outside her ministry's building. To dramatize her exclusion from the center of government activities she addressed the National Assembly in her raincoat. After several weeks she was given an office in the building.

The case of Françoise Giroud is perhaps the most revealing. Not only was her new post of Secretary of State for the Status of Women deprived of an independent budget, but there were also fundamental questions concerning the status of the new office and its authority. In addition to opposing the idea of creating a ministry for women's affairs, Chirac also objected to Giroud on the political grounds that she had supported François Mitterand – the opposition candidate – during the presidential elections. In the end, however, Giroud was confirmed in office and empowered to 'move toward integration of women into contemporary society and advance them on every level of responsibility' (*The New York Times*, August 26, 1974).

Giroud made considerable progress during her two years in office. By February 1976 she had submitted 111 proposals to the premier designed to eliminate the most obvious forms of inequality in French law. While in office she succeeded in initiatives changing divorce laws, outlawing job discrimination on the basis of sex or family status, and setting up measures to improve the condition of widows, unmarried mothers, and women heads of family (French Embassy, 1975).

Among the legal measures that she introduced were proposals to give women the right to sign a declaration of income, to open all university competition to both sexes, and to raise the maximum age for civil service examinations to 45, so that women who had interrupted their studies or careers to raise children would not be excluded from government careers. She also proposed a maternal indemnity to permit one parent to remain at home until a child was old enough to attend nursery school.

On August 27, 1976 Giroud was transferred from the post of Secretary of State for the Status of Women to the post of Secretary of State for Culture by the new premier – Raymond Barre. At the same time Barre created a Delegation for the Status of Women, replacing the state secretariat established in 1974 (French Embassy, 1976). The present Delegate to the Premier for the Status of Women and Family Affairs is Monique Pelletier.

Simone Veil was appointed Minister of Health after serving as Secretary of the Higher Council of the Courts from 1970 to 1974. During her career as secretary general she drafted important legislation concerning the rights of prison inmates, mental patients, and adopted, retarded, and illegitimate children. She has a degree in law and is a graduate of the Institut d'Etudes Politiques. The only woman to reach full ministerial rank in the Fifth Republic, Veil has made her mark in the areas of birth control and abortion. In June 1974 the National Assembly gave overwhelming approval to a Bill, sponsored by the government and presented by Veil, that authorized the general distribution of contraceptives and provided that the social security system pay for the costs. The nearly unanimous approval given to the Bill – only one vote was against – demonstrated the reversal of previous attitudes toward birth control and replaced a 1967 law that permitted the distribution of contraceptives only on medical orders with a specific time limit. The new law also eliminated the restriction that women under 18 had to have the written permission of their parents as well as a doctor to obtain contraceptives. Veil promised a vigorous public-information campaign on birth control to publicize the fact that birth control was now a matter of 'common right,' freely available.

In addition to birth control reform Veil has also played a major role in the passage of recent abortion legislation. The subject of abortion had been avoided in Catholic France. In 1974 the Pompidou government intended to introduce a Bill to liberalize abortion, but it dropped the Bill without debate when it ran into opposition from powerful sources.[2] The new law, drawn up and defended by Veil with the support of the Giscard government, gave women the right to abortion within the first ten weeks of pregnancy. The Bill permitted any permanent resident 'distressed' by a pregnancy to have an abortion, provided it was performed by a doctor in an established hospital. Women under 18 had to have parents' permission. The law ended the prohibition of abortion in France; but it is still a matter of controversy, and many doctors are refusing to perform abortions. The public, however, strongly favors abortion. In a poll for the Ministry of Health, taken by the French Institute of Public Opinion, 73 per cent of those questioned favored the right of abortion during the first ten weeks of pregnancy (*The New York Times*, November 28, 1974).

Public opinion is indeed in favor of the programs and measures adopted by the Giscard government as regards women's rights. In January 1975 a Figaro-Sofres poll indicated that a large majority of the French believed the status of women to be the most positive aspect of the president's program. Moreover, they replied to the question 'To whom would you like to give greater responsibilities?' by placing Simone Veil first, ahead of the premier, followed by Françoise Giroud, ahead of the Ministers of State, Finance, and Foreign Affairs.[3]

Veil retained the post of Minister of Health until June 1979, when she was elected to the presidency of the first directly elected European Parliament. At present, there are four women in the Cabinet of Prime Minister Raymond Barre: Alice Saunier-Seité, Minister for Universities; Monique Pelletier, Minister Delegate to the Prime Minister for the Status of Women and Family Affairs; Nicole Pasquier, Secretary of State to the Ministry of Work and Participation and, in particular, Women in the Labor Force; and Hélène Missoffe, Secretary of State to the Ministry of Health and Social Security. Thus, of the four women in the Barre government, one is a full-ranking minister, one a minister delegate, and two are state secretaries (French Embassy, *The Third Barre Cabinet*, 1979).

BRITAIN

In contrast to France's rather late acceptance of women in politics, the British government included a woman Cabinet minister as early as 1929. Margaret Bonfield was appointed Minister of Labour in the Labour government of 1929. Women were first allowed to stand for Parliament in 1918, and one of the seventeen women standing – Lady Astor – was elected. Between 1918 and 1971 ninety-four women were elected to Parliament and twenty-seven attained ministerial rank, eight as full ministers. The Life Peerage Act, 1958 admitted women to the House of Lords, and twenty-six women have been created peeresses for life. (*British Information Services*, 1971, 1975).

The Labour Party has consistently placed more women in executive level positions than the Conservatives, who did not appoint a female minister until 1951, when Dame Florence Horsbrugh was named Minister of Education. Margaret Thatcher – former Secretary of State for Science and Education in the Conservative government of Edward Heath (June 1970 to March 1974) – was only the second woman in the history of the Conservative Party to hold a full Cabinet position. Lady Tweedsmuir served as minister in the

Scottish Office in Prime Minister Heath's government, but this was not a full Cabinet post. In addition, Peggy Fenner was Parliamentary Secretary of State in the Ministry of Agriculture, Fisheries, and Food in 1973.

Included in the Labour government of Harold Wilson (March 1974 to March 1976) were two women in full Cabinet positions: Barbara Castle, Secretary of State for Social Services; and Shirley Williams, Secretary of State for Prices and Consumer Protection. Another woman was a minister but not in the Cabinet – Judith Hart, Minister for Overseas Development. In the Labour government headed by James Callaghan (April 1976 to May 1979), Shirley Williams was the only woman to serve in a full Cabinet position: Secretary of State for Education and Science and Paymaster General. Judith Hart retained her position as Minister of State for Overseas Development under Callaghan.

There has been less dramatic progress in women's rights in Britain than in France during the mid-1970s, obviously because Britain made substantial progress many years earlier. Birth control is generally accepted as an integral part of family welfare. The National Health Services Act, 1967 provides for family-planning services under the authority of local health departments. Over 10,000 clinics exist for family planning, run by voluntary family-planning associations. The Abortion Act, 1967 permits abortion if the continuation of a woman's pregnancy involves a greater risk than its termination in view of the dangers to the mother's life, to the physical or mental health of her or her existing children, or to the physical or mental health of the unborn child. Two doctors must approve the operation, which must be performed within the first twenty-eight weeks of pregnancy.

In an effort to end discrimination in employment, Barbara Castle – then Secretary of State for Employment and Productivity – introduced and piloted through Parliament the Equal Pay Act, 1970. This measure was designed to eliminate discrimination between men and women in both the terms and the conditions of employment by the end of 1975. According to the provisions of the Act:

> Where men and women do the same or broadly similar work for the same or related employer, or where they do different jobs recognized by job evaluation schemes as equivalent, women will qualify for equal pay. The Act also removes the effects of any obvious discrimination there may have been in the actual process of job evaluation. (British Information Services 1971, 1975)

The Equal Pay Act gave employers five years in which to implement its provisions. It came into full effect on December 29, 1975.

Barbara Castle was one of the Labour Party's 'regulars.' She was a member of the government throughout Wilson's two terms in office: 1964–70 and 1974–6. Castle's first position was Minister of Overseas Development from 1964 to 1965. She was then named Minister of Transport from 1965 to 1968 – the first woman to hold this office. In this position she was responsible for the most comprehensive Transport Act ever enacted in Britain. Subsequently, she was appointed Secretary of State for

Employment and Productivity in 1968, and she remained in this position until Labour's defeat in the March 1970 elections. It was in this position that she carried through Parliament the Equal Pay Act, 1970. From April 1975 until April 1976 she held the Cabinet post of Secretary of State for Social Services. In this capacity Castle was concerned with a broad range of social welfare issues, including pensions, social security, and national insurance benefits. Castle lost her post as Secretary of State for Social Services in April 1976 when James Callaghan took over the Labour government after Wilson's resignation.

Shirley Williams, the only woman Cabinet minister in the previous Labour government, rose rapidly in party politics, attaining ministerial rank (but not on the Cabinet level) only two years after being elected to Parliament in 1964. She was a member of the Labour government from April 1966, first as Parliamentary Secretary of State in the Ministry of Labour, then as Minister of State in the Department of Education and Science (1967–8), and subsequently as Minister of State in the Home Office (1969–70).

After the election of Wilson in 1974 Williams was appointed to the Cabinet as Secretary of State for Prices and Consumer Protection. In September 1976 she was transferred to a different ministerial position – Secretary of State for Education and Science. She also held the Office of Paymaster General. In May 1979, Williams lost her Cabinet position as well as her seat in the House of Commons as a result of the Conservative victory in the British general election. Williams had been regarded as a possible successor to Prime Minister Callaghan.[4] A respected and competent politician, Williams remains an important political figure to watch in Britain.

Margaret Thatcher is certainly the most prominent woman in British politics today. In the former Conservative government Thatcher served as Minister of Education and Science for almost four years. The public image that she projected during this period was far from popular, exemplified by such epithets as the 'Iron Lady'. She supported the principle of meritocracy against the open-enrollment school policy of the Labour government. Moreover, in another unpopular move she raised the price of school lunches and eliminated the distribution of free milk to schoolchildren. In some ways Thatcher appears to be typical of the classic Conservative politician: middle-class, Oxford educated, a member of the meritocracy, an upholder of traditional values. She stands for law and order, individual enterprise, and traditional moral values.

From February 1974 until her election as party leader she served in the Shadow Cabinet and was the spokesperson on Treasury and Economic Affairs. On February 12, 1975 Thatcher was elected head of the Conservative Party, becoming the first woman to lead a major British political party. Thatcher's emergence on the British political scene was surprising: she acknowledged that she did not think that the Conservatives would be ready for a woman leader in her lifetime.

On May 3, 1979 Margaret Thatcher and the Conservative Party won a decisive victory in Britain's general election. Thatcher thereby became the first woman Prime Minister in European history. The Conservatives won a comfortable majority of forty-three seats in the House of Commons, reflecting a shift to the right in the British electorate. The Conservative victory can be attributed in large part to Labour's failure to deal effectively with Britain's economic problems, including a series of strikes in the winter of 1978–9. Thatcher appointed an all-male Cabinet of twenty-two members. Thatcher did appoint two women Ministers of State (without Cabinet rank): Sally Oppenheim, Minister of State for Consumer Affairs in the Department of Trade and Baroness Young, Minister of State in the Department of Education and Science.

It is doubtful that Thatcher would do more to advance the cause of women in politics than would a male Labour Prime Minister. When asked her opinion of the women's liberation movement, she responded: 'What's it ever done for me?' (*New Statesman*, October 7, 1977). Historically, the Conservatives have placed fewer women in positions of influence and power. In fact Thatcher's voting record in the House of Commons over the past twenty years has been consistently right-wing conservative, especially on social reform issues. For example, she has voted in favor of restoring the death penalty and has opposed abortion reform laws.

The election of Thatcher as Prime Minister is a significant development in female executive leadership in Britain and Europe. Although there have been a few individual women of influence, British politics has never fully integrated women. Historically, of course, Britain has accepted female monarchs who came to the throne by succession, but it has not accepted them as actual contenders for political power. For this reason both Margaret Thatcher and Shirley Williams are important figures to watch in British politics. It is interesting that the two women contenders for political leadership are so different; neither stands for a feminist platform,[5] but each represents opposing political philosophies and programs that will affect the basic direction and tenor of British society.

Two significant legal advances in the area of women's rights in Britain warrant special attention: the Equal Pay Act, 1970, and the Sex Discrimination Act, December 1975.

The Sex Discrimination Act, 1975 has been considered one of the most radical pieces of social legislation of modern times (*Sunday Times*, February 20, 1977). The Act made it unlawful to treat one person less favorably than another on grounds of sex in the following areas: employment; training and related matters; education; and the provision of housing and goods, services and facilities to the public. The Act also applied to discriminatory advertising in these areas.

The Equal Pay Act, 1970, as indicated previously, came into force in December 1975 after allowing employers five years to comply with its requirements. This Act complemented the Sex Discrimination Act by ending sexual discrimination in terms of employment. The Act covered basic pay as well as such other forms of additional payments as overtime pay, bonuses, holiday pay, and sick pay.

In order to ensure implementation of the equal rights legislation the Sex Discrimination Act also established and gave statutory powers to an Equal Opportunities Commission. The tasks of the commission are to work toward the elimination of discrimination, to promote equality of

Table 3.3 *Average weekly earnings, including overtime (£).*

Year	Men	Women
1971	32·9	18·3
1976	71·8	46·2

Source: Equal Opportunities Commission (1977), p. 7.

opportunity between men and women, and to monitor the implementation of the Sex Discrimination Act and the Equal Pay Act. The current chairperson is Betty Lockwood.

In November 1977 the Equal Opportunities Commission issued a report based on evidence to the Royal Commission on Income Distribution and Wealth, entitled *Women and Low Incomes.* The report discusses the status of women in Britain, with particular attention to sexual inequality in terms of income and state benefits. The commission found that, while the Equal Pay Act had to some degree reduced the relative gap between male and female basic wage rates, the gap remained significant (Table 3.3).

The commission has urged the distribution of women throughout all sectors of the economy. It has recommended that women be guaranteed equal access to all fringe benefits and be provided with training facilities to enable them to acquire new skills. As regards social security and state benefits, the commission has recommended a revision in social security laws and regulations, specifically the elimination of the dependency principle in favor of the principle that women are equal with men in terms of social security contributions and benefits. (Social security legislation presently treats the man as the automatic head of household and the woman as the dependent party who is not in need of full social-security benefits).

FEDERAL REPUBLIC OF GERMANY

West German attitudes toward leadership have probably played a decisive role in limiting leadership possibilities for women. For historic reasons West Germans have tended to favor strong authoritarian male leadership. In the order of West German society women traditionally have been tied to their 'natural' place: the kitchen, children, and the church. Although the image of women has changed considerably in recent years, otherwise progressive West German politics has been rather slow in accepting women in roles of political leadership (*German International*, March 1975).

These national tendencies have manifested themselves in several ways and contributed to existing prejudices and discrimination against women. For example, in 1971 only 28·4 per cent of all students at universities were women. In 1971 women held only 3·5 per cent of the posts in the higher service of the Federal Administration, and in the Bonn ministries, including representation abroad, only 5·5 per cent (Federal Republic of Germany, 1973). In the December 1976 elections thirty-eight women were elected to the Bundestag (lower house) compared with 438 men. This represents a slight increase in representation compared with the 1972 election results, from 5·8 per cent to 7·3 per cent (*Sozial Report*, August 1976).

However, women have made some significant advances, especially in areas such as divorce and family law. In addition three of the four Vice Presidents of the Bundestag are women: Katharina Focke, Annemarie Renger, and Lisolette Funke. At present there is also one woman Cabinet minister: Antje Huber, Minister of Health, Youth, and Family Affairs. In 1977 Marie Schlei held the Cabinet post of Minister of Economic Cooperation.

The first woman Cabinet minister in the history of West German government was Elisabeth Schwarzhaupt of the Christian Democratic Union (CDU), appointed by Adenaur to the newly created Ministry of Health in November 1961 in response to pressure by women members of the Bundestag. From 1967 to 1976 there were two women 'regulars' in the Cabinet: Kate Strobel and Katharina Focke, who were both Ministers of Health – a ritually female appointment. The social insurance system falls within the jurisdiction not of the Ministry of Health but of the Ministry of Labor, which is headed by a man.

Kate Strobel was in the Bonn government for almost six years as Minister of Health from 1967 to 1972, first in the Kiesinger government and later in the Brandt government. She was replaced by Katharina Focke in 1972. Focke was elected to the Bundestag in 1969 and in the same year was appointed Parliamentary State Secretary in the Federal Chancellery. During this period she was responsible for European affairs, education and science, and co-operation between the federal government and the Landers. She was named Minister for Health, Youth, and Family Affairs in 1972 and held this position until 1976. Dr Focke is presently a Vice President of the Bundestag.

As Minister of Health, Family, and Youth Affairs Focke was active in promoting women's rights, especially independent social security for women and recognition of women's work in the family and of their contribution to family maintenance. Additionally, the improvement of educational and vocational training for women was given a high priority.

In an effort to facilitate reform in these areas the Bundestag appointed a commission to study the role of woman at all levels of society. In November 1976 the commission released a preliminary report on 'Women and Society' (Deutsche Bundestag, 1976). The report identified problems faced by women in areas of employment and education and concluded that West German women earned less and had fewer educational opportunities, fewer professional opportunities, and less chance for advancement than men (*The New York Times*, January 18, 1977). The commission also offered suggestions to correct these inequities and stressed the need for educational reforms, increased professional opportunities, increased job training, and an effective public relations campaign to make women more conscious of their rights. It is now up to the Bundestag to take specific measures to deal with the problems identified by the commission.

An important recent change in the legal status of women is in the area of family law. A new marriage and family law, called the First Act for Reform of Marriage and Family Law, came into effect on July 1, 1977. Unlike previous family laws the new law does not give guidelines for marriage; for example, it does not state that a husband should work and a wife should take care of the home. Both husbands and wives are now jointly respons-bible for family income, education, and housework. Prior to this Act, if a wife wanted to work, she needed the permission of her husband. The new law provides for legal equality in marriage and family life (*Sozial Report*, July 1977).

Another important aspect of the new law is the amended divorce law, which allows for divorce on grounds of irreparable marriage breakdown. The former 'guilt principle' has been replaced by a no-fault concept. After divorce all assets, including pensions, are divided between the partners, and each is responsible for his or her own maintenance. (Only the financially weaker partner who is unable to earn a living can be granted alimony.) Child support is awarded to the one who receives custody of children.

Perhaps the most prominent woman in the Bonn government is the former President and current Vice President of the Bundestag – Anne-Marie Renger. The President of the Bundestag is accorded a formal position just below that of the President of the Republic. Renger, of the Social Democratic Party (SDP), was elected President in December 1972, becoming the first woman president of a West European parliament. She held this position until December 1976, when she lost her post to a Christian Democrat – Karl Carstens – following the Social Democrats' defeat in the October 1976 elections (*New York Times*, January 18, 1977).

Renger has directed her efforts toward equalizing employment oppor-tunities for women. She has edited a book entitled *Equal Opportunities for Women* (1977), which consists of selected letters received from women employees describing instances of sexual discrimination at work. Although the principle of 'equal pay for equal work' has been recognized on paper in West Germany, it has not been consistently applied. A parliamentary commission on law reform found that on average women earned 30 per cent less than men. 'Nowhere is there such a wide divergence between men and women and day-to-day reality than in working life,' said Renger (*Sozial Report*, June 1977). Renger has also deplored the small number of women in politics and criticized the major parties for not placing more women on their electoral lists.[6] Yet, she is opposed to the more radical proposal of a constitutional amendment to assure women proportional representation in the Bundestag or in the Länder parliaments.

Despite Renger's prominent position in West German politics it is extremely unlikely that she will ever become chancellor. In fact, given traditional attitudes toward women, the likelihood of a woman chancellor, at least within the next generation, is remote.

The third woman Vice President of the Bundestag is Lisolette Funcke of the Free Democratic Party (FDP). A member of the Bundestag for twenty years, she is head of the Bundestag's financial committee and has been active in abortion reform legislation.

In June 1975 the Bundestag passed a law permitting abortion on demand during the first ten weeks of pregnancy. However, on February 25, 1975, the Federal Constitutional Court ruled that the law transgressed the Basic Law's principle that 'everyone shall have the right to life and inviolability of person' (*German Tribune*, March 13, 1975) and declared the law unconstitutional. Funcke said that West German women 'would not accept or abide by such a decision' (*Sozial Report*, July 1976). Subsequently, on February 12, 1976 the Bundestag adopted a new Bill, which permits abortion on medical and emergency grounds. The new law does not permit abortion on demand but specifies conditions under which abortion is legal (*Sozial Report*, July 1976): where there is a risk to the life or health of the pregnant woman or to the physical or mental health of the child; in cases of rape; or where there is the risk of other serious disadvantage to the pregnant woman.

Before an abortion can be obtained, a woman must receive medical and social advice from a doctor or recognized advisory service. She must also obtain a doctor's certificate indicating that the medical conditions have been fulfilled. The abortion must then be performed in a hospital by a doctor other than the one providing the certificate. Insurance companies and state assistance programs cover all costs incurred in abortion. The Bundestag has also addressed the issue of birth control by providing free advice on contraception and free provision of contraceptive devices under social assistance schemes.

Another prominent woman in the present West German government is Marie Schlei – the first woman to head the Ministry of Economic Co-operation. Prior to her appointment she served in the chancellor's office. In her new role Schlei has created a new department concerned with women's affairs, in particular with the advancement of women in developing countries.

One last woman in West German politics deserves mention, namely, Dr Hildegarde Hamm-Brucher – Parliamentary State Secretary for Foreign Affairs. Widely regarded as the only woman with even a faint chance of achieving government leadership, she is one of the more liberal women politicians and believes that, although women in West Germany have made some psychological advances, they have not yet become integrated into politics.

Dr Helge Pross – a woman sociologist member of the parliamentary commission on 'Women and Society' – has also emphasized the importance of attitudinal change in West Germany. Referring to the status of women in West German society she stated in 1977 that, although the position of women was changing slowly, it would take 'to the end of the century' before women achieved true equality, especially in terms of psychological and attitudinal equality. 'The problem isn't the law,' she said, 'the problem is the way people think' (*The New York Times*, January 18, 1977).

This paper has discussed two separate yet closely related issues: women in politics, and women's rights. More specifically, it has discussed the role that women in politics have played in advancing women's rights. The final question to be answered is whether progress has been made in relation to both these issues. The question of 'progress' is a thorny one. The term is relative and must be viewed within the context of a particular society.

It could be argued that women have indeed made considerable progress in terms of increased numbers, greater representation, and greater influence. In France women have made inroads in the realm of government. In West Germany there are now three women Vice Presidents of the Bundestag and a woman minister. Most significantly, a woman has become Prime Minister in Britain. Given these facts, it can be concluded that women certainly have made gains in government during the past few years in all three countries. (See the summary in the appendix to this paper.)

On the other hand, relative to the total population and to the composition of the government as a whole, women cannot be considered adequately represented or well integrated into politics. Given the fact that women represent over half of the total population of each country, they are seriously under-represented in the political processes in both the legislative and the executive branches of government. In the next generation, perhaps, women will become more fully integrated in politics. For the time being, however, women in government are the exception rather than the rule. The role that women in politics have played in improving the status of women is more impressive. Substantial progress has been made within the last few years in all three countries in regard to women's legal rights to employment, to education, and in the family. These legal rights are in fact prerequisites for meaningful political integration.

Although the legal status of women has improved considerably, attitudinal changes have been slower, but they are evident nevertheless: '(T)hings are changing slowly. Already there are big differences in expectations and in education, in life styles, between men and women under 30 and those over 30' (*The New York Times*, January 19, 1977). This observation was borne out by a poll conducted by the Commission of the European Communities in May 1975 (European Community Information Service, 1976). The poll, conducted in the nine member countries – Belgium, Denmark, France, West Germany, Ireland, Italy, Luxemburg, the Netherlands, and the United Kingdom – was the most extensive international poll on sex roles and men's and women's attitudes toward social problems. One of the findings was that politics was still considered to be a 'masculine field' by both men and women *but much less so by young women and by well-educated individuals*. In fact the poll concluded that sex affected attitudes less than did age differences (i.e. 'the generation gap') and the effects of national culture and history.

Of the individuals questioned, 35 per cent thought that politics should be left to men – a view most pronounced in West Germany, Belgium, and Luxemburg. Also, 38 per cent of those polled (42 per cent of the men and 33 per cent of the women) expressed a preference for a male representative in parliament. The most favorable attitude toward women's participation in politics was found in those countries where women have participated in the electoral and political process the longest, a prime example being the United Kingdom. Although the issue of women's participation in society was not considered a very great problem in the United Kingdom, it was in contrast considered particularly important in France.

Overall, the poll underscored the importance of age and education in the formation of attitudes, especially as they related to women in politics. The fact that younger and better educated individuals more readily accept women in positions of leadership is a sign that societal attitudes have in fact begun to change. It is realistic to expect that this trend will continue, especially as equal rights legislation is more fully implemented and more individuals receive better educational opportunities. Moreover, recent legislative reforms – marriage law, family law, abortion, social security provisions, etc. – will very much affect the lives of the younger generation. It is in both their immediate and their future impact that legal reforms are inextricably linked to changes in attitudes and, ultimately, to the status of women.

As women benefit from greater educational and professional opportunities, they will assume more – and more important and influential – positions in government. Despite national variations it is possible to generalize that the advances made in the sphere of women's rights have been to a considerable extent the result of the actions and influence of women in positions of political leadership. The continued expansion and implementation of women's rights can best be ensured by women themselves; and if past performance is an indication of future progress, women in roles of executive political leadership will undoubtedly be instrumental in the creation of a more equal society.

NOTES

(1) Humanities cover such fields as archeology, history, languages, letters, library science, philosophy, psychology, and theology. Education includes pedagogy (including subjects studied at teacher-training institutes) and physical education.
(2) *The New York Times* (November 28, 1974), p. 30. For an account of the first victory in the abortion debate, see *L'Express* 'Pour la loi Simone Veil,' (25 November to December 1, 1974), pp. 30–3.
(3) *L'Express* (December 30, 1974 to January 5, 1975), p. 59. The results were: 55 per cent of the respondents chose Veil as first choice; 49 per cent Chirac; 45 per cent, Giroud; 41 per cent, Pontatowski; 30 per cent, Lecamuet; and 28 per cent, Fourcade.
(4) Both *Punch* and *Time* have tipped Shirley Williams as a future prime minister, and *L'Express* has made references to this possibility as well. See 'Madame le futur premier ministre,' *L'Express* (February 17–23, 1975), pp. 68–9. (This article is primarily about Margaret Thatcher.)
(5) In contrast, there exists in Belgium a special women's party – the Parti Féministe Unifié (PFU). In the election of March 1974 Belgian voters were the first to have an option of a female candidate in all major cities. The PFU was founded in September 1972; and its platform, which accepts men but not for office or to stand for election, is for equal pay, opportunity, education, and social security.
(6) *German International* (March 1974), p. 14. Half of the members of the Bundestag are drawn from lists made up by the parties; the other half are elected directly.

REFERENCES AND FURTHER READING

British Information Services (1971, 1975) *Women in Britain* (New York).
British Record (New York: British Information Services, 1974–5).
Christian Science Monitor (Boston, 1974–5).
Current Biographies (New York: H. W. Wilson, January 1967).
Current World Leaders: Biographies and News (Pasadena, Calif.: M. R. Cranshaw, 1974–5).
Deutsche Bundestag (1976) *Zwischenbericht der Enquete-Kommission Frau und Gesellschaft gemass Beschluss des Deutschen Bundestages* (Bonn, November 11).
Equal Opportunities Commission (1977) *Women and Low Incomes* (London, November).
European Community Information Service (1976) *European Community: Background Information* (New York, March 5).
Federal Republic of Germany, Press and Information Office (1973) *The World of Women* (Bonn).

French Embassy, Press and Information Division (1974) *Chirac Cabinet* (New York, May).

French Embassy, Press and Information Division (1975) *Giroud, Françoise* (New York).

French Embassy, Press and Information Division (1976) *Delegation for the Condition of Women* (New York).

French Embassy, Press and Information Division (1977) *The Second Barre Cabinet* (New York, March 30).

French Embassy, Press and Information Division (1979), *The Third Barre Cabinet* (New July).

German International (Bonn, 1975).

German Tribune (Hamburg, 1964, 1975).

International Who's Who, 38th edn (London: Europa Publications, 1974–5).

International Yearbook and Statesmen's Who's Who (London: Mercury House Reference Books, 1965–76).

Le Monde (Paris, 1974–7).

L'Express (Paris, 1974–7).

Le Soir (Brussels, Spring 1975).

Ms (New York, 1974–7).

New Statesman (London, 1977).

Punch (London, 1974–5).

Regner, Annemarie (ed.), *Equal Opportunities for Women* (Heidelberg, 1977).

Sozial Report (Bonn: Inter Nationes, 1975–7).

Sunday Times (London, 1977).

The Bulletin (Bonn: Federal Republic of Germany, Press and Information Office, 1974–5).

The Europa Yearbook (London: Europa Publications, 1965–79).

The New York Times (New York, 1969–77).

The Statesman's Yearbook (New York: St Martin's Press; London: Macmillan, 1969–70 to 1978–9).

The Times (London, 1974–5).

Time (New York, 1974–7).

United Nations Educational, Scientific, and Cultural Organization (UNESCO) (1976) *Statistical Yearbook, 1975* (Paris).

APPENDIX

Number of posts on executive level occupied by women/total number of posts (and percentage of women occupying executive level positions).

	1965	1966	1967	1968	1969	1970	1971	1972	1973	1974	1975	1976	1977	1978	1979
France															
Ministers	0/22 (0%)	0/21 (0%)	0/21 (0%)	0/22 (0%)	0/20 (0%)	0/19 (0%)	0/18 (0%)	0/21 (0%)	0/22 (0%)	0/22 (0%)	1/14 (7%)	1/16 (6%)	1/15 (7%)	2/20 (10%)	2/20 (10%)
Secretaries of state	0/4 (0%)	0/5 (0%)	0/10 (0%)	0/6 (0%)	1/10 (10%)	1/13 (8%)	0/13 (0%)	1/15 (7%)	1/14 (7%)	1/13 (8%)	3/22 (14%)	3/23 (13%)	3/25 (12%)	2/25 (8%)	2/20 (10%)
United Kingdom															
Cabinet Members	1/23 (4%)	1/23 (4%)	1/22 (5%)	1/21 (5%)	1/23 (4%)	1/21 (5%)	1/18 (6%)	1/17 (6%)	1/18 (6%)	2/20 (10%)	2/23 (9%)	2/20 (10%)	1/24 (4%)	1/24 (4%)	0/22 (0%)
Ministers not in Cabinet	2/31 (6%)	2/31 (6%)	5/27 (19%)	3/26 (12%)	3/21 (14%)	5/24 (21%)	1/20 (5%)	1/22 (5%)	1/28 (4%)	1/26 (4%)	1/25 (4%)	1/28 (4%)	1/23 (4%)	1/26 (4%)	2/23 (9%)
West Germany															
Ministers	1/22 (5%)	1/22 (5%)	1/20 (5%)	1/20 (5%)	1/20 (5%)	1/23 (4%)	1/16 (6%)	1/17 (6%)	1/17 (6%)	1/18 (6%)	1/16 (6%)	1/16 (6%)	2/16 (13%)	1/16 (6%)	1/14 (7%)
Parliamentary State Secretaries	0/19 (0%)	0/19 (0%)	0/19 (0%)	0/19 (0%)	0/23 (0%)	2/23 (9%)	2/15 (13%)	1/15 (7%)	1/15 (7%)	1/18 (6%)	1/20 (5%)	1/20 (5%)	0/20 (0%)	1/20 (5%)	1/16 (6%)

France: De Gaulle (RPF-UNR-UDT-Vᵉ République-UDR)* is president from December 1958. Pompidou (UDR-Gaullist) assumes office in November 1970. D'Estaing (Republican Party) assumes office in May 1974.

United Kingdom: Wilson (Labour) is prime minister from October 1964. Heath (Conservative) assumes office in June 70. Wilson (Labour) assumes office in March 1974. Callaghan (Labour) assumes office in April 1976.

West Germany: Kiesinger is chancellor from December 1966. Brandt (SPD) assumes office in October 1969. Schmidt (SPD) assumes office in May 1974.

* De Gaulle's party label shifted frequently:
(1951) 1st party label – RPF (Rassemblement du Peuple Français)
(1958) 2nd party label – UNR (Union pour la Nouvelle République)
(1962) 3rd party label – UDT (Union Démocratique du Travail)
(1967) 4th party label – Vᵉ République
(1968) 5th party label – Union de Démocrats pour la République

Sources: International Yearbook and Statesmen's Who's Who, 1965–1977;
The Europa Yearbook, 1965–1977;
The Statesman's Yearbook, 1969/70–1978/79; and (for 1977) information also provided by embassies' information services.

4

Women in the Economic, Political, and Cultural Elites in Finland

ELINA HAAVIO-MANNILA

The classical elite theorists Pareto and Mosca distinguished between 'elite' and 'mass' in order to substitute them for Marxist concepts of class relationships. In place of the Marxist juxtaposition of class society and classlessness they substituted the idea of the cyclical replacement of elites *in perpetuo* (Giddens, 1973, p. 106). The term 'elite' can be used in a very broad sense to include all those who occupy important privileged positions in hierarchies, whether in terms of wealth or prestige (Aron, 1970, p. 154). But it is often useful to separate the decision-making 'power' elite from groups who hold a high rank in society without, however, direct influence in managing the society. Anthony Giddens has remarked that the term 'elite' may refer to those who lead in any activity – actors and sportsmen, as well as political or economic leaders. The former lead in fame or achievement, whereas the latter head specific social organizations possessing an internal authority structure – the state or an economic enterprise (Giddens, 1973, pp. 119–20).

In his analysis of social class and power in Canada, *The Vertical Mosaic*, John Porter (1965) has defined those who have power to make major decisions for the society as elite and those who do not have such power as non-elite (p. 25). According to him, 'power arises because of the general social need for order, and power roles are essential to all forms of social organization' (p. 202).

This paper describes and analyzes the participation of Finnish women in the decision-making elites, in the Porterian sense, employing historical, statistical, and survey data. Women's role in some strategic elites (Keller, 1963) is investigated, partly using the classification of Porter (1965) who has written

> In the modern complex society the power functions have been broken up into separate but interrelated systems or sub-systems. These sub-systems, it has been suggested, are the economic, the political, the administrative, the defensive, and the ideological . . . People in power roles belong to an elite. Thus in each of these interrelated systems of power there is an elite. The fused power roles of earlier societies give way, with social development, to separate elite groups at the top of separated institutional orders . . . Specialization of function is a factor limiting interchange . . . [It] is also a reason for the bringing together of elites at the level of a national power structure, because . . . some kind of over-all co-ordination of the social system is necessary. (pp. 202–9)

The economic, administrative, political, and ideological (and/or cultural) elites of Finland are each discussed separately, from the point of view of women's participation in them. This does not deny the existence of centralized power nuclei in Finland that combine the highest elites of different sectors of society. Within such centralized power groups women suffer a special disadvantage because of informal segregation of the sexes and the ambiguous rules governing these power centers.

With the development of modern societies ascribed statuses are losing importance and achieved statuses are gaining it. At the same time elites have become more important: 'The development of industrial societies can properly be depicted as a movement from a class system to a system of elites, from a social hierarchy based upon the inheritance of property to one based upon merit and achievement' (Bottomore, 1970, p. 171).

The importance of sex, as ascribed status, has greatly declined in the educational systems of the developed countries. There seems not, however, to be a similar decline of sex differences in such social rewards as occupational status and income. Men and women have not had an *equal* chance of entry into elite positions, and the representation of the sexes is certainly not random at the elite level of society. We may, however, expect some levelling off of the impact of sex differences as women are further emancipated in other social sectors.

In the following pages an attempt is made to show how women's participation in decision-making elites has proceeded in Finland during this century. Compared with other Scandinavian countries Finland has a tradition of a high proportion of women in education, the labor force, and politics (see Table 4.1 and Haavio-Mannila, 1970). It is interesting to see what effects this has had on the participation of women in the management of Finnish society.

Table 4.1   *Percentage of the total population of men and women aged 15–64 years with some vocational education, with academic education, and with full time employment: Scandinavian countries, 1972*

Education and employment		Denmark	Finland	Norway	Sweden
Has some vocational	M	38	33	57	46
education	W	27	34	42	36
With academic	M	4	3	8	7
education	W	1	5	1	3
Is full time employed	M	79	54	75	70
	W	33	51	20	26
(N)	M	(497)	(477)	(496)	(497)
	W	(498)	(517)	(509)	(508)

Source: Allardt (1975).

PROPORTION OF WOMEN IN DIFFERENT ELITE GROUPS

Economic Elite

Before examining women's participation in economic decision-making in Scandinavia, it is important to note their relatively low level of income. According to Erik Allardt's (1975) study on welfare and need satisfaction in Scandinavia, in 1972 Finnish women working full-time for twelve months a year earned on average 64·9 per cent of the incomes earned by men, as can be seen from Table 4.2. Women very seldom belonged to high income

Table 4.2 *Individual incomes of men and women and women's income as a percentage of men's income among full-time all-year workers:*[b] *Scandinavia, 1972.*

Income[a]	Denmark		Finland		Norway		Sweden	
	Men	Women	Men	Women	Men	Women	Men	Women
No income	5	41	8	30	6	51	4	28
Low	16	35	27	40	17	33	20	49
Medium	34	18	29	20	42	15	55	20
High	45	6	35	10	34	1	21	3
Total	100	100	99	100	99	100	100	100
(*N*)	(457)	(463)	(463)	(480)	(494)	(504)	(488)	(491)
Women's income as % of men's incomes	61·4		64·9		60·4		67·5	

a In Denmark, Norway, and Sweden, low = 1–19,999 crowns, medium = 20,000 –39,999 crowns and high = 40,000 + crowns a year; in Finland, low = 1–7,999 marks, medium = 8,000–13,999 marks, and high = 14,000 + marks a year (coding instructions used by Research Group of Comparative Sociology, University of Helsinki),
b Family workers and farmers excluded.

Source: Unpublished material for Allardt, (1975).

groups on the basis of their own earning power. This large disparity is only partly explained by the high percentage of women without any income at all. Of the four Scandinavian countries, Sweden had the smallest income difference between the sexes and Norway the largest.

Statistical information on the incomes of men and women in Finland is consistent with the survey data. However, when occupational categories are controlled, sex differences in income diminish. Women's wages then vary between 70 and 90 per cent of men's wages (Prime Minister's office, 1975).

The very low proportion of women in the economic decision-making elite can clearly be seen from Tables 4.3 and 4.4. These tables are based on two studies: one that investigated the role of women among the Finnish economic leadership (Hernesniemi, 1968), and another that studied elites in the *Who's Who* in Finland (Kartovaara, 1972).

Table 4.3   *Percentages of women among leaders of economic life:*
Finland, 1968.

Field of Occupation	% of women	No. of persons
Industry	3·1	3,000
Commerce	2·0	6,500
Pharmacies	49·5	535
Banks and insurance:		
Merchant banks	2·3	950
Co-operative banks	4·4	478
Savings banks	3·2	342
Insurance companies	2·0	200
State administration	3·2	1,300
Local administration:		
Towns and market towns	2·3	1,000
Parliament and communal councils:		
Parliament members	17·0	200
Communal councilors:		
Whole country	7·9	12,325
Towns and market towns	14·3	2,491
Helsinki	31·2	77
Foundations and associations:		
Foundations	6·0	33
Labor market organizations and unions	3·5	400
Other economic associations	5·0	120
Other fields or occupations:		
University professors	3·6	590
Chief physicians	8·9	119
Economy chiefs of hospitals	2·5	80
Solicitors	4·2	313
Architects (owners of offices)	13·0	468
Main editors of newspapers	1·0	104
Directors of personal service organizations		
restaurants, travel agencies, etc.)	2·4	500
Total (communal councilors excluded)	4·5	16,592

Source: Hernesniemi (1968).

The percentage of women in the *Who's Who* was analyzed for the years 1909, 1934, and 1970 and was at its highest in 1934 (Table 4.4). According to Figure 4.1, there were relatively many women listed in the book in the 1920s, 1930s, and 1950s. Since 1966 the percentage of women has declined, contrary to expectations based on the increasing numbers of women in higher education, in the labor force, and in politics. The decline of women's participation in the Finnish elite may be related to changes in the very structure of that elite. According to Kartovaara, three groups have gained major importance since 1909: the economic, the scientific and educational, and the military elites. In all these groups the proportion of women is low.

In Hernesniemi's study of economic elites the only fields in which

Table 4.4   *Percentage of women in different elite groups in* Who's
Who: *Finland, 1909, 1934, and 1970.*

Nature of group	1909 %	(N)	1934 %	(N)	1970 %	(N)
Politics	12·5	(8)	20·0	(10)	20·7	(29)
Civil service	—	(40)	6·4	(47)	8·4	(83)
Labor market organizations	—	(2)	—	(3)	—	(5)
Economic life	—	(24)	3·3	(60)	1·8	(111)
Arts	32·0	(25)	34·9	(43)	42·9	(49)
Science and education	7·1	(42)	12·5	(72)	7·7	(143)
Church	3·1	(32)	—	(17)	6·3	(18)
Health care	—	(14)	—	(14)	8·7	(20)
Mass media	—	(21)	7·7	(13)	5·9	(17)
Agriculture	—	(5)	—	(5)	—	(4)
Army	—	(4)	—	(10)	—	(20)
Total	7·3	(217)	11·7	(294)	10·2	(499)

Source: Kartovaara (1972), app. 5.

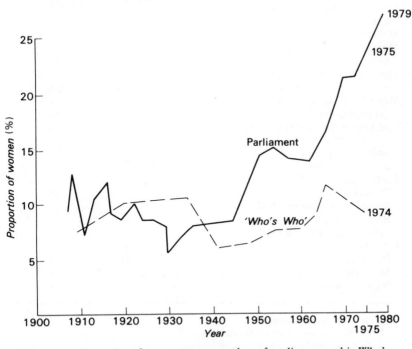

Figure 4.1 *Proportion of women among members of parliament and in* Who's
Who: *Finland, 1907–79.*

Sources: Report of the Committee (1973), p. 133; and Haavio-Mannila (1968), p. 76,
completed by the author with reference to later years.

women had a relatively high representation (49·5 per cent in 1968) was pharmacy – owning and operating a drugstore. There is a very high proportion of women among pharmacists in Finland; of the 1973–4 graduates in pharmacy, 87 per cent were women.

Table 4.5 *Percentage of women among decision-making bodies of some economic and labor market organizations: Finland, 1974.*

Organization and position		% of women	No. of persons
Co-operative concerns			
Delegates of the conference	OTK[1]	15	68
	KK	13	72
	SOK	10	199
Members of the council	OTK	2	40
	KK	2	40
	SOK	17	18
Members of the government	OTK	9	11
	KK	9	11
	SOK	—	8
Central Union of Agricultural Producers			
Members		37	33,976
Members on the boards of local farmers' associations		13	4,040
Members on the boards of regional farmers' unions		4	224
Members of the delegation of the central union		5	61
Members of the executive board		—	14
Employers' confederations			
Finnish Employers' Confederation:			
Delegates		—	58
Members in governing body		—	16
Body of leaders		—	7
Confederation of Commerce Employers:			
Delegates		4	54
Members in governing body		7	14
Body of leaders		—	9

1 OTK = Osuustukkukauppa
   KK = Kulutusosuuskuntien Keskusliitto
   SOK = Suomen Osuuskauppojen Keskusliitto
   These are the three central organizations of co-operative concerns, which take care of a large part of retail trade in Finland.

Source: Prime Minister's Office (1975) pp. 97–9.

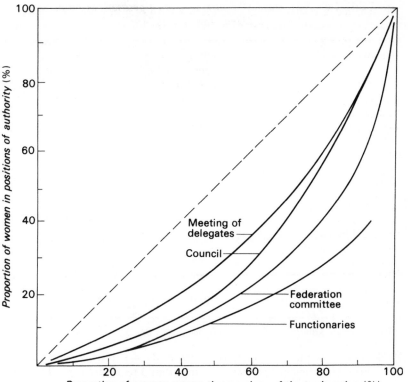

Figure 4.2 *Proportion of women among the total membership and among persons in positions of trust in the Central Federation of Trade Unions: Finland (SAK), 1975.*

Source: Räsänen (1976), p. 6.

The tiny proportion of women in decision-making bodies of both the employers' organizations and the unions is obvious when Table 4.5 and Figure 4.2 are considered. There are also few women in the highest organs of the co-operative concerns in Finland.

In state administration the proportion of women seems somewhat higher than in the economic elite. Table 4.6 presents the percentage of women who held leading positions (salary class B) in various Finnish government departments in 1974. The average percentage of women in government posts was 10·0, compared to the 4·5 per cent in 1968 found by Hernesniemi in her study on economic elites (see Table 4.3). According to several studies, professional women often go into government work because they are less deterred than men by relatively low civil-service incomes and because they prefer the stability and open rules of recruitment and advancement in the state bureaucracy to the system that usually prevails in private business.

The number of women in leading positions in government in 1974 (Table 4.6) was much larger than it was in 1968 (Table 4.3). One reason for this is the rapid development of the state administration between 1968 and

Table 4.6 *Percentage of women in leading positions in ministries: Finland, January 1974.*

Ministry	% of leading positions held by women	No. of positions
Cabinet office	13·0	23
Foreign affairs	2·1	94
Justice	0·6	359
Interior	9·9	252
Defense	0·2	413
Finance	3·7	240
Education	23·8	953
Agriculture and forestry	3·9	439
Communications	1·4	291
Trade and industry	4·1	222
Social and health affairs	15·9	170
Labor	4·1	49
Attorney general	—	10
Total	10·0	3,515

Source: Prime Minister's office (1975), p. 38.

1974. As a consequence women were able to advance into leading positions in government, their proportion growing from 3 to 10 per cent. They are represented mostly in the leadership of the Ministries of Education and of Social and Health Affairs. The large number of top positions in the Ministry of Education account for most of the women in state administration. In most other departments their role is limited (less than 5 per cent in 1974), as is the case in most economic elite groups.

Political Elite

Finnish women do not differ in political activity from their Scandinavian sisters (see Table 4.7). However, compared with Finnish men, women's activity is high because men's is relatively low. Similar results have been observed for education and economics. Finnish women have high activity rates in comparison with Finnish men but not in comparison with other Scandinavian women.

In 1974 the percentage of women among members of Finnish political parties varied between 26 and 60 per cent (Table 4.8), but men dominated as one ascended the party hierarchy. At the top the percentage of women fluctuated between 8 and 25 per cent. In most parties one in nine or ten executives is a woman. Slightly more women are found in the governing circles of bourgeois parties than of socialist parties.

The representation of women in the democratically elected political decision-making bodies (i.e. Parliament and the communal councils) has traditionally been higher in Finland than elsewhere in Scandinavia (Haavio-Mannila, 1972, p. 162). However, Sweden is approaching the

Table 4.7   *Political activity of men and women: Scandinavian
countries, 1972 (%)*

Political activity		Denmark	Finland	Norway	Sweden
Voted in the last general election	M	83	76	81	85
	W	80	78	74	84
Belongs to a party organization	M	17	10	19	14
	W	9	4	4	8
Belongs to some club or organization	M	85	69	81	89
	W	57	56	63	71
Not easily replaced in the organization (members only)[a]	M	8	11	7	11
	W	5	9	4	8
Has asked for the floor in a meeting of an organization or association	M	45	46	54	65
	W	15	30	28	34
Has contacted a politician in order to influence a decision[b]	M	21	22	26	21
	W	8	9	10	12
(N)	M	(457)	(483)	(494)	(488)
	W	(463)	(480)	(504)	(491)

a   Considers that it would be difficult to fill one's place without special organizational arrangements.
b   Has tried to influence a decision in a community or on a political question by making a personal contact with a politician, an official, or some other person in a decision-making capacity.

Source: Allardt (1975).

Finnish percentage in Parliament and has already passed it in the communal councils. Compared with the position of women in legislative parties elsewhere, the 26 per cent of women (in 1979) in the Finnish Parliament – the country's true decision-making body – is quite high. As Figure 4.1 shows, the proportion of women there has considerably increased since the early 1960s. How can we account for this? One reason may be the lively sex-role discussions in the country, which have made female voters aware of the importance of voting for women candidates. According to a survey, only 10 per cent of men voted for women candidates in communal elections in 1976; 44 per cent of the women did so (Haavio-Mannila, 1978, p. 22).

There is not much difference among the parties as regards votes cast for women candidates. The agrarian parties and the Swedish-speaking party, representing an ethnic minority, send the lowest proportion of women to

Table 4.8 Percentage of women among members of political parties and governing bodies of parties: Finland, November 1974.

Party	Members Total	Members Women (%)	Last party conference Total	Last party conference Women (%)	Party council Total	Party council Women (%)	Party government Total	Party government Women (%)
National coalition party	81,500	50	893	24	61	20	17	18
Swedish People's Party in Finland	43,500	32	212	17	130	21	28	14
Liberal Party	18,000	34	268	27	48	27	20	25
Finnish Rural Party	30,000	30	900	22	60	17	16	12
Unification Party of the Finnish People	15,000	40	1,500	40	46	20	15	13
Finnish Christian Union	11,000	60–70	341	30–40	60	15	24	12
Center Party	164,500	45	1,791	9	133	24	24	12
Social Democratic Party of Finland	88,000	33	324	10	60	5	13	8
Democratic League of the People of Finland	56,000	29	243	20	45	13	24	12
Finnish Communist Party	41,000	26	494	11	—	—	35	9

Source: Prime Minister's Office (1975), table 68.

parliament and also generate relatively few votes for women candidates. The proportion of women candidates to elected Members of Parliament is very similar, indicating that it is advantageous to have many women candidates run for parliamentary seats.

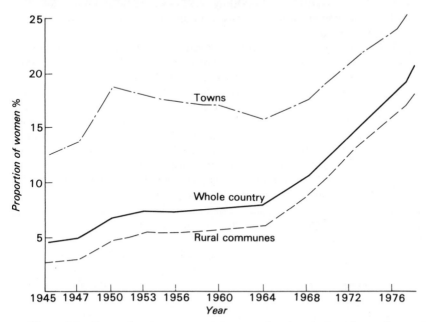

Figure 4.3 *Proportion of women among persons elected to communal councils in the whole country, in towns, and in rural communes: Finland, 1945–76.*

Sources: Haavio-Mannila (1970 in 1972), p. 163; Central Statistical Office of Finland (1974), p. 15; data collected by Suomen Naisjärjestöjen Keskusliitto for 1972 and 1976.

In Finland women have traditionally held more important positions in urban than in rural areas (Figure 4.3). Urbanization thus means increasing numbers of women in political decision-making bodies. We find that women themselves have more options for influence in political rather than in economic life, where advancement to higher positions comes by appointment, not by election. It is in politics – the studies show – where the proportion of women has increased most in this century.

Ideological and Cultural Elites
We shall next investigate the participation of Finnish women in the ideological elite. Porter (1965) has designated as an ideological elite:

> ... those at the top of ideological institutions, specifically in the modern period, the mass media, the educational system, and the churches. Although the ideological elite does not have the control over human and material resources that the economic elite has, it does have some power over people's minds. Thus the ideological elite may at times be in coalition with, and at other times in conflict with, other elite groups. (p. 460).

Let us first look at the mass media. In 1968 there was only one woman among the 104 senior editors of Finnish newspapers (Table 4.3). In *Who's Who* a declining percentage of women has been represented in the mass media (Table 4.4). However, women often head women's magazines, and some women executives hold leading positions in radio and television. But there are no women among the boards of directors of the state-owned radio and television corporations.

The relatively low percentage of women among holders of doctoral or licenciate's degrees (12 per cent) does not totally explain the low proportion of women among higher education faculties. Table 4.9 shows that in 1970 women were only 3 per cent of full professors and 7 per cent of assistant professors and docents. At the lower level of university teaching, women counted for one-fifth of the teaching staff. Women are still a small minority in academe, even though 48·5 per cent of the students at the universities and equivalent institutions were women in 1973–4, as were 49.5 per cent of the graduates of these schools and 40·1 per cent of holders of academic degrees. The leadership of higher education still lies in the hands of men, but women dominate the teachers' positions in primary and secondary education.

Table 4.9 *Percentage of women among teachers at universities, etc.:*
Finland, end of spring term 1970

Whole country	% of women	Total no. of teachers
Professor	3	648
Assistant professor	7	364
Docent	7	770
Lecturer and teacher	21	451
Assistant and amanuens:		
whole time	19	1,595
part time	22	140
Part time teacher	17	1,115
Other teacher	17	83
	14	5,166
University of Helsinki		
Professor	2	217
Assistant professor	7	110
Docent	8	495
Lecturer and teacher	22	144
Assistant and amanuens:		
whole time	26	539
part time	33	60
Part time teacher	21	251
Other teacher	9	34
Total of teachers	16	1,850

Source: Central Statistical Office of Finland (1973), pp. 150–1.

Porter (1965) has also mentioned *church* leadership as an intellectual elite. One of the few survivals of sex discrimination in Finland is the exclusion of women from the Lutheran clergy. In a survey in 1976 individual parishes were asked to comment on this question; 73 per cent of the parishes supported women's right to become ministers of the church, and only 13 per cent opposed it. Women are hopeful of change, because they constitute almost half of the students at the theological faculty but may be appointed only to lecturer's positions in the parishes.

The decision-making power of artists is limited, but they are often recognized as among the sophisticated *cultural elite* of a country. In this role they influence the general intellectual climate.

Table 4.4 indicates that the percentage of women in the arts elite is much higher than in other elite groups cited in *Who's Who*. In contrast to most other elite groups, except in the sphere of politics, women have increased their representation in the artistic elite since 1909. Their presence is concentrated in the performing arts – singing, dancing, and acting – but there are a few women composers, directors, sculptors, painters, and writers (see Table 4.10). Creative art is still largely male dominated.

Table 4.10   *Percentage of women among members of artists' associations: Finland, 1965.*

Type of artists	% of women	Total members in the association
Composers	2·2	45
Stage managers	6·6	61
Graphic artists	20·8	96
Sculptors	21·4	70
Musicians	25·0	120
Architects	27·2	736
Theater directors and producers	27·4	124
Painters	28·3	233
Writers	39·2	332
Actors	48·6	677
Soloists	57·4	115
Industrial designers	69·4	447
Reciters	70·0	120
Dancers	81·4	264

Source: Suolinna (1965, p. 34.

The proportion of women painters and architects has not increased over time (Tables 4.11 and 4.12). As shown in Suolinna's (1965) study, there were more women artists in the 1930s and 1940s than in the 1950s; later data are unfortunately lacking. An historically interesting finding is that the proportion of women painters was larger in the late nineteenth century than in this century.

In contrast with the other elite groups (see Tables 4.13 and 4.14) female artists are more often married than male artists. Kartovaara (1972) has

Table 4.11   *Percentage of women among painters according to year of first art exhibition: Finland, 1650–1962.*

Year of first art exhibition of the painter	% of women	total no. of artists
1650–99	—	4
1700–49	10·0	10
1750–99	—	12
1800–49	14·8	27
1850–99	38·4	146
1900–09	13·9	109
1910–19	14·8	155
1920–29	15·1	139
1930–39	30·9	149
1940–49	25·2	127
1950–59	20·0	90
1960–62	50·0	4
Total	22·5	970

Source: Suolinna (1965), p. 35.

Table 4.12   *Percentage of women among graduates in architecture at the Helsinki Technical University, 1901–64.*

Year	% of women	Total no. of graduates in architecture
1901–09	16·1	56
1910–19	19·7	71
1920–29	29·2	65
1930–39	30·3	152
1940–49	38·7	137
1950–59	28·6	325
1960–64	21·1	180
Total	27·6	986

Source: Suolinna (1965), p. 27.

analyzed this by referring to the low incomes of artists and to the provider role of men; a woman can be active in the arts while supported by her husband, but a male artist is prevented from marrying because he cannot support a family. Thus, the high proportion of women in the arts elite may be partly explained by the low economic rewards of artistic activity. Economically, the artist belongs to a 'leisure class' and is supported by somebody else. Wives of wealthy husbands sometimes belong to that class.

Apart from artists, women's opportunities in the ideological elite seem to be almost as limited as those in the economic elite.

BARRIER AGAINST WOMEN'S ADVANCEMENT TO ELITE
POSITIONS

A notable obstacle in a woman's career is the resistance of many persons to
working under a female boss. Even though general sex-role attitudes in
Finland became more equality oriented between 1967 and 1970, there was
little change in the preference for male supervision:[1]

In 1967 only 23% of the women and 7% of the men and in 1970 23%
of the women and 11% of the men would choose the job where the boss
is a woman. Male bosses were preferred by 58% of the men and 43% of
the women in 1967: by 52% and 44%, respectively, in 1970. The
attitudes of women on this matter did not change much; even 'no
difference' answers increased only from 29% to 31%. Among men,
both the willingness to work under a woman and 'no difference' replies
increased a little (the latter from 31% to 35%). Furthermore, it should
be pointed out that among women, the willingness to work under a
woman is most common in the lower occupational groups, in the rural
areas, and among older women. Choosing a woman as a boss may thus
be a symptom of willingness to *retain* sex segregation at work places,
not an indication of a modern egalitarian orientation. The equality
orientation is probably represented by the 'no difference' responses. It
is most common among women in leading positions, in high income
and educational groups, in large towns, and in Southern Finland.
    Among men, the traditional preference for male bosses is greatest in
the highest status occupational groups. This indicates that the
competition between men and women is most intense there. Farmers
and workers accept women as bosses better than white collar
employees do. The liberal attitude of peripheral Finnish men towards
women's emancipation is again interesting to note. (Haavio-Mannila,
1972, pp. 102–3).[2]

According to a 1967 study in two Valkeakoski factories, the men
particularly opposed women acquiring power in society. They supported
statements like: 'women should not have leading positions, the husband
should have more power in important family decisions;' 'women should
stay away from discussions about politics and society matters;' and 'it is
good for peace in the family that male and female jobs are kept separate'
(first factor in Table 4.13).
On the other hand, some sex-role attitudes were related more to social
class and occupation than to sex. Equality-of-the-sexes statements were
supported more by white collar employees, almost regardless of sex, than
by manual workers. Examples of such white-collar attitudes were: 'boys as
well as girls should learn how to keep house;' 'girls should be encouraged to
choose technical occupations;' 'women should have as good possibilities for
leading positions in work life as men;' 'it is unnecessary to divide jobs
according to sex;' 'a married woman has as equal right for employment as
an unmarried one;' and 'a girl should get as good an education as a boy
does' (third factor in Table 4.13).

Table 4.13 *Strength of some sex-role attitudes among workers in two factories in Valkeakoski according to sex and type of work, 1967 (mean factor scores).*

	Men		Women	
Attitude dimension	*White collar*	*Manual workers*	*White collar*	*Manual workers*
I No power to women	0·49	0·49	0·40	0·42
II Women should participate in managing the society	0·40	0·37	0·45	0·51
III Equal and similar roles for men and women	0·46	0·41	0·50	0·37
IV Women should stay at home	0·49	0·46	0·42	·42
V Women may drink, smoke, and be unfaithful in marriage	0·43	0·53	0·52	0·47
(No. of interviewees)	(63)	(65)	(64)	(62)

Source: Unpublished results from a survey conducted by Veronica Stolte-Heiskanen and Elina Haavio-Mannila.

As regards women's participation in organizations (second factor) and the right of women to be employed (fourth factor), women were clearly demanding more rights than men were willing to give them, again regardless of social class. However, in attitudes towards women's emancipation on the dimension of 'male bad habits' (i.e. drinking, smoking, unfaithfulness), female white-collar workers and male manual laborers seemed to be the most liberal (fifth factor).

Also, data on six Finnish professional groups – architects, agronomists, academic foresters, lawyers, physicians, and engineers – show that the men in them are more reluctant than the women to give power to women (Eskola and Haavio-Mannila, 1975). Although 71 per cent of the professional women agreed with the statement that 'in order for the affairs of society to be managed, there should be equal numbers of men and women in its decision-making circles,' only 35 per cent of the men did so. Similar differences in response occurred with other questions. The only exception was the reaction to female bosses; 48 per cent of both male and female professionals agreed with the statement that 'it is kind of degrading for a man to have to work under a woman and take orders from her.' These seem to indicate deeply rooted prejudices against women in leading positions, even among women themselves.

SEX SEGREGATION

Another obstacle against women's advancement into the elites is formal and informal segregation of the sexes, particularly in careers. Men and women largely work in different kinds of occupations. In many companies (e.g. banks) men are recruited into jobs that lead directly into higher positions. They get leadership training and are free to participate in the informal gatherings of the decision-making male elite, from which women are usually barred. Women remain segregated and are usually ignored when career advancement is considered.

The limited informal communication at work across sex lines contrasted with same-sex shop talk has often been remarked (HS-Gallup, 1976). Women and men often belong to different categories at work, even when they have similar educations and even similar work positions. Not only does recruitment into elite positions presume a particular social background, but it also seems to require a male gender. Women are trapped in a vicious circle. Because they have for so long been excluded from elite positions, they find it difficult to gain access to them. As Porter (1965) remarked in his discussion on elites:

> Because their decisions are taken either in co-operation or in conflict with each other, they enter into a scheme of social relationships, and thus acquire a degree of social homogeneity which the masses do not have. Elites are more than statistical classes. Common educational background, kinship links, present and former partnerships, common membership in clubs, trade associations, positions on advisory bodies and philanthropic groups, all help to produce a social homogeneity of men in positions of power (p. 230).

This homogeneity might be threatened if a new element were introduced.

PRIOR EXPERIENCE OF SUCCESSFUL MALE AND FEMALE PROFESSIONALS

From studies of different experiences prior to assuming leadership roles it has been found that female Finnish economic leaders are older than equivalent males – on average 57 years old compared with 54 years old. Advancement into leading positions occurs later in life among women than men – at 42 years on average compared with 37 for men. Women leaders tend to have lower educational levels than men, related to the fact that they manage smaller enterprises in which the educational level of leaders in general is fairly low. Also, women leaders hold, according to Hernesniemi (1968), fewer positions of trust (i.e. board memberships, presidencies) in voluntary organizations than men – on average 1·1 compared with 2·1 for men.

According to the above-mentioned study of six professional groups – architects, agronomists, academic foresters, lawyers, physicians, and engineers – women in male-dominated academic professions have achieved more higher honors and degrees on the average than their male colleagues. Only women with very high educational attainments have the courage to enter male professions. Educational success is also an important predictor of later career advancement among women, but not among men. Here, in condensed form, are the factors contributing to career success for both men and women, as measured by income and by appropriateness of professional placement, according to this study (Eskola and Haavio-Mannila, 1975, p. 198):

For both sexes
(1) Broad scope of professional activity (extra jobs, committees organizations).
(2) Graduate academic degree.
(3) Contact with male coworkers outside working hours.
(4) Freedom from home-making obligations.
(5) Settled down in job and satisfaction with one's own work.

For women
(1) Good performance in secondary school.

(2) Organizational activity at school and university.
(3) Faithful service to same employer and advancement in this job.
(4) Contact with male coworkers during working hours.
(5) Contact with women coworkers during working hours.
(6) Location in eastern Finland.[3]
(7) Location in urban locality.
(8) Progressive attitude toward woman's role in working life.

For men
Good academic performance and motivation for achievement at university.
High prestige of father's profession.
Job changes.

Keeping up with professional literature.
Working overtime.

Married, wife not working.

The correlation analysis also included the following variables, for which no statistically significant connection with either income or appropriate placement could be observed: type of locality and region of secondary school; rapid completion of academic studies; spouse with same education as oneself; long work week in chief job; much time spent following developments in one's field; much time spent preparing lectures and articles; absence from work; more time at work spent with male rather than female coworkers; voted for women at parliamentary elections; has experienced discrimination due to sex; and attitudes toward changes in sex roles generally (not at work). Here are the conclusions based on these results:

> Without enumerating over again all the individual findings, we may note that the conditions necessary or contributing to the career success of men and women differ somewhat. For those interested in the success of women, it would seem to be necessary to aim at dividing the burden of housework more evenly between the two sexes and at reducing their number, to encourage women to adopt new sex role attitudes, and to make contact between men and women both at work and outside less

difficult. On the other hand, we are not sure that it is a good thing for women's career advancement to depend only on academic performance and on remaining steadily in the same job; on the contrary, we believe that women might also, to a greater extent than at present, change jobs, follow professional literature and take post-graduate degrees, and thus succeed under the same conditions as men. The connection between working overtime and the career success of men is probably dysfunctional from the point of view of men's health; it is highly probable that the higher mortality rates of men are due in part to their need to work overtime thus acquiring symptoms of stress in order to succeed. Another condition of a man's success is that he has a wife at home, taking care of the house and family. This is an advantage hardly likely to be obtained by women, even if the number of 'house-husbands' were to increase. The emancipation of women and their flight from the home may thus form a handicap to men's careers. The liberation of women will involve a reduction in the privileges of men. We may ask: is our society ready for such a change? (Eskola and Haavio-Mannila, 1975, p. 200)

DIFFERENCE IN THE MARITAL STATUS OF THE MALE AND FEMALE ELITE

The marital status of elite Finnish men and women differs considerably, according to several studies (Tables 4.14 and 4.15). Women are much less likely to be married than men, and the disparity seems to have increased during the twentieth century, especially in the proportion of women and men who have never married. One-quarter to one-third of women in elite groups are single, compared with 2–3 per cent of the men. Women seem to find it more difficult to combine marriage with a successful career than do men. No difference has been found between the career success of married and non-married professional women. Married men, on the other hand, advance further in their careers than unmarried.

One reason for the high proportion of unmarried elite women is the old

Table 4.14 *Marital status of Finnish men and women in* Who's Who, *1909, 1934, and 1970 (%).*

	1909		1934		1970	
Marital status	*Men*	*Women*	*Men*	*Women*	*Men*	*Women*
Unmarried	25	29	8	46	2	23
Married once	72	57	78	43	84	45
Married twice or more	3	7	8	3	12	4
Divorced	—	—	1	3	1	14
Widowed	1	7	5	6	1	14
Total	101	100	100	101	100	100
(*N*)	(148)	(14)	(264)	(35)	(449)	(51)

Source: Kartovaara (1972).

Table 4.15 Marital status of men and women in the economic elite 1968, professionals 1967–8, Who's Who 1964, and the over-25 Finnish population 1960 (%)

Marital status	Economic elite, 1968		Professionals,[a] 1967–8		Who's Who 1964		Total population 1960	
	Men	Women	Men	Women	Men	Women	Men	Women
Unmarried	3	34	5	25	2	36	17	17
Married	96	48	91	66	87	57	78	63
Widowed or divorced	1	18	4	9	11	7	6	20
Total	100	100	100	100	100	100	100	100
(N)	(198)	(133)	(230)	(223)	(4,533)	(447)	(1.3 million)	(1.3 million)

[a] Persons with degrees in agricultural science, architecture, architectural science, engineering, law, medicine, and forestry. An equal number of men and women were selected randomly from the six professional groups. Data were collected by written questionnaire, which was returned by 80 per cent of the persons in the sample.

Source: Eskola and Haavio-Mannila (1975), p. 180; Hernesniemi (1968), p. 26.

notion that women should marry 'upward.' But if this tradition is maintained, not many eligible men are available for educated women. According to a comprehensive survey on sexual life in Finland, a strong correlation exists between levels of education and marriage among both men and women, but in opposite directions; high education correlates positively with probability of marriage among men but negatively among women (Sievers, Koskelainen, and Leppo, 1974).

The problem is why so many educated Finnish women choose to remain unmarried, or perhaps we should not consider it a problem. But the question in Finland is interesting, because the proportion of university-trained women is high by international standards, even in the older age brackets. In 1970 Finnish women comprised 49·8 per cent of the over-55 population with university degrees, compared with 40·6 per cent in Sweden, 34·4 per cent in Poland, and 37 per cent in the USSR, where the percentage is counted on the basis of persons aged 60 and older (*United Nations Demographic Yearbook, 1973*, table 34).

The tendency of women to marry upwards, or at least on the same educational level, was perceived in a study on professional women, of whom 92 per cent had husbands on the same or higher educational levels, whereas only 37 per cent of the men had college-educated wives (Eskola and Haavio-Mannila, 1975, p. 180). In this area men have available a larger field of marriage eligibles than women do. Among the Finnish lower classes it is common today for wives to have more comprehensive general education than their husbands; girls form a majority of almost 60 per cent in secondary schools. It may be expected that the old tradition of wives choosing husbands with similar or higher education levels or social positions will disappear when more women attain higher positions.

Another explanation for the low proportion of married women in the elite is that the family obligations of a married woman prevent her from applying herself sufficiently to her career to achieve a top position. One of the most strongly correlating variables with career success of professionals is freedom from home-making obligations, whether by means of a helping spouse, outside help, or absence of such obligations.

CONCLUSION

The distribution of elite positions largely favors males, particularly in fields where holders of top jobs are recruited by private arrangements, which make those jobs closed and self-perpetuating. This method is found more in private business than in state bureaucracies and more in ideological than in political bodies. In the latter people are recruited by either open selection or public election; consequently, in these elites relatively many women are found. In private institutions and among ideological elites, however, an ingroup closed-society type of recruitment predominates, and the proportion of women in them remains small.

Women have difficulty entering elite groups for many reasons, examples being the traditional distraction of household duties, sexist attitudes among men especially but often among women too, and the formal and informal segregation of the sexes in most social institutions. It seems especially difficult for women to combine marriage and an elite position; a third of the Finnish female elite has never married, compared with 2–3 per cent of the male elite.

According to Paavo Seppänen (1965), the emancipation of Finnish women has occurred in stages, not linearly. There was a rise in the social participation of women after both world wars, simultaneously with the loosening of certain moral norms (e.g. an increase in divorce rates and white collar criminality). Unfortunately, the time trends presented in this paper do not indicate very clear patterns of development; thus, we cannot arrive at firm conclusions about trends in the advance of women to elite positions.

The sharp increase in the success of women as political representatives, starting in the latter half of the 1960s, indicates a new wave of emancipation. However, it is not reflected in the proportion of elite women included in *Who's Who*, which has recorded percentage declines since 1966. In education the percentages of female students and master's level graduates have stabilized, but there has been a clear increase in the percentage of women Ph.D.s (Figure 4.4). It remains to be seen how the attainment of the highest academic degrees will affect women's opportunities to enter elite positions. I doubt the importance of education in the recruitment of elites. Women today are quite able and willing to obtain higher and graduate education, but many subtle informal barriers are still in their way and obstruct their progress.

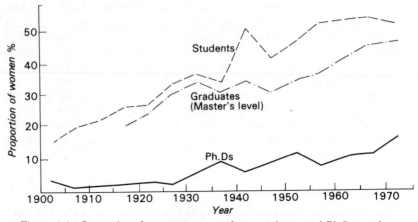

Figure 4.4   *Proportion of women among students, graduates and Ph.D.s at the University of Helsinki, 1900–75 (five-year averages).*

Sources: Kertomukset Helsingin Yliopiston toiminnasta, laatinut Yliopiston rehtori, 1965–75; *Helsingin yliopiston luettelot,* 1964–75; and Commission of Women of Suomen Kulttuurirahasto (1966).

NOTES

(1) Results of a Gallup study on the attitudes of a representative sample of the Finnish population. The question was: 'If you were to choose between two similar jobs in which the work, salary, and working conditions were the same and the bosses had the same education and practical experience, would you choose the one with a man or a woman as boss?' (Haavio-Mannila, 1972, pp. 102–3).

(2) This greater egalitarianism on the part of working class men may stem from the fact that they need not compete with women for jobs, which at that level are for the most

part sex segregated. Women thus present no threat regarding job acquisition. Furthermore, although there is equal pay for equal work, this sex segregation in jobs results in a situation where men are paid on average more than women – a fact that enhances their security.

(3) This finding is consistent with those results which show that women are elected as political representatives more frequently in eastern Finland than in the western and more patriarchal parts of Finland (Haavio-Mannila, 1970).

REFERENCES

Allardt, Erik (1975) *Att ha att alska att vara – om valfard i Norden* (Lund: Argos).

Aron, Raymond (1970) 'Social class, political class, ruling class,' in Marvin E. Olsen (ed.), *Power in Societies* (London: Collier-Macmillan).

Bottomore, T. B. (1970) 'Elites and society,' in Marvin E. Olsen (ed.), *Power in Societies* (London: Collier-Macmillan).

Central Statistical Office of Finland (1973), *Official Statistics of Finland*, Vol. 37, No. 4: *Higher Education, 1969–1970* (Helsinki).

Commission of Women of Suomen Kulttuurirahasto (1966) *Finnish Women: Doctoral Degrees and University Appointments* (Helsinki).

Eskola, Irja and Haavio-Mannila, Elina (1975) 'The careers of professional women and men in Finland,' *Acta Sociologica*, vol. 18, no. 2–3, pp. 174–201.

Giddens, Anthony (1973) *The Class Structure of the Advanced Societies* (London: Hutchinson University Library).

Haavio-Mannila, Elina (1968) *Suomalainen nainen ja mies* (Porvoo: WSOY).

Haavio-Mannila, Elina (1969) 'The position of Finnish women: regional and cross-national comparisons,' *Journal of Marriage and the Family*, vol. 31, no. 2, pp. 339–47.

Haavio-Mannila, Elina (1970) 'Sex roles in politics,' *Scandanavian Political Studies*, vol. 5, pp. 209–39. Also in Constantina Safilios Rothschild (ed.), *Toward a Sociology of Women* (Lexington, Mass.: Xerox College Publishing, 1972), pp. 154–72.

Haavio-Mannila, Elina (1971) 'Convergences between East and West: tradition and modernity in sex roles in Sweden, Finland and the Soviet Union,' *Acta Sociologica*, vol. 14 no. 1–2, pp. 114–25. Also in Martha T. S. Mednick, Sandra S. Tangri, and Lois W. Hoffman (eds) *Women and Achievement* (Washington and London: Hemisphere Publishing, A. Halstead Press Book, John Wiley, 1975), pp. 71–84.

Haavio-Mannila, Elina (1972) 'Sex-role attitudes in Finland, 1966–1970,' *Journal of Social Issues*, vol. 28, no. 2, pp. 93–110.

Haavio-Mannila, Elina (1978) 'How women become political actors,' Working Paper 6, Department of Sociology, University of Helsinki (Helsinki).

Helsingin yliopistonluettelot, 1964–1975 (Helsinki, University of Helsinki, 1964–1975).

Hernesniemi, Marja (968) *Suomalainen nainen talouselämän johtoportaassa vuonna 1968* (Ekenäs: Naisjärjestögen Keskusliitto).

HS-Gallup (1976) *Survey Conducted by the Finnish Gallup, Spring 1976* (Helsinki: Helsingen Sanomat).

Kartovaara, Leena (1972) 'Suomalainen eliitti Kuka Kukin On-teoksen valossa vuosina 1909, 1934, ja 1970,' (University of Helsinki, Master's thesis).

Keller, Suzanne (1963) *Beyond the Ruling Class* (New York: Random House).

Kertomukset Helsingin yliopiston toiminnasta laatinut Ylioposton rehtori, (Helsinki, 1964–75).

Porter, John (1965) *The Vertical Mosaic* (Toronto: University of Toronto Press).

Prime Minister's Office (1975) *Statistics about the Position of Women in Finland*, Publications of the Prime Minister's Office 1975:5 (Helsinki).

Räsänen, Leila (1976) *Naisten asuus työmarkkinajarjestöjen ja puolueiden jäsenistöstä sekä päättävistä elimistä vuoden 1975 lopussa* (Helsinki: Tasa-arvoasiain neuvottelukunta).

Report of the Committee 1970 on the Position of Women in Finnish Society, A8 (Helsinki, 1973).

Seppänen, Paavo (1965) 'Muuttuva yhteiskunta,' *Sosiologia*, vol. 2, no. 2, pp. 73–89.

Sievers, Kai, Koskelainen, Osmo, and Leppo, Kimmo (1974) *Suomalaisten sukupuolielämä* (Porvoo: WSOY).

Suolinna, Kirsti (1965) *Naise asema Suomen taiteessa. Suomen Kulttuurirahaston Naistoimikunnan taiteen jaoston toimeksianto* (Helsinki: Suomen Kulttuurirahasto).

United Nations Demographic Yearbook, 1973 (New York: UN, 1974).

5

Progress for Women:

Increased Female Representation in Political Elites in Norway

TORILD SKARD,
WITH THE ASSISTANCE OF HELGA HERNES[1]

As in all male-dominated societies, the most striking fact about the participation of women in political elites in Norway is that there are so few of them. But the women participating in Norway's political elites are not quite as rare as in many other Western countries, and during the last decade they have shown a marked increase.

That is what this paper is about.

Some reservations must be stated concerning the scope of what is usually considered as 'political activity.'

First, in a patriarchal society like the Norwegian one there exists a fairly clear division between the public sphere of production – the labor market, the economy, organizations – and the private sphere of reproduction – the family, housework, child-rearing, sexual life. Political activity is mainly preoccupied with the public sphere. Consequently, 'politics' is primarily concerned with the undertakings of men, and political activity is generally considered proper for men, not women (Albrektsen, 1977, pp. 21–30).

Second, in a capitalist society like that of Norway the economy is mixed, with public, co-operative, and private enterprises all operating within the capitalist structure. This means that political institutions have some power within the economic field, but it is clearly limited. Important decisions are made by economic elites, especially within the private sector, and these decisions are not usually considered as political activity. The activities of these economic elites, which in Norway are nearly completely male dominated, remain outside the scope of this paper.

Third, the public authorities and political parties are at the center of what is ordinarily considered political activity and the political elites are many and varied. In this paper two kinds of elites are studied:

(1) assemblies elected directly by popular vote – the local and county councils and Parliament; and
(2) appointed committees – the commissions, boards, and councils working for the different ministries.

The two groups of institutions represent two different channels for political participation and influence.

ELECTED ASSEMBLIES: THE NUMERICAL CHANNEL[2]

In Norway, as in other Western democracies, it is a general phenomenon that citizens on the whole are very rarely politically active. Less than one-tenth of them engage in political activities demanding more than a minimum of time and energy. Further, it is generally true that women are less active politically than men; and when one moves upward in the political hierarchies, the differences in participation between women and men become striking. The political elites are dominated by men (Millbrath, 1965; Martinussen, 1973; Albrektsen, 1977).

Up to the end of the last century women in Norway were not considered real citizens, and they were not permitted to participate in the public political system. In 1901 women were allowed to vote for the first time; that is, those women having certain economic means could vote in local elections. In 1913 women achieved the general right to vote in national elections. Norway was among the first countries in the world to give women this right.[3]

The number of women using their right to vote has increased as the years have passed, and today electoral participation is almost identical for women and men. This is true of both national and local elections (Tables 5.1 and 5.2).

Table 5.1   *Participation in local elections (%)*

Year	Women	Men
1901	21	45
1937	67	77
1955	70	74
1975	70	72

Source: Means (1973), p. 121, and Central Bureau of Statistics

Table 5.2   *Participation in national elections (%)*

Year	Women	Men
1915	54	70
1936	81	88
1957	76	80
1977	82	84

Source: Means (1973), p. 33, and Central Bureau of Statistics.

But the picture changes as soon as we turn to the question of who holds political office. Political leadership is still reserved for men, although the participation of women in local and county councils and Parliament has increased in the past decade (Tables 5.3 and 5.4).

County councils were elected by direct popular vote for the first time in

Table 5.3   *Female representation in local councils (%)*

1901	0·8
1937	2·5
1955	6·6
1959	6·0
1963	6·3
1967	9·5
1971	14·8
1975	15·4
1979	22·0 (approx.)

Source: Central Bureau of Statistics

Table 5.4   *Female representation in Parliament (%)*

1915	0
1936	0·7
1957	6·7
1961	8·7
1965	8·0
1969	9·3
1973	15·5
1977	23·9

Source: Central Bureau of Statistics

1975, and female representation was then 24·9 per cent. In 1979 it increased to about 29 per cent.

Female participation does not differ greatly now on the various levels of elected assemblies. After the elections in 1979 women account for approximately 22 per cent of the members of the local councils, 29 per cent of the members of the country councils, and 24 per cent of the members of Parliament.

At the top of the Norwegian political system, among the ministerial heads, there recently were four women – more than ever before. But the party in power, the Social Democrats, had considerable losses at the local elections in September 1979 and after this reduced the number of women ministerial heads to two, or 12 per cent of this top leadership.[4] There are some more women among the assistant secretaries of state, but very few among the high administrative officials.

HOW DID IT HAPPEN?

As the tables show, since the mid-1960s female representation in local councils and in Parliament has tripled. How did it happen? What made such a sudden increase take place? We don't know all about this yet, but we know that a systematic and extensive campaign was organized to mobilize women and increase female representation in the elected bodies.

It can be said to have started in 1967 with the creation of a committee aimed at increasing the number of women in the local councils. It was a top level committee with high prestige; the then prime minister, Per Borton (Agrarian), was chairman, and a former prime minister, Einar Gerhardsen (Social Democrat), was vice chairman. All the political parties were represented, as were a great number of women's organizations. The committee launched a broad propaganda campaign about the participation of women in politics, asking for the nomination of women candidates by the political parties and urging the electorate to support female candidates. The campaign did not result in a landslide, but female representation was increased.

Then, the new feminist movement came to Norway. Very much inspired by the movement in the United States, a considerable number of young women started organizing new feminist groups in 1970, and the traditional women's organizations discovered that the struggle for women's rights was no longer in an 'ice age.' Things were beginning to happen; there was a new sort of 'spring thaw.'

The top level political campaign was not repeated before the local elections of 1971, but now women at the grass roots started activities on a broad scale to increase the number of women in local councils. The largest traditional woman's organization launched a widespread propaganda campaign, and the new feminist groups, having studied ways of gaining political influence, urged women to use the most effective voting techniques in favor of women. At the same time women within all the political parties created pressures for women to be nominated and elected in greater numbers than before.

The results exceeded the expectations. There was not only a general increase in female representation in the local councils; in three municipalities – Asker, Oslo, and Trondheim – women became a majority of the council members, and in six other municipalities they obtained more than 40 per cent of seats. In many small municipalities women entered the political scene for the first time. After 1971 only twenty-two of the 444 local councils were without any female representatives at all.

The response was an uproar in Norwegian political circles. Although there had been no public opposition to women's claims before the elections, these results were more than many male politicians could accept. Leading male politicians from different political parties accused women of using 'undemocratic procedures' – those previously only employed by men. The newly elected women were declared to be 'incompetent' in spite of the fact that all had been accepted as candidates by their political parties, and countermeasures against the women were announced.

'Why is it "strategy" when some people do it, but a "coup" when others do it?' was the comment (by women) in a popular song.

But the male-dominated political system acted. Not long after the 1971 elections the electoral law was changed, diminishing the influence of voters on the choice of candidates representing the political parties,[5] and at the next local elections, in 1975, results were *status quo* in the representation of women in the local councils. Even if the number of women increased on some councils, there was no longer a female majority anywhere, and in only two municipalities did women obtain 40 per cent or more of council seats.

The 1971 elections had other consequences, not so easily counteracted by supporters of the patriarchal system. The most important was probably the change in attitude that was evident in many women, especially women interested in politics.

I had been active in party politics for many years, and I knew that I was accepted, in spite of being a woman, if I did not stress the fact that I was a woman and did not press women's interests and values. All of a sudden women were supporting women candidates *because they were women*. It felt like a revolution! Now I could engage in politics as a woman, and I could fight actively for women's issues. Many women felt as I did and gained new courage, self-confidence, and spirit. Also, those elected to the local councils for the first time often discovered that everyday political work in a body like this was not too difficult and that they could manage it in spite of discrimination and other problems.

The events of 1971 also influenced the attitudes of many Norwegian men. They began to realize that women were serious about their demands – so serious that they were willing to act and use their votes to accomplish their aims – and as women constituted half the electoral body, they were a bit of a threat! On the other hand, men also discovered that it probably wasn't as dangerous as they had thought to have women in the local councils. They were evidently capable of doing an efficient job, and in the councils where women had obtained a majority there was no catastrophy nor revolution (unfortunately, some would add).

Since 1971 women have continued to put on pressure both within the political parties and outside them, and the political parties have responded positively to a certain extent. Consequently, the number of women elected to Parliament increased in a marked way, first in 1973 and then again in 1977, the number of women elected to the county councils increased in 1975 and in 1979, and in 1979 the female representation in the local councils increased once more. Although voters can influence the choice of candidates representing the different political parties in the local elections, this is not the case on county and national elections. Thus, the increase in female representation here is due to action of the political parties, not the voters. The parties have recognized that there is now a risk that poor female representation among their candidates can influence the voters' choice of party.

APPOINTED COMMITTEES: THE CORPORATE CHANNEL

In addition to the legislative bodies elected by popular vote, modern industrial democracies have developed other forms of access and other forms of participation in public-policy decision-making. Although there are some cross-national variations, there is a striking similarity among modern administrative systems in the extent to which they depend on large numbers of committees – commissions, task forces, boards, councils, and special delegations – in the process of making and executing public policy. Since other and more clearly defined organized interests are represented here than in the elected bodies, this has been called 'corporate pluralism.'[6] Compared with other Western systems (e.g. those in Great Britain and the

United States) the Norwegian one is officially and legitimately more 'corporate' in that there is relatively more organizational representation (Hallenstvedt and Moren, 1975; Hernes and Voje, 1977; Olsen, 1977).

Although recruitment to the public committees always happens by appointment through the responsible ministry, there are differences among individual members in terms of their mode of selection. Some are appointed as administrative officials, some serve by virtue of their expertise, and some come as representatives of organizational interests. The latter may be elected within their organizations or appointed by the organizational leadership. Thus, recruitment to public committees is based on one's occupational status, one's organizational membership, and one's position in the public hierarchies. Political affiliation is relevant but not decisive.

Table 5.5   *Female representation in public committees (%)*

1966	6·9%
1971–2	10·5
1974–5	11·2

Sources: Likestillingsrådet (1974, 1976).

The representation of women in the public committees is shown in Table 5.5. Since the mid-1960s the number of women in public committees of different kinds has incresed by more than 100 per cent, but the starting point was low, so that by the end of 1977 only just under 17 per cent of committee members were women.

By the end of 1975 there existed 1,155 different public committees in all. Some of these were delegations and temporary committees, but most were permanent. These were established at various times, and only a few were appointed or reappointed each year.

From studying the committees in greater detail a clear pattern of sexual differences is found. First, there are differences in status. Of the chairpersons of the committees that were active at the end of 1975, only 3·3 per cent were women; and of the reporting secretaries only 1·2 per cent were women (Hernes and Voje, 1977). This means that men dominate the most important positions within the committee system.

The relative participation of women also varies greatly, depending on the area of public policy covered by a committee and whether it is perceived as a 'male' or 'female' field. This is shown in Table 5.6. The highest percentage of women is found in committees concerned with matters traditionally considered 'typically feminine' – consumer affairs and social services. Women have little or no say in questions concerning defense, agriculture and fisheries, industry, transport, commerce, foreign policy, environmental protection, labor, and finance. No ministry has appointed more than 25 per cent women to its public committees, and 61 per cent of the public committees are without any female representation.

The relatively high percentage of women in the committees of the Ministry of Justice may in part be explained by the fact that many of them

Table 5.6   *Percentage of female members in the public committees with each ministry, 1974–5 (%).*

Consumer Affairs	24·8
Social Services	23·5
Justice	19·4
Education and Religion	14·7
Prime Minister's Office	14·2
Finance	10·7
Labor	10·3
Environmental Protection	9·3
Foreign Office	6·2
Transport and Traffic	4·5
Commerce and Shipping	3·6
Industry	2·7
Fisheries	2·5
Agriculture	2·4
Defense	2·3

Source: Likestillingsrådet (1976).

are boards of overseers for prisons, on which women sit as lay representatives in their role as socially concerned citizens who are believed to be especially suited for caretaking functions.

The fairly low percentage of women in the committees of the Ministry of Education and Religion, despite the prevalence of women in this sector, can be explained. Even in committees dealing with education and religion, economic organizations hold 90 per cent of the organizational representations, whereas religious organizations hold only 1 per cent and cultural organizations 6 per cent (Hernes and Voje, 1977; Olsen, 1977); and women are vastly under-represented in the leadership of economic organizations.

WHAT HAS BEEN DONE?

Women's pressure for increased political participation has aimed at greater representation on the different public committees, even if this field has not created as much interest as women's role in the elected assemblies. In December 1973 the government passed a resolution asking for more equal representation of women and men in the public committees. This was to be achieved in the following way. Before the appointment of a public committee the organizations and bodies to be represented should submit a list of candidates containing twice as many names as needed and equal numbers of women and men. The Ministry of Consumer Affairs was supposed to be informed about the appointments.

The procedure thus decided on was not made a binding rule, only a 'guideline,' and in the following two years the appointment of women to the public committees did not increase much.

In 1974 and 1975 the percentage of women appointed to the public committees stayed between 15 and 17 per cent all the time (Table 5.7). In November 1976 the government adopted a new resolution calling for

Table 5.7   *Percentage of female members of the public committees
appointed by the government, 1974 and 1975.*[7]

January–June 1974	14·8
July–December 1974	17·1
January–June 1975	15·1
July–December 1975	16·6

Source: Likestillingsrådet (1976).

increased female representation. Now the demand was extended to include *all* public committees, not only the new ones but also existing committees at the time of reappointment. In addition the Ministry of Consumer Affairs had to evaluate the proposed appointments before the government could approve the membership.

It is too early to see the results of the latest resolution, but the appointments made during January–June 1977 show a more positive tendency than before. In the sixty-one public committees appointed during this period the membership averaged 27·1 per cent women (Likestillingsrådet, 1977). The Norwegian Council for Equality between Women and Men is, however, of the opinion that rules must be adopted that assure both women and men on *all* committees, if necessary by adding female members to the existing committees. Each committee should also include more than one single woman. County and local authorities should assist the government by procuring lists of female candidates for the public committees (Likestillingsrådet, 1976).

Different feminist groups have demanded clear rules fixing quotas for the representation of women and men. They have, for example, urged that a minimum of 40 per cent of each sex be named to all committees. A reappraisal of the criteria for participation in the public committees has also been demanded (Sandberg, 1977). Under the present system the participants from public administrative bodies are recruited from high level positions, in which there are very few women, and the participants from economic organizations to a great extent come from the large labor and industrial organizations, where the representation of women is weak.

SOCIAL CONDITIONS

The increase in female representation in the political elites that we have studied has been the result of a conscious and planned effort. Under what social conditions did this effort take place and yield results?

Norway is a small country with only about 4 million inhabitants. The population is dispersed, with a little more than half of the people living in densely populated areas. The country belongs to the rich capitalist industrialized part of the world; and besides agriculture, forestry, and fishing the main economic activities are industry, business, and services. As a part of the European culture the country is influenced by a patriarchal tradition that has lasted for many centuries.

In spite of differences all the Protestant Western countries have had a roughly parallel industrial development, and with this have come changes in the position of women. The Nordic countries in particular share a fundamentally democratic tradition; the societies are relatively egalitarian, and their socialist and feminist movements are comparatively strong.[8]

The organization of women has roots going back to the 1880s in Norway; but during the Second World War, the reconstruction period afterwards, and then the cold war the climate was not positive for women's liberation causes. During the 1960s, however, interest in the position of women again started to grow. International tension was decreasing, radical ideas were spreading, and economic conditions in Norway were good. There was especially an increasing demand for women in the labor force.

Compared with other western European countries, Norway for many years had a relatively small number of women working outside the home. In 1960 less than one-fifth of adult women were engaged in the labor force. Since then the numbers have increased rapidly, especially among married women, and in 1977 about half of the adult female population was active in the labor force, some full time, others only part time. Three-quarters of the employed women are working in the service sector (Hoem *et al.*, 1975; Skard, 1977).

During the postwar years Norway's people, particularly its women, have been receiving more education than before, on both a primary and a secondary level. Compulsory schooling now lasts nine years, and in 1970 about 25 per cent of adult women had achieved more education than this, compared to 35 per cent of men.

The women in Norway's labor force are discriminated against. Generally, the higher positions – those implying qualified and independent work, responsibility and influence, and good wages – are obtained by men. Women usually obtain the routine and monotonous work, often subordinate and nearly always poorly paid. With the same qualifications women obtain poorer jobs and lower pay then men, and they have not secured equal pay for jobs of equal value. In 1970 women in the Norgwegian labor force on average earned half as much money as men did.

During the last few decades Norwegian women have gained increasing control over reproduction. Modern means of birth control are becoming widespread, and the abortion law was practiced in a liberal way, before abortion on demand was accepted in 1978. On average each family now has two children, and they are usually born while the woman is in her twenties. About half of adult women have housework and childrearing as their main occupation. Many of these would like to work outside the home as well, but they are prevented by limited job opportunities in many places and by the small number of facilities for preschool children. In 1977 only 10 per cent of all preschool children could go to kindergarten. Some men, especially younger ones, are starting to take part in housework and child-rearing, but the basic sexual division of labor in the home is still untouched. Whatever work the woman may do elsewhere, the work at home is hers.

FACTORS INFLUENCING POLITICAL ACTIVITY

Within the framework of the present Norwegian society, what do we know about the factors influencing women's political activity? We can only give a few glimpses.

Kirsten Voje (1975) studied the representation of women in local councils after the election in 1967 and found that the number of women varied with the municipalities' labor market, educational level, and regional location. She has stated that the municipalities that had a differentiated labor market, including the service sector, that had a high educational level, and that were situated geographically in the central and most industrialized regions had the greatest probability of a relatively high female representation in their local councils. But, Voje has noted, this does not mean that an economically advanced community automatically promotes the political influence of women, nor that increased female participation in politics is impossible elsewhere.

To be able to pursue a political career the individual must have certain political resources at her disposal, among others time and economic means, information and skills, contact with other people, and prestige (Martinussen, 1973; Means, 1973). But it is difficult for many women to acquire such resources.

The sexual division of labor in society forms the basis of many of women's problems. A full time housewife is socially isolated, and taking care of small children for twenty-four hours a day doesn't leave much opportunity for political activity. Women working outside the home nearly always have a double workload, as they are obliged to do the work in the home also.

Having interviewed women in Parliament and the local councils in Bergen, Tromsø, and Volda in 1970, Ingunn Norderval Means (1973) has concluded that:

> As a group the women are caught in a dilemma. Working outside the home is the best way of achieving the skills and contacts needed for political success. But few women have enough resources and endurance to participate in political activity at the same time as they work both outside and in the home. Those women who have the necessary skills and contacts for political success, therefore, don't have time for political activity – and those who have time don't have the necessary qualifications. (pp. 64–5, 169)

This conclusion has been supported by an investigation made by Beatrice Halsaa Albrektsen (1977) in Jevnaker, Odda, and Tinn in 1974. She analyzed women and discovered that women working full time outside the home were the least active politically. Full time housewives were a bit more active, but women working part time outside the home were by far the most active; their political activity was more than twice as great as that of full time workers outside the home. Why was this? Albreksten has pointed out that women working part time outside the home have both contact with the economic life of the community *and* a certain amount of time, whereas other women lack one or both (p. 168).

The financial burdens of political participation are not as heavy for the individual in Norway as in many other Western countries. The political parties and public authorities to a great extent pay not only for work in political office but also for electoral campaigns.

Being a Member of Parliament is a full-time paid job, but participation in local councils and public committees is supposed to be in addition to whatever job the individual may have. Ingvild Baklid and Astrid Rangnes Bråten interviewed women in the local councils in Asker, Bærum, and Oslo in 1971 and noted that the political work demanded a great deal of time – on average three evenings a week and up to five in the most hectic seasons. (It is less, though, in small municipalities). They have concluded that:

> To be active in politics you must be in good financial condition. It is hard to be a single family provider. You must have a telephone and preferably a car. You must be able to read documents during working hours and participate in meetings and inspections without financial loss or extra cost. You must be able to telephone people during office hours to get information. (Skard, 1979, pp. 66–7)

But even if women have the necessary political resources, their political activity is often hampered by traditional attitudes and reactions.

The upbringing of Norwegian girls and women usually stresses kindness, helpfulness, passivity, and self-denial. But participation in politics demands a certain amount of initiative, persistence, boldness, and self-confidence. Means (1973) has observed that 'The better a woman has learnt the traditional female role, the less suited she is for becoming an able politician' (p. 163).

Beyond the brakes inside themselves women also experience oppositon and discrimination in the male-dominated political world. Traditional patriarchal ideas about politics being a men's affair still exist, and by means of various mechanisms men try to keep women in their powerless position. Men make women invisible; they forget women, ignore them, and underestimate them; they make fun of women and hold back information from them; they divide women and give them guilt feelings (Ås, 1975). When women run for office, they are evaluated differently from men. No matter what skills they have or what interests they represent, they are always judged primarily as *women*; and as one woman put it, 'If a woman is to be nominated, she must be more competent than a man.'

The more important a political position, the harder it is for a woman to win it; and the smaller the number of representatives to be elected or appointed, the harder it is to get a woman among them. Thus, an electoral system with one-person districts gives women very few chances of becoming elected. In Norway the first woman in Parliament was elected after the introduction of proportional elections, and there is a clear tendency today for most of the women elected as representatives to come from the large political parties. When a party is sure of getting several representatives elected from a district, it can 'afford' nominating women in addition to the men among those to be elected (Means, 1973, pp. 40–7).

It is sometimes said that women are less willing than men to run for office. With the workload that many women have and the attitudes that they meet this would be understandable. But the Central Bureau of Statistics did an extensive investigation in connection with the local elections of 1971 and discovered that, among the women and men who were willing to accept political positions on the local level, twice as many men as women had obtained such positions. However, Means (1973) has underlined that the modesty and insecurity of many women call for a far more active and systematic recruitment work with women than with men to engage them in political activities. Whereas men often come by themselves, women often need to be asked, persuaded, and encouraged, even when they are capable of doing an excellent job (p. 169).

PRESENT PROBLEMS

The increase in the participation of women in different political elites in Norway has brought the interests of women more to the foreground, but it has not yet created any fundamental changes in public policy. So far the number of women is still too low; 50 per cent is still a little in the future.

On the other hand, even in the local councils where women obtained a majority of the members in 1971, policy has not drastically changed. Why? It is because the leading positions in the councils, the political parties, and the local administrations have been held by men; because the party programs have been decided by male majorities and the women have been split by loyalty to their respective parties; and because the women have concentrated their efforts in the traditional female fields of health and social work, whereas the men have dominated in the traditionally male fields of economics and technical advancement – fields implying more power over the development of the community.

It is clear that progress for women cannot be achieved by increasing the female participation in only a few political fields and elites. A great number of women must participate in decision-making on a large scale.

But with more women engaged in political activities, and with a broader scope of politically active women, the obstacles to female political activity are more clearly felt. There are more active women than before, but there are also more exhausted women than before – exhausted because of practical problems and social and psychological resistance. So, whether women elected or appointed to political positions can obtain help is a crucial question – practical help in taking care of a family and getting necessary work done, and psychological support to counteract discrimination and promote the interests of women.

The political world is dominated by the male culture in our society. The female culture is different, with different interests and values and different ways of speaking, thinking, and feeling. Being a woman is hard in the political world, and many women only manage to survive and succeed by functioning politically as males. They give up functioning as females and working as feminists.

In the short run women must help and support each other. Outside the political system an active, independent, and strong feminist movement must create woman power and raise issues, put forward demands, create pressure, and, if necessary, act directly politically. Inside the political system women must find ways of co-operating across party lines, and members of each political party must create feminist policy-making and supporting groups.

In the long run the sexual division of labor in society must change. Men must take their share of housework and child-rearing, so that women can take their share of political activities and power. This again means changing the structure of economic life, so that both women and men of all social classes can combine work outside the home with work inside the home and still have opportunity for political activity.

Political life also must change. The definition of political activity must be extended to include more of the domestic sphere, and these activities must change character to give room to the female culture and to serve women's as well as men's interests.

NOTES

(1) Helga Hernes has assisted especially with material and views concerning female representation in public committees.

(2) Stein Rokkan (1970) has presented the terms 'numerical channel' and 'corporate channel.'

(3) Women obtained the right to vote for the first time in the state of Wyoming in 1869. Other states followed the example of Wyoming, but the first independent nation to give women this right was New Zealand in 1894. Australia followed in 1902 and Finland in 1906. Then came Norway.

(4) The two ministerial heads are: Labor and Local Affairs, Inger Louise Valle; Consumer Affairs, Sissel Rønbeck.

(5) The voters vote for political parties, not individuals, and each party can obtain one or more representatives. On the party ballot is a list of names, and according to certain rules the voters can influence the chances that each person on the list has to be elected as one of the party's representatives. For example, a name can be crossed or given additional weight.

(6) The term has been used by Stein Rokkan (1970).

(7) Note that the percentages are higher than in Table 5.5 and 5.6 because the existing committees appointed in previous years are not included.

(8) The similarity between the Nordic countries can be illustrated by the percentage of women in the various Parliaments. In 1977 the figures were: Sweden 23·0 per cent, Finland 22·9 per cent, Denmark 17·1 per cent and – the exception – Iceland 5·0 per cent (Ekenvall, 1976). Sweden has achieved 28 per cent of women in Parliament at the time of writing.

REFERENCES

Albrektsen, Beatrice Halsaa (1976) 'Kvinners politiske aktivitet' (The political activity of women), in Støren and Wetlesen, (eds) *Kvinnekunnskap* (Knowledge about Women), (Oslo: Gyldendal), pp. 197–219.

Albrektsen, Beatrice Halsaa (1977) *Kvinner og politisk deltakelse* (Women and Political participation) (Oslo: Pax).

Ås, Berit (1975) 'On female culture: an attempt to formulate a theory of women's solidarity and action,' *Acta Sociologica*, vol. 18, no. 2–3, pp. 142–61.

Ekenvall, Asta (1976) *Kvinnen i Norden* (The Woman in the Nordic Countries) (Stockholm: Nordisk Råd).

Hallenstvedt, Abraham and Moren, Jorolv (1975) 'Det organiserte samfunn' (The organized society), in Natalie Rogoff Ramsøy and Vaa (eds), *Det Norske samfunn* (The Norwegian Society) (Oslo: Gyldendal), pp. 323–62.

Hernes, Helga and Voje, Kirsten (1977) *The Representation of Women in Public Policy-making: the Norwegian case* (Bergen: Universitet i Bergen, mimeo).

Hoem, Ragnhild *et al.* (1975) 'Kvinners stilling i samfunnet' (The position of women in society), in Natalie Rogoff Ramsøy and Vaa (eds), *Det Norske samfunn* (The Norwegian Society) (Oslo: Gyldendal), pp. 444–511.

Holter, Harriet (1970) *Sex Roles and Social Structure* (Oslo: Universitetsforlaget).

Likestillingsrådet (1974) *Fakta om likestilling* (Facts about Equality) (Oslo).

Likestillingsrådet (1976) *Representasjon av kvinner i offentlige utvalg, styrer og råd: utviklingen fra 1971 til 1975* (Female Representation in Public Committees: Development from 1971 to 1975) (Oslo, mimeo).

Likestillingsrådet (1977) *Ifølge offisielt fra statsråd 1. januar–30. juni 1977 har regjeringen foretatt følgende oppnevninger* (Government Appointments from January 1st to June 30th 1977) (Oslo, mimeo).

Martinussen, Willy (1973) *Fjerndemokratiet* (The Distant Democracy) (Oslo: Gyldendal).

Means, Ingunn Norderval (1973) *Kvinner i Norsk politikk* (Women in Norwegian Politics) (Oslo: Cappelen).

Milbrath, Lester W. (1965) *Political Participation* (Chicago: Rand McNally).

Olsen, Johan P. (1977) 'Organizational participation in government' (Bergen: Universitetet i Bergen, draft).

Rokkan, Stein (1970) *Citizens, Elections, Parties* (Oslo: Universitetsforlaget).

Sandberg, Tone (1977) *Kvinnelig representasjon i offentlig oppnevnte utvalg, råd, styrer mv* (Female Representation in Public Committees) (Bergen: Universitet i Bergen, mimeo).

Skard, Torild (1977) *Halve jorden* (Half of the World) (Oslo: Socialistisk Opplysningsforbund).

Skard, Torild (ed.) (1979) *'Kuinnekupp' i kommunene* ('Women's coup' in the Municipalities) (Oslo: Gyldendal).

Voje, Kirsten (1975) *Kvinnelig representasjon i kommunestyrene* (Female Representation in the Local Councils) (Bergen: Universitet i Bergen, mimeo).

6

Women in Decision-Making Elites:

The Case of Poland

MAGDALENA SOKOŁOWSKA

Poland is a country with a long turbulent history, whose strong national culture has helped the Polish people to survive. In the years 1795–1918 Poland lacked both statehood and an independent political organization; thus, its culture, in which the Roman Catholic Church and the family played an important role, provided the very basis of national existence. In the nineteenth century Poles as Roman Catholics developed a strong feeling of identity with both 'Polishness' and Catholicism, and the family – the patriarchal family – became the basic national institution of a society that remained primarily agricultural (Sokołowska, 1977).

Poland was liberated from German occupation in 1945 by the Soviet army, with Polish divisions fighting at its side. As a result Poland changed its political system and became in Western parlance a 'communist country.' Under this new political and economic system Poland achieved its industrial revolution largely within one generation. This dramatic change from a backward rural economy to industrialization occurred in a country devastated by a war in which 220 people were lost out of every 1,000.

Sexist attitudes are an ingredient of Polish cultural tradition and heritage, typical of Polish men and women, including intellectuals and political leaders. Poles are not aware of the meaning of the word 'sexist' as now used in the West. Its only connotation in Polish is sexuality, and sexuality, associated with striptease and bed, is not considered to be a part of the gallantry and romantic chivalry that are principal traits of the traditional Polish male personality.

Therefore, Poland is an interesting place for studies in social change and cultural continuity. It is these processes and patterns of behavior that throw light on the complicated phenomenon of women's elites in contemporary Poland. There are no systematic studies in this area and almost no relevant statistical data.

GENERAL INFORMATION

In Poland there are at least two areas where the postulate of equal rights for both men and women has been implemented: the law and education.

The Law

'Equality before the law is not yet equality in life,' said Lenin. However, equality before the law is a *sine qua non* for further actions aimed at implementing the law. The fundamental legal norms based on Marxist-

Leninist doctrine and formulated in the constitution assume equality of men and women as one of the basic values. The constitutional provisions and guarantees of equal rights are expanded and concretized in the family code.

Table 6.1   *Educational levels of women and men aged 18–24 and 50 and over: Poland, 1970 (%).*

Education	18–24 years		50 years and over	
	Women	*Men*	*Women*	*Men*
Higher, including not completed	6·8	4·5	1·5	4·8
Secondary, including not completed	53·7	55·5	9·1	15·3
Primary completed	36·4	35·8	36·4	35·0
Primary not completed	1·9	3·2	36·3	37·2
Self-taught	—	—	6·3	3·7
Only able to read	—	—	2·5	0·5
Illiterate	0·2	0·2	6·4	3·3
No data	1·0	1·1	1·2	0·9
Total	100·0	100·3	99·7	100·8

Source: Central Statistical Office (1975), p. 11.

Table 6.2   *Educational levels of women and men aged 25–29 Poland, 1970 (%).*

Education	*Women*	*Men*
Higher, including not completed	6·7	7·9
Semi-higher*a*	4·4	1·8
Secondary, including not completed	22·5	17·2
Basic vocational	10·1	22·9
Primary completed	51·1	45·5
Primary not completed	4·6	3·8
No data	0·6	0·9
Total	100·0	100·0

a Schools of nursing, for instance.

Source: Central Statistical Office (1975).

Education

Table 6.1 presents the dramatic rise in the educational level of Polish men and women, in a country with a 30 per cent illiteracy rate before the Second World War. These data also show that differences in the educational levels of men and women are being obliterated. Table 6.2 shows the present situation in this area related to the 25–9 age group. However, the educational structure is not identical for both sexes; for instance, the percentage of men with a basic vocational training is much higher than that of women, which partly explains the persisting higher wages of men, as jobs requiring a basic vocational training, mostly technical, are usually well paid (Table 6.2).

Poland's efforts to change the traditional division of education and occupation into male and female areas should be mentioned. Systematically, both national and local educational authorities, as well as several other organizations, have been attempting to change traditional views and to form new ones (Sokołowska, 1976a). The spectrum of study areas chosen by women is broader and contrasts with 'traditional' female preferences. However, there are visible differences in the occupational structure of academically trained women and men; whereas some 45 per cent of women with such training are concentrated in health fields and the humanities, almost the same proportion of men is involved in engineering (Table 6.3). Nevertheless, the broad participation of women in the professions must be stressed.

Table 6.3   *Occupational structure of women and men with higher educations: Poland, 1970 (%).*

Subject area	Women	Men
Medicine, dentistry, pharmacy	22·0	8·5
Humanities	23·2	11·7
Economics	13·4	11·9
Law, administration	5·7	8·3
Mathematics, physics, chemistry, biology	11·8	5·6
Engineering	11·5	41·5
Agriculture	6·8	8·6
Fine arts	4·0	2·3
Other	1·6	1·6
Total	100·0	100·0

Source: Central Statistical Office (1975), p. 17.

In spite of their undoubted educational achievements the relationship between women's education and their economic, occupational, and social advancement remains weak,

> ...as if men had agreed to the broad access of women to better secondary schools and to higher education while keeping for themselves better opportunities for advancement, higher wages, and managerial positions. Undoubtedly, urban women in particular gained much in the educational sphere; however, their educational advancement is not accompanied by a correspondingly open socio-occupational advancement. (Kozakiewicz, 1973, p. 256)

Occupation

In 1974 the proportion of women in the labor force was 46·2 per cent.

Women constituted 57 per cent of those in nationalized agriculture and 70 per cent of those on private farms (Central Statistical Office, 1975). The feminization of the private agricultural sector is reflected in Table 6.4, which reveals the significant excess of women among 'non-qualified service

Table 6.4 *Women per 100 men in selected socioeconomic groups: Poland, 1972.*

Non-agricultural occupations	73·8
Employees:	72·9
Clerical personnel	274·4
Technical management	7·2
Other engineers and technicians	23·6
Foremen and similar	42·0
Specialists of higher level in non-technical occupations	174·8
Other specialists in non-technical occupations	465·6
Workers in industrial and similar occupations	44·3
Workers in construction	4·9
Workers for various simple jobs	41·9
Employees in transportation	15·6
Employees in sales and other non-industrial services	201·2
Non-qualified service personnel	788·0
Working on the private account	33·6
At-home work	541·5
Agricultural occupations	127·8
Employees	36·1
Individual (private) farmers	141·8

Source: Central Statistical Office (1975), p. 51.

personnel,' 'specialists in non-technical occupations,' 'clerical personnel,' 'employees in sales and other non-industrial services,' and those doing 'at-home work.' But interesting too is the relatively high number of women among 'foremen and similar personnel,' 'engineers and technicians,' and even 'technical management.' Table 6.5 presents levels of 'feminization' of selected branches of the national economy.

Earnings
The disparate rates of men's and women's pay are clear evidence that the postulate of female equality in labor has not yet been realized (Tables 6.6, 6.7 and 6.9). Women's average wages are about 30 per cent lower than men's. Since the principle of equal pay for equal work most often is observed, pay inequality must be attributed to inequality of positions within the occupation (Łobodzińska, 1970). Table 6.4 partly mirrors this phenomenon. Differences in earnings are to a great extent associated with the employment structures of men and women. As Table 6.5 shows, most working women are grouped in fields where pay rates are relatively lower. A man with a secondary vocational training is most often a technician; his female counterpart is a nurse, school teacher, or clerk.

Table 6.5   *Percentage of women in selected branches of the economy:*
Poland, 1970.

Health services, social welfare, physical culture	77·7
Finance	72·2
Education	71·7
Trade[a]	67·6
Culture, arts	56·6
Administration[b]	53·8
Housing, community administration	36·8
Science[c]	35·5
Industry	35·4
Agriculture	24·5
Transportation	21·2
Construction	16·1
Forestry	15·8

a   Mostly sales girls.
b   White collar categories.
c   All sciences (not only natural).

Source: Central Statistical Office (1975), p. 36.

Table 6.6   *Monthly wages of women and women: Poland, 1973 (%)*

Zloty	Men	Women
Below 1,000	0·4	1·4
1,001–1,200	0·3	2·3
1,201–1,500	1·7	8·2
1,501–2,000	6·8	24·1
2,001–2,500	14·9	29·4
2,501–3,000	19·5	19·1
3,001–5,000	44·3	14·4
Above 5,000	12·1	1·1
Total	100·0	100·0

Source: Central Statistical Office (1975), p. 44.

Working Life Pattern

Table 6.8 presents participation rates of urban married women in four age groups in the labor force in 1960 and 1970. Although the percentage of married women had risen in 1970 in each of the four age groups, it is interesting that this trend was the sharpest in the age groups 25–34 and 35–44 – those years in which domestic chores are greatest. As much as 75 per cent of the working women in Poland are married, and most of them are mothers. Neither the number of children nor their ages exert great influence on the percentage of women's vocational activity. Thus, in 1968, 64 per cent of mothers with children up to the age of 3, 71 per cent of those with youngest children between 4 and 7, and 74 per cent of those with

Table 6.7 *Percentage of persons with low (below 1,500 zloty) and high (above 3,000 zloty) monthly wages in selected occupations: Poland, 1973.*

Occupation	− 1,500 zloty	3,000 + zloty
Education	25·2	17·7
Construction	12·1	27·6
Industry	7·1	14·8
Sciences	6·3	37·3

Source: Central Statistical Office (1975).

Table 6.8 *Participation rates of urban married women in the labor force in four age groups: Poland, 1960 and 1970 (%).*

Age group	1960	1970	Difference
20−24 years[a]	51·3	65·5	+ 14·2
25−34	43·8	68·5	+ 24·7
35−44	39·2	66·0	+ 26·8
45−54	29·9	53·7	+ 23·8

a   for 1960, age group 18−24 years.

Source: Estimated on the basis of National Censuses, 1960 and 1970. See Central Statistical Office (1975), pp. 66−7.

children of 14−18 were working, as were 77 per cent of mothers with one child and 63 per cent of those with three children (Piotrowski, 1969). Only approximately 6 per cent of women worked part time.

Most women resume work after childbirth. But although the general proportion is high, there are striking differences depending on kind of job and educational level, so that there is a direct relationship between schooling and continuation of work after childbirth. All other factors are of minor importance (Table 6.10).

Table 6.10 shows that among white collar employees there is no clear relationship between average wages in any given occupation group and the percentage of married women who continue to work. For example, school teachers, who earn less than bookkeepers, more often take a job after childbirth than the latter. The wages of kindergarten nurses are in the low group, at the level of salesgirls or bartenders, but still many kindergarten nurses return to work. Other experiences show, too, that the level of education and occupation decisively influence the decision of a working woman to continue or quit work after childbirth. More educated women are less eager to accept maternity and family benefits – for instance, a system of maternity leave introduced in 1974 permits women to stay off the job until a child is 3 years old – and they forgo them more frequently

Table 6.9 Percentage of jobs open to men and women according to wages offered: Poznań district,[a] 1966, 1969, and 1971

Year	below 1,000 zloty		1,001–1500 zloty		1,501–2,000 zloty		above 2,000 zloty		Total
	Men	Women	Men	Women	Men	Women	Men	Women	
1966	16·6	45·9	36·5	43·9	34·5	9·9	12·4	0·4	100·0
1969	8·9	24·4	30·3	72·7	43·4	2·6	17·4	0·3	100·0
1971	8·8	22·2	19·9	64·9	41·1	12·8	30·2	0·1	100·0

a An industrialized district in western Poland.

Source: Rogusąska-Klupść (1975), p. 104.

Table 6.10 *Married urban women continuing work after childbirth (after six months following the end of maternity leave) by occupation and education: Poland, 1964 (%).*

Occupation	All educational levels	Academic education	High school education	Other education
White collar workers				
Teachers	94·7	90·9	95·7	50·0
Physicians, pharmacists	94·2	94·2	—	—
Kindergarten nurses	84·9	100·0	77·8	23·0
Engineers, technicians	84·2	82·1	84·1	—
Nurses	83·2	—	83·9	76·0
Bookkeepers, economists, planners	80·5	45·5	78·8	84·0
Secretaries, typists	73·7	—	68·4	74·0
Foremen, draftsmen	72·7	100·0	68·2	80·0
Shop and restaurant or cafe managers	67·3	—	63·2	68·0
Salesgirls	54·3	—	46·5	55·6
Bartenders, waitresses	49·0	—	75·0	64·4
Laborers				
Skilled workers in industry and construction	70·0	100·0	72·2	70·0
Unskilled workers in industry and construction	49·0	—	—	49·0
Physical laborers outside industry	50·2	—	62·5	49·2

Source: Kurzynowski (1967), p. 130.

than other mothers. All the other variables in the 1960–4 study investigated by Kurzynowski (1967) – such as occupation, husband's income and education, woman's age, marital standing, number of children, kind of housing and job, branch of employment – turned out to be insignificant or of only minor importance to the decision on whether to resume work. Fondness for the job was reported as the first and most important motive to work by 84·9 per cent of physicians, 73·6 per cent of teachers, and 67·5 per cent of nurses. However, whatever the reason, the working life curve of Polish women differs from women's career patterns in the West. Figure 6.1 presents the striking similarity between the working life curves of Polish men and women.

Living Conditions
The fact that Polish wives and mothers have jobs has not much influenced the distribution of domestic responsibilities. Although in the families of working women domestic contributions of husbands and other household members are twice as high as in homes of women who do not work, it remains meager. A relatively small proportion of women benefit from such

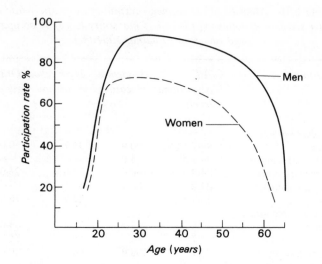

Figure 6.1   *Participation roles of urban females and males in the labor force,*
by age: Poland, 1970

Source: Based on National Census, 1970 (see Central Statistical Office, 1975)

communal services as canteens and laundries. The bulk of household work continues to be the responsibility of the working woman.

In more than 80 per cent of urban households all meals are eaten at home. Laundry is washed at home, and few have automatic washing machines; the bulk of the laundry (e.g. bed linen) must be ironed. Daily shopping for food is one of the most time-consuming and burdensome activities. Approximately one-third of urban families own a small garden, usually at a distance from the home, where vegetables are planted for family consumption. Paid domestic help is employed part or full time by approximately 5–6 per cent of urban families (Markowska, 1976). An average apartment inhabited by four to six family members consists of two rooms plus bathroom and kitchen; it will usually contain approximately 40 square meters (Andrjejewski, 1976).

The Polish birthrate fell from 30·7 in 1950 to 18·4 in 1974. In 1968, out of the total number of working women with children up to age 16, 36 per cent had one child, 32·8 per cent had two children, 8·1 per cent had three, and 13·1 per cent had four or more (Piotrowski, 1969).

The use of contraceptives in Poland is slow to gain acceptance. It has been estimated that about half of married couples have adopted some method of contraception and that among this group about half depend on *coitus interruptus* or the rhythm method. The most common contraceptive used is the condom, used by approximately 10 per cent of couples. Only 1 per cent of women in the prime child-bearing ages – 15 through 49 – use the pill (Sokołowska and Łobodzińska, 1971). Legal abortions have been available since 1956. According to official statistics, one abortion occurs for every two live births. However, it seems that this figure is far from accurate.

Attitudes toward Women's Societal Positions.
Adopting the usual stance of sociologists that norms, attitudes, expectations, or beliefs exist prior to the person and so govern behavior, data have
been sought on changes in expectations about women's roles and the roles
of husbands and wives. The responses indicate that at this point the
normative state of the society is complex and multidimensional (Mogey and
Piotrowski, 1976).

Of the respondents of a nationwide random sample of the adult population
(Otawska, 1974) 36 per cent declared themselves to be for the traditional limi-
tation of married women to the duties of wife and mother, and 20 per cent
stated that women should combine gainful employment with full responsibility for the household. A decided majority of respondents, women as well as
men, believed that child care and upbringing were exclusively the woman's
job; even the matter of taking sick children to the doctor or staying at home
with them found few advocates of a mother's and father's common responsibility in such cases. A much larger group favored common responsibility for
shopping (53 per cent), but other studies on marketing showed that women
did the shopping in 75 per cent of households. Of another group of
respondents, 41 per cent declared that household responsibilities should be
equally shared, but 45 per cent of these were of the opinion that the wife
should prepare breakfast even when both partners worked.

Views on women's professional opportunities were not consistent either.
Of a group of respondents, mostly male, 67 per cent considered that women
had many such opportunities. More men (60 per cent) than women (51 per
cent) were convinced that Polish women were paid as much as men for the
same work. Among those who declared that opportunities for advancement
were equal for both sexes, as many as 35 per cent stated that women
occupied controlling positions more rarely than men because 'they are not
permitted to.' Most respondents (45 per cent), both men and women,
explained that women rarely occupied directing positions because of their
reluctance to undertake such responsibility. Of the respondents, more men
than women referred to women's presumed lack of qualifications for
managerial posts ('Don't know how to direct people').

The above findings attest to a high degree of traditionalism in attitudes
about women. But the question arises whether these findings reflect a
generally conservative outlook or frustration and conflict arising from the
difficult living conditions of most Polish families.

Since 1945 Poland has actively attempted through law and employment
to achieve equality between women and men in all sectors of society. The
direction of change in the family is toward equality in household tasks and
joint decisions by both husbands and wives (Mogey and Piotrowski, 1976).
The couples who have changed most in this direction are those who have
gained most from the new social structure and have greater education and
income. Changes in roles of either husbands or wives will require structural
changes in the society and in individuals' participation in society.

Table 6.11   *Women in political elites: Poland.*

(a) Polish United Workers Party (PUWP), 1975.

Position in party	Women %
Members	23·6
Members of the central committee	5·6 (7 persons)
Members of the secretariat	—
Members of the politburo	—
First secretaries of the provincial PUWP	2·1 (1 person)
First secretaries of the local PUWP	7·0
First secretaries of the basic organizations	15·3

Source: Wieruszewski (1975), p. 230.

(b) Government administration, 1975.

Government position	Women (no.)
Council of State[a]	1
Council of Ministers[b]	—
Ministers	—
Deputy ministers	2
Foreign service: ambassadors	—

a   Composed of president, fourteen deputy presidents, secretary, and eleven members.
b   Composed of president (prime minister), six deputy presidents, and twenty-two ministers (the number is subject to change).

(c) Sejm (the single-chamber parliament).

Year	%	No. of women
1953	17·4	74
1957	4·1	19
1961	13·0	60
1965	12·4	57
1969	13·5	62
1972	15·9	73
1976	20·6	95

Source: Central Statistical Office (1975), p. 95.

Managerial Positions in Administration, Industry, Academia and the Mass Media

Tables 6.11 and 6.12 reflect the discrepancy between the percentages of women at the top levels of management (i.e. among directors, presidents, and chairmen) and the percentages of women among experts, specialists, legal advisors, and advisors to the top levels. Although the proportion of women visibly at the top is generally small at all levels −10 per cent), their proportion among 'invisible' advisors and highly qualified senior or chief specialists is comparatively high (19−35) per cent). Thus, it is not a lack of competence that prevents women from being directors and presidents. There is a remarkably high proportion of female chief accountants (87 per

Table 6.11 continued.

(d) *Selected unions, 1972.*

Union	Women members (%)	Women members of boards (%)
Health workers	76·2	37·1
Teachers	76·2	41·4
Writers, press, radio, television	58.9	8.6
Culture and arts	51·7	29·8
Agriculture (socialized)	22·2	23·6

Source: Central Statistical Office (1975), p. 97.

e) Other political parties and youth organizations, 1973.

Organization	Women members (%)	Women members of boards (%)	Women (no.)
Unified Peasants Party	22·2	18·0	17
Democratic Party	29·2	11·2	9
Union of Socialist Youth	47·7	24·3	28
Union of Rural Youth	49·4	30·5	26

Source: Wieruszewski (1975), p. 163.

cent in non-industrial institutions). Table 6.13 shows that in industry this proportion is much smaller and decreasing, whereas at the level of senior financial consultant it is rising.

In 1974 women constituted 48·6 per cent of those holding master's degrees or the equivalent (e.g. physician) and 27·7 per cent of those with Ph.D. degrees or the equivalent (e.g. Doctor of Medical Sciences). But it is rather the docent degree[1] that is decisive for academic career and advancement. In 1974 women constituted 11·7 per cent of docents, and about 10 per cent of professors were women (Central Statistical Office, 1975) (Table 6.14).

For several decades the proportion of women among Polish physicians has been higher than in many other countries. After 1945 many Polish men chose technical rather than medical careers; engineering was considered more 'productive' than medicine, and, moreover, the newly developing and attractive technical professions paid better than medicine. Thus, medicine became feminized (Table 6.15). It is interesting to note that the prestige of this profession remains very high – second only to that of university professor and higher than that of engineering. No research has been done in this field, but it seems that the sex variable does not influence the authority

Table 6.12   *Women in various managerial non-industrial positions:*
Poland, 1973.

Position	Women	
	%	No.
Ministries		
Directors and vice-directors of departments; chief specialists outside the department; chairmen of independent ministerial units	4·6	66
Chief specialists in departments; chairmen of ministerial units; legal advisors; senior specialists and specialists	21·5	774
Local state administration		
Chairmen of the presidium of the province council; mayors of cities and towns and their vice-chairmen	9·8	218
Chairmen of the smallest (village) territorial units	4·1	97
Chief accountants	87·1	3,169
Management and employees of the various central state and co-operative institutions		
Directors (presidents); vice-directors (vice-presidents)	3·6	105
Advisors to directors (presidents); directors and vice-directors of bureaus and departments; chief specialists; chief accountants; chairmen (vice-chairmen) of the units	23·4	3,574
Central Co-operative Union		
Directors and vice-directors of sectors (bureaus); chief accountants; chairmen of independent units	8·8	24
Chairmen of departments; chief specialists; specialists; chairmen of departmental units	19·0	95

Source: Central Statistical Office (1975), pp. U5–U7.

of a doctor. In spite of the feminization of medicine both male and female MDs enjoy high social prestige, perhaps because people are used to the idea of the woman doctor, which in Poland has a long tradition. It seems that the high prestige of the medical profession derives mainly from the doctor's function as individual healer (Sokołowska, 1976b), and that being perceived as a good or bad doctor counts much more than gender. It should be added that qualifications of male and female doctors, measured by proportions of specialists, do not greatly differ.

Table 6.16 shows the distribution and proportion of women with doctoral and docent dissertations in selected medical specializations, where women predominate (pediatrics, ophthalmology, and microbiology), where they constitute almost half of the numbers (biochemistry, biophysics, and medicine), and where their proportion is the smallest (obstetrics, gynecology, and surgery). These data indicate the wide range of specializations chosen by female physicians and docents. Even in surgery – the most prestigious area of medicine – the proportion of women is quite impressive (16 per cent).

Table 6.13 *Percentage of women in higher work positions in industry: Poland, 1964 and 1968.*

Position	1964	1968
Director	1·9	1·5
Chief engineer, vice-director for technical affairs	2·2	2·3
Vice-director for management	3·6	4·6
Chief mechanic, chief power engineer, chief technician	2·7	4·2
Head of production section:		
section mechanic	8·2	7·1
power engineer, technician	9·7	13·9
Senior foreman	1·7	4·0
Foreman	3·9	5·0
Chief accountant	38·2	30·6
Director of finance section	17·5	23·6
Senior financial consultant	37·6	58·2
Financial consultant	50·8	76·9

Source: Wrochno (1971), p. 27.

Table 6.14 *Percentage of women among people occupying various academic positions: Poland, 1960–1 to 1974–5.*

Position	1960–1	1965–6	1970–1	1974–5
Full professors[a]	5·5	5·1	6·6	6·7
'Extraordinary' professors[b]	8·4	8·9	9·7	10·2
Docents[c]	14·4	15·3	13·2	14·5
Adjuncts[d]	22·1	28·2	32·8	33·4
Assistants	33·7	33·5	35·0	37·1
Lecturers	10·6	20·8	26·6	30·7
Others	42·7	51·8	54·8	63·2

a So-called 'ordinary'
b Equivalent to associate professor.
c Special Polish degree (see explanation, note 1).
d Roughly corresponds with senior lecturer.

Source: Central Statistical Office (1975), p. 41.

The proportion of women physicians holding the degree of medical doctor and docent increased markedly between 1968 and 1973 (Table 6.17), and it is much higher than the proportion of women in all disciplines holding doctoral and docent degrees. Undoubtedly, the decisive factor is the 'supply' of a large number of women physicians; their upward pressure has resulted in their breaking through the barriers to higher levels.

On the contrary, however, no similar passage exists between the occupational and managerial structures in the Polish health services (Sokołowska, 1976b). There has never been a female Minister or

Table 6.15 Number of physicians, dentists, and pharmacists of both sexes and the percentage of women in these professions: Poland, selected years 1921–74.

Year	Total no. (thousands)			% of women		
	Physicians	Dentists	Pharmacists	Physicians	Dentists	Pharmacists
1921	5,464	2,537	3,558	12·0[a]	51·1	16·0
1960	28,708	9,316	7,924	38·4	78·2	73·9
1970	49,283	13,611	12,298	47·6	81·3	80·7
1974	54,930	15,091	13,845	50·2	81·3	83·1

a Twenty per cent of doctors in 1931 were women.

Source: Statistical yearbooks. See Sokołowska (1976b), p. 141.

Table 6.16 *Total number of dissertations for doctor and docent degrees in medical sciences and the percentage of women, by selected specializations: Poland, 1960–9.*

Speciality	Doctoral disserations		Docent dissertations	
	Total no.	% of women	total no.	% of women
Pediatrics	293	74·1	39	74·3
Ophthalmology	93	66·6	27	51·8
Microbiology	129	62·7	33	39·3
Biochemistry, biophysics	139	46·7	41	17·0
Medicine	723	38·8	135	22·2
Obstetrics, gynecology	276	20·2	48	12·5
Surgery	666	16·6	129	6·2

Source: Statistical Yearbook of Science, 1971, p. 12.

Table 6.17 *Percentages of women physicians holding doctoral and docent degrees and being nominated professors: Poland, 1968 and 1973.*

Year	Professors[a]	Docents	Doctors
1968	13·8	20·8	32·7
1973	12·0	25·7	36·9

a Between 40 and 55 years of age usually.

Source: Census of Personnel, 1968 and 1973, p. 10.

Deputy Minister of Health and Social Welfare, of which there are four. No women are directors of departments in that same ministry nor heads of the provincial departments of health and social welfare. In this hierarchy women first appeared as heads of newly established administrative units aimed at unifying all health services at the provincial level. In 1973 – the first year of this new organizational system – women were 6·5 per cent of the directors of these units.

In 1973 women formed 38·6 per cent of directors of hospitals and outpatient clinics – an unexpectedly high proportion, representing an interesting trend that should be studied. It may reflect a relatively low level of decision-making in institutions subject to a centrally planned bureaucracy or the fact that these posts may be located in a grey area between the professional structure and the managerial one.

Let us not forget that decision-making in medicine often involves questions of life and death. The physician functions at a dramatic decision level, even if life or death is not always involved, and that is precisely why the doctor enjoys such high prestige in modern society. That prestige is still very high in Poland compared to that of a government minister (Sarapata, 1965). The high proportion of female physicians in the socialist countries and their growing percentages in other countries means that women are now gaining access to the unique powers and rights granted by society to its medical healers (Sokołowska, 1976b).

FACTORS PROMOTING CHANGE

The initial impulse that set in motion profound changes in the situation of women in the socialist countries came from political decisions grounded in ideological premises. The driving force of these changes was Marxist-Leninist ideology and the political criteria based on it.

Marxist-Leninist Doctrine Regarding the Position of Women under Socialism
The Marxist classics saw woman's role in two dimensions: in the family and in society. They did not restrict the function of women to the sphere of domestic life but emphasized their role in social production and anticipated that their mass participation in the social economy would effect a fundamental change in women's position in the society as well as in the family. They considered that the capitalist system separated women from the currents of social life, rendering them immobile and backward, whereas the socialist system would free women from the burden of household chores, involve them in social production, and enable their active participation in public life. Socialism would thus create the necessary conditions for women's full and harmonious development as full-fledged members of society. The Marxist classics did not identify the household with the family. They considered woman's changed position under socialism as an essential factor of change in the family, but the family of the new type was to continue to be the basic social group enjoying the protection of the state. Engels argued that the emancipation of women would become possible only when women were enabled to take part in production on a large social scale and when domestic duties required their attention to only a minor degree. This has become possible only as the result of modern large-scale industry, which not only permits the participation of women in production in large numbers but actually calls for it and, moreover, strives to convert private domestic work into a public industry (Engels, 1972, 1902).

Marxists considered the participation of women in public service and political life as indispensable to building a socialist society. 'Without drawing women into the public services, into political life, it is not possible even to build democracy, not to speak of socialism,' wrote Lenin (1962). This pertained to women occupying managerial posts in enterprises and acting in all organs of Soviet power. 'It is necessary that women take ever greater part in the management of public institutions and in government' (Lenin, 1962).

This 'initial impulse' of Marxist-Leninist ideology set in motion political decisions affecting the lives of Poland's women. Legislation was the first step, and the next was the industrialization of Poland.

Industrialization of Poland
The changes introduced by the new government – such as the socialization

of industry and other economic sectors, the radical agrarian reform, accelerated industrialization, widely accessible education, and other cultural advances – all transformed the country and gave it a new image in a brief few years. One such fundamental change was the phenomenon of 'women leaving the four walls of the home' and undertaking employment. By creating a demand for labor industrialization implemented the basic constitutional guarantees of equal rights for women. Expansion of the number of occupations and of places of work and their differentiation opened up new possibilities for satisfying family needs by gainful employment outside the home. During Poland's Six Year Plan of 1950–6, marked by an especially rapid rate of development of industry, an organizational and educational effort was made to induce the largest possible number of women to take jobs. Women were inclined to go to work. Since average earnings per employee in the socialized economy were inadequate to maintain a family, an additional breadwinner was required. In this period the need to build nurseries, kindergartens, day care centers, and other facilities was strongly stressed, liberating women from 'household slavery.'

Education
The education of women is one of the great achievements of socialism. Education is a driving force for change in the lives of individuals and groups; it creates new choices and shapes the direction of life. It is to the credit of socialism that the mass of Polish women can for the first time share this priceless good.

BARRIERS[2]

Historical and Cultural Heritage

Familial Importance in Polish Culture   It may be said that 'Poland endured because of the family,' particularly during the period of the country's partition (i.e. 1795–1918). The family was then the only national institution – both the cradle and bastion of national spirit. Women's position in the family varied in character in peasant, working class, and gentry-intelligentsia families, but the traditional image of Polish women during this period presents them as an enlightened stratum.

Polish conditions demanded fortitude. Polish wives and mothers were often their husbands' advisors; and compelled by circumstances, when the husband was at war, in prison, or in exile, or if he had perished, the woman often became head of the family, conducted affairs, and directed the children's future. The ideal of woman was praised to the skies: fortitude and adherence to duty were demanded of her; her importance in bringing up the children and in the household was emphasized. Feelings of public responsibility arose among women and embraced ever-widening circles of them. Wives and daughters of the gentry secretly taught Polish language and history in villages, opened nurseries, and conducted courses in household management and hygiene for rural women. Healing the village sick was often the women's function (Jabłonowska, 1975).

After 1945 it appeared to some people – including myself, as one of the founders of the Polish industrial health service – that because of the position traditionally occupied by women in the family they would automatically play leading roles in the new occupational, professional, and political structures. But there was no bridge between the two, just as there is none between philanthropic and voluntary work and gainful employment in the modern economy. 'Serving' leaves women outside the centers of government, decision-making, and planning.

Underdevelopment of Democratic Patterns of Family Life (Sokołowska, 1976c). Conditions during the Polish partition militated against the development of inner family democracy. Education and preparation for constructive citizenship were neglected. Although women of all classes traditionally occupied high positions in the family and in informal circles, these were their only areas of activity. They were assigned a strictly feminine role by the patriarchal social order. The patriarchal family is typical of agrarian society. It is characterized by the authority of the father-head of the family, who represents force and compulsion and protects other family members. From the beginnings of the Polish state all ordinances emphasized the role of the father.(Sokołowska, 1976a).

Owing to the preponderance of the agricultural population the patriarchal famly was the dominant form of Polish family life. The father played the leading role economically and socially, and the other family members enjoyed more individual rights, but here too there reigned a strict differentiation of family roles based on sex. The wife-mother occupied an important position in the household, and literature of the period made frequent reference to 'matriarchy' in the family. But this matriarchy was limited to the home and divorced from contact with the world, which was totally the male's domain. Women enjoyed relative levels of emancipation among the intelligentsia, in which changes in life patterns were visible. But in 1939 the intelligentsia constituted only 6 per cent of the Polish population.

The Roman Catholic Church.   In the interwar period (i.e. 1918–33) more than half of the Polish population was agricultural. The patriarchal structure and its patterns were especially strong. This situation was reinforced by the Roman Catholic Church – a powerful force in the country for the last 1,000 years.

The church in Poland is the irreconcilable advocate of a social life based on the strict separation of the sexes, with the woman's role severely limited to the home and family. Although all religions share that attitude toward women, Roman Catholicism is considered to be the most conservative in this respect (Daly, 1970).

Sexist Attitudes   The majority of Poles in the 40–65 age group today stem from the peasantry or working class and were deeply imbued in their childhood and youth with a prevailing 'ideal' image of women. In conversation on this question with men in leading positions one is struck by the fact that their conception of woman is still so similar to that 'ideal' model. It is an image encompassing all 'female wisdom.' She is brave, hardworking, economical, self-denying, and devoted; the guardian angel of the children, the aged, and the sick in the family; the ruler of pots, pans, and the washtub; the confidante of man's troubles; and his life companion. It is difficult for them to accept a different idea of woman – not that she should not have an education and a washing machine, but that she is a true and equal partner in family, professional, social, and political life instead of someone's 'life companion' (Sokołowska, 1978).

Jan Szczepański (1970), writing of Polish personality types in his work *Polish Society*, has observed:

> The traditional Polish personality ideal was derived from the culture of the nobility and was composed of such traits as readiness to defend the Catholic faith and the fatherland, a highly developed sense of personal dignity and honor, a full-blown individualism, an imposing mien, chivalry, intellectual brilliance and dash. This personality ideal, developed by the nobility, was in some degree assimilated by the peasants, whose sense of attachment and fidelity to religious faith, to their fathers' heritage, and to old customs proved to be a vital factor in maintaining national consciousness in the nineteenth century. The intelligentsia also accepted this traditional personality ideal, with only the urban population of small entrepreneurs being somewhat closer to the ideals of the Western middle classes. Some nineteenth-century ideological currents sought to reshape this traditional personality ideal into something more work-oriented and businesslike, for economic growth was perceived as the necessary condition for the regaining of independence. But in spite of these currents, most of the intelligentsia was inclined to maintain the traditional and romantic idea of armed struggle, and the chivalrous personality was better suited to this purpose. (p. 167)

Certain generally-accepted persisting norms regulate male–female relations and behavior. The male, traditionally, has to play the role of 'cavalier.' He kisses the woman's hand at home, at work, and at professional meetings, as an expression of welcome, farewell, sorrow, gratitude, and so on. Political leaders also observe this custom. A man is expected to bring women flowers for any number of occasions, which occur every day. Perhaps this is the reason for Poland's warm acceptance of the International Woman's Day on March 8. It has become a veritable 'flower day,' on which men swamp 'their' women with flowers: wives, sisters, girlfriends, mothers, grandmothers, daughters, female colleagues, friends, supervisors, subordinates, and so on (Sokołowska, 1978).

Fluctuations of the Declared Models of Women's Position in Polish Society
There are two main policy trends regarding the societal position of Polish women: one aimed at raising their occupational positions, and the other aimed at guaranteeing conditions to enable them to perform domestic duties better. These two trends do not contradict each other; however, they are visible in practice in differing degrees. Such differences are most

evident among women without professional qualifications; the higher the level of education, the less evident these differences become. Nevertheless, they play an important role in shaping social consciousness and public attitudes.

In the last thirty years there has been a polar change in the models for women's position in Polish society, as expressed in the press and elsewhere (Piotrowski, 1963). Four main viewpoints have emerged. (1) The years 1947–54 were characterized by a desire to achieve maximum activization of women, in which connection their role as members of a socialist society was emphasized. (2) In 1955–7 a new model was projected, primarily stressing women's family role and thus automatically lowering their vocational or professional role. (3) From about 1958 to the end of the 1960s the tendency appeared to be to harmonize both viewpoints. (4) At the beginning of the 1970s a new approach focused on a pronatalist population policy. It seems that recently a still new trend has been emerging marked by the growing availability of individual options. From each viewpoint different principles of social policy have flowed. In the first period the need to build nursery schools was strongly stressed, as well as kindergartens and other facilities liberating women from the household. In the second period resources were limited for those facilities and directed toward increased wages and higher family allowances. In the third period the approach was rather undecided, but the expansion of creches and kindergartens was still checked. In 1973 about 20 per cent of urban working mothers with children up to the age of 3 sent their children to a day nursery. About 48 per cent of urban working mothers used kindergartens (Kurzynowski, 1977).

The fourth period has been characterized by a new trend aimed at limiting the employment of certain groups of women for demographic reasons – to increase the birthrate. The press devotes ever more space to the problems of the family, which is regarded purely as the woman's domain. Biographies of mothers with many children are being published, and a system of incentives has been created to encourage leaves from work after childbirth. The molding of opinion on the upbringing of children leaves no doubt that it is regarded as the mother's responsibility. 'Family policy' is one of the most propagated slogans in Poland today, but it is seen primarily as part of the 'woman's question.' That 'woman's question' takes a different emphasis in different parts of the world. For Poland it centers on the question of nurseries, kindergartens, other child-care services and social welfare benefits, care for the aged and handicapped, services facilitating housework and household management (e.g. restaurants, laundries, frozen food), and recreational facilities. It has become a commonplace that these form a specifically woman's sphere and that society provides women with them in order to lighten their burdens. The mass media often use the slogan 'let us help the workingwoman,' taking for granted that the double role – family and work – is a purely woman's affliction. However, there have been further changes in the past few years. On one hand, there are several new regulations making it easier for mothers to stop working periodically; and on the other hand, the number of helping institutions is increasing. Besides, the pronatalist propaganda in its former shape is clearly decreasing (Sokołowska, 1978).

The Polish mass media have for some time been projecting the model of the incomplete family – one deprived of a father. Actually, the proportion of families with so-called single mothers is approximately 11 per cent. The great majority have both a father and a mother, but the father remains in the background where family and household matters are concerned.

Not much more was required of the traditional father than to provide maintenance and punish the children. The 'good' husband and father is still considered by many to be one who does not drink or brawl and brings home the money that he earns. If he also helps his wife to take out the garbage, for instance, or make minor repairs, he is considered almost ideal. Traditional prescriptions for the father role say very little about child upbringing. The most important decisions regarding the children were once his prerogative. Today, all such matters are handled in common or, as in most families, are the exclusive domain of the mother. Matters affecting children and the family are relegated to women. This is why the Polish press publishes pictures of mothers often but of fathers relatively seldom. This is why, when reading about women's professional achievements, we are usually told that they have children; with men we learn only of their professional achievements. A regulation issued a few years ago equalized mothers' and fathers' rights to leave from work to care for a sick child. Yet the situation now is practically the same as before the regulation; that is, a father can get such leave only in exceptional circumstances.[3]

The present period is transitional. The existing prejudices and stereotypes can only inhibit the tempo of change; they cannot stop it.

Important changes are occurring in the roles of husband and wife. They are most rapid in urban families and among women and husbands with relatively high levels of education. They are pioneers of new patterns of family relationships. New life styles have traditionally been modeled by the educated class in Poland. It can be expected that these new patterns will be accepted and adopted by society at large. They arise as a result of the rationalization and individualization of the social behavior of both individuals and families. Underlying them are far-reaching changes in the value systems cherished by men as husbands and fathers and by women as wives and mothers (Sokołowska, 1975).

Examples of such processes of change have been provided by a study (Łobodzińska, 1970) of a group of married couples in which both partners are engineers, living and working in Warsaw ('dual career families' in Western terms). Here, there is a partnership of the spouses, expressed in a more equal division of domestic duties, shared child care, and shared holidays and pastimes. An important place in the marriages of young engineers is occupied by professional discussions and by mutual help in domestic matters. The women engineers have no thought of permanently quitting their jobs, since they see their professional activity as an indispensable element in their lives.

Young couples, both of whom are scientific workers, constitute a similar group. This category of the intelligentsia, enjoying high social prestige, was prominent among the respondents to a 1967 questionnaire entitled 'My Weekdays' for readers of a popular daily, *Zycie Warszawy*. Remarkable in the responses was the lack of sex differentiation in descriptions of burdensome time-consuming household chores. Sunday washing and cleaning, shopping after work, meals cooked for the next day, standing in line for consumer goods, washing diapers, walking the children to school or kindergarten, and dozens of other tasks were performed in haste and tension by wives and husbands alike. All this indicates that the traditional division of household labor between wives and husbands will become obsolete (Chylińska, 1967).

CONCLUSIONS

A top managerial post is practically unattainable for most Polish working women because they must at the same time run a household – a difficult and absorbing task, given Polish conditions. Experience indicates that an ordinary job – even one requiring a higher education – can somehow be reconciled with the performance of domestic duties, but managerial positions mean irregular job hours, concentration on work, and the subordination of other aspects of life to it. For a married woman and mother to undertake a managerial post would require a fundamental reorganization of the present family and professional structures. The Polish revolution transformed class relations but did not automatically change relations among family members. Patterns of family life change much more slowly, and this is aggravated by underdeveloped services and child care and educational institutions (Sokołowska, 1975, 1977). However, time is passing rapidly indeed.

The coming years will bring further changes. In Poland there appear to be favorable conditions for such changes. (1) Most working women are employed during their whole lifetimes, like most working men. This is a basic precondition if women are to avoid marginal work roles and become important members of staffs with opportunities for advancement. (2) The influence of classic Freudian theories is weak in Poland, as are other conservative orientations on child-rearing; Dr Spock is unknown, for instance. (3) There are high percentages of women in the professions. Women as physicians, dentists, lawyers, and even engineers can be met every day in Poland, and the population is already used to this image. (4) There is a general recognition of women as individual performers at senior levels (e.g. medical specialists, research scientists) where demonstrable skills and qualifications are required.

The achievement of leading positions in management is the last link in the chain of equal rights for women – the last 'fortress' to be 'conquered.' It is the area in which masculine prejudice operates most strongly and where men's judgement of what women can be expected to achieve is furthest from reality (Fogarty, Rapoport, and Rapoport, 1967).

There exists a vast number of bright, well-qualified, and determined women. It is such people who make for a growing part of decision-making elites. Many such women already serve as deputies, advisors, consultants, and specialists. Barriers of every kind will gradually disappear as relics of the past. This is an irreversible process and an inevitable development.

NOTES

(1) The degree of docent roughly corresponds with the title of associate professor in the United States. Some people get nominated to the position of docent on the basis of their Ph.D. and scientific and/or practical achievements, without accomplishing a dissertation, which otherwise must be published in book form. A docent with the dissertation can obtain a professorship.
(2) Much of the material in this and the following section appeared in Sokołowska (1978).
(3) Interview with the editor-in-chief (Barbara Sidorczuk) of the women's weekly *Kobieta i Życie* (Woman and Life) in the weekly 'Kultura' (February 1, 1976).

REFERENCES

Andrzejewski, Adam (1976) 'Social aspects of housing policy,' in A. Rajkiewicz (ed.), *Social Policy* (Warsaw: Panstwowe Wydawnictwo Ekonomiczne), p. 259.
Census of Personnel, 1968 and 1973 (1969, 1974) (Warsaw): Central Statistical Office).
Central Statistical Office (1975) *Kobieta w Polsce* (Women in Poland) (Warsaw).
Chylińska, Kamila (1967) 'Twilight of a hookworm,' *Zycie Warszawy* (May 22).
Daly, M. (1970) 'Women in the Catholic Church,' in R. Morgan (ed.), *Sisterhood is Powerful* (New York: Random House).
Engels, Friedrich (1972) *The Origin of the Family, Private Property and the State* (New York: International Publishers, 1972; originally Chicago: Charles H. Kerr, 1902).
Fogarty, Michael, Rapoport, Rhona, and Rapoport, Robert (1967) *Women and Top Jobs: An Interim Report* (London: Political and Economic Planning).
Jabłonowska, Zofia (1975) 'The family in the 19th and beginning of the 20th centuries,' in J. Komorowska (ed.), *Changes in the Polish Family* (Warsaw: Instytut Wydawniczy CRZZ), pp. 52-71.
Kozakiewicz, Mikołaj (1973) *Barriers to the Promotion by Education* (Warsaw: Instytut Wydawniczy CRZZ).
Kurzynowski, Adam (1967) *Ciągłość Pracy a Macieryństwo* (The Continuity of Work and Maternity) (Warsaw: Państwowe Wydawnictwo Ekonomiczne).
Kurzynowski, Adam (1977) 'Genesis and perspectives of the gainful employment of married women in Poland,' unpublished dissertation (Warsaw: Higher School of Statistics and Planning).
Lenin, Vladimir I. (1962) 'O proletarskoj milicii' (On the proletarian militia), *Połnoie Sobranie*, vol. 31, Moscow, Gosizdat pp. 35-47.
Łobodzińska, Barbara (1970) *Urban Marriage* (Warsaw: Pánstwowe Wydawnictwo Naukowe).
Markowska, Danuta (1976) 'The contemporary family in the light of the social science findings,' unpublished paper presented at the conference on Summary of the Scientific Findings on Women, Maternity, and Family, Polish Academy of Sciences, Warsaw.
Mogey, John and Piotrowski, Jerzy (1976) 'Changes of family forms in Poland,' unpublished paper presented at the Fourth World Congress of Rural Sociology, Torun, Poland, August 9-13.
Otawska, Elzbieta (1974) 'Not only about women,' Radio-TV *Current Events* (Warsaw).
Piotrowski, Jerzy (1963) *Women's Gainful Employment and the Family* (Warsaw: Książka i Wiedza).
Piotrowski, Jerzy (1969) *Family Needs Resulting from an Increased Employment of Married Women* (Warsaw: Institute of Social Economy).
Roguszka-Klupść, Maria (1975) *Premiany Spoleznej Pozycji Kobiety Prącującej Zawodowo (Changes of Social Position of Working Woman) (Poznań: Wydawnictwo Poznańskie),* p. 104.
Sarapata, Adam (1965) *Studies of the Stratification and the Social Mobility in Poland* (Warsaw: Książka i Wiedza).
Sokołowska, Magdalena (1975) 'The role and status of women in Poland,' *Studies in Comparative Development*, vol. 3, no. 10, pp. 71-87.
Sokołowska, Magdalena (1976a) 'Women's emancipation and socialism: the case of the People's Republic of Poland,' *International Journal of Health Services*, vol. 1, no. 6, pp. 35-51

Sokołowska, Magdalena (1976b) 'Women in decision making in health,' in *Proceedings of International Conference on Women in Health, June 16–18, 1975* (Washington, DC: US Department of Health, Education, and Welfare.

Sokołowska, Magdalena (1976c) 'The woman in the awareness of contemporary Polish society,' *The Polish Sociological Bulletin*, no. 3/35, pp. 41–50.

Sokołowksa, Magdalena (1977) 'Poland: women's experience under socialism,' in J. Zollinger Giele and A. Chapman Smock (eds), *Women: Roles and Status in Eight Countries* (New York: Wiley), pp. 347–81.

Sokołowska, Magdalena (1978) 'Poland,' in Sheila B. Kamerman and Alfred J. Kahn (eds), *Family Policy: Government and Families in Fourteen Countries* (New York: Columbia University Press), pp. 239–69.

Sokołowska, Magdalena and Łobodzińska, Barbara (1971) 'Contraceptives and termination of pregnancy,' *Problemy Rodziny*, no. 1/57, pp. 50–5.

Statistical Yearbook of Science, 1971 (1972) (Warsaw: Central Statistical Office).

Szczepański, Jan (1970) *Polish Society* (New York: Random House).

Wieruszewski, Roman (1975) *Equality of Women and Men in the Polish People's Republic* (Poznań: V. Wydawnictwo Poznańskie).

Wrochno, Krystyna (1971) *Problemy Pracy Kobiet* (Problems of Women's Work) (Warsaw: Interpress).

7

Women and Political Power in a Revolutionary Society

The Yugoslav Case

BOGDAN DENITCH

This study of women in the Yugoslav revolution was inspired by a short quotation from Schumpeter (1942, 1947) with which I have been in dispute for the last five or six years:

> Social structures, types and attitudes are coins that do not readily melt. Once they are formed, they persist, possibly for centuries, and since different structures and types display different degrees of ability to survive, we almost always find that the actual group and national behavior more or less depart from what we would expect it to be if we tried to infer it from the dominant forms of the productive process.

I do not agree. I think that national types, attitudes, and values do melt and change when the proper degree of heat is applied continually over a protracted period of time. It is very much like the issue of whether one can abolish racism only by changing the minds and hearts of the persons who are racists or whether one can set up structures and legal sanctions that make it impossible for the practice to continue.

Yugoslavia is an interesting social laboratory and should be especially so for feminists; sociologists could not have invented a better one. To begin with, Yugoslavia has a wide variety of economic and historic development, ranging from that of central Europe to that of central Asia; it has, for example, an illiteracy rate in Slovenia in the north of 2 per cent for both women and men and an illiteracy rate in the south of 41 per cent for women and 21 per cent for men, all within the same polity. There are three religious traditions—Catholic, Orthodox, and Moslem—which are an intimate part of ethnic identity and share an historically rooted mutual hostility much as in Northern Ireland. There is a high degree of decentralization and diversity, over which a set of policies has been imposed since the wartime revolution with the aim of modifying and modernizing Yugoslavia's society and state. These conditions enable one to ask which factors act as barriers to social and political modernization and which do not. Is it the religious factor? Is it degree of development? Is it the urban or rural issue?

What is particularly interesting about the political culture underlying the Yugoslav reality is that much of the country was dominated for centuries by the Turks. Thus, in addition to the other factors mentioned the legal and political traditions of Islam were imposed over centuries on a subject European population and were adopted by much of that population. They were traditions based on the most exaggerated form of *machismo* known to Europe. In Montenegro, for example, female infanticide was practiced until not too long ago.

The modernizing policies of the party and state have often been viewed as an attack on the culture and religious traditions of a specific subgroup. For example, in the province of Kosovo, which is Albanian and Moslem, there is enormous resistance on the part of parents in rural areas to sending women to secondary school. They are not marriageable within the community once they have completed secondary school. Does the state send police? How should it enforce an unwanted social policy in a mountain area that is armed to the teeth and has a tradition of guerrilla warfare? How much external pressure is appropriate, or should the society wait for internal pressures favoring modernization to develop? This is just one of the many constraints faced by national policy in the Albanian region, because its tradition is Islamic, with very specific and subordinate roles assigned to women.

A few background points are necessary. Critical to Yugoslavia's course of development is the fact that the social revolution that occurred there took place within the framework of a bitter civil war. Most of the barriers against this social revolution, eliminated only gradually elsewhere in eastern Europe, were smashed in Yugoslavia in a very compressed amount of time. Thus, the regime, after consolidating power, could develop a more popular and broader base than the other eastern European regimes; it remained more responsive to this base, in good part because it was left with a residue, which still exists, of an armed rural population that sets rather rigid limits on what can and cannot be done.

Yugoslavia's wartime resistance was much like that of Vietnam—a guerrilla resistance combined with mobile larger military units—but the guerrilla resistance imposed two sociologically interesting factors. The most successful guerrilla resistance was in the most backward areas—those regions that are the most mountainous, the most distant from the cities, and thus the most traditional and patriarchal. Therefore, the population that looked for a deserved reward from the social system after the revolution was in good part the most traditionally formed population in Yugoslavia. It made up a large part of the new elite, which did not, as is widely assumed, consist only of workers and intellectuals from the industrial centers.

Further, the guerrilla resistance imposed a pattern of organization, continued for twenty years, of a dual military and civilian arm, which was often female. As the guerrilla movement grew, the underground organizational structure – its network – had to be organized in the rural villages. Therefore, unlike the rest of eastern Europe the social revolution began in the traditional patriarchal Yugoslav villages before the communists conquered the cities. In order to win the civil war they had to smash conservative attitudes in the villages that were their strongholds. A new power pyramid was created in the village in the early stages of the movement;

instead of leadership by the wealthier aged peasants, who were the heads of household and traditional holders of village power, the new party organization right after the war was young and poor – the exact opposite of the traditional model. Fortunately, or unfortunately, this coincided with a bias against the countryside on the part of the new leaders. Since they themselves were of peasant origin, they had little romanticism about the desirability of peasant life, and they thought that the greatest single reward that the revolution could bring the peasants was to elevate them from rural neglect and abolish them as a class. That is, they wanted to reduce the rural population as quickly as possible. Yugoslavia's rural population, which was approximately 80 per cent of the country at the time of the war, declined to approximately 34 per cent in a period of twenty-five years. As a result the overwhelming majority of the population of Yugoslav cities comes from peasant communities and peasant backgrounds and norms.

Postwar birth-control policies did not lead to the same strife in Yugoslavia that was seen in Poland, primarily because the Catholic Church was organizationally crippled because of its extensive wartime collaboration with the foreign occupiers. Thus, it was in the name of patriotism rather than antireligiosity that the party could wage a relatively popular campaign against the social and political influence of the organized religious groups. The Catholic hierarchy had collaborated with the Germans, and the Moslem and Orthodox churches had backed the losers in the civil war.[1] The churches were thus forced to keep a low profile for the next twenty years. But the new government introduced the most marvelous and effective of all contraceptive devices, namely, small apartments, which had the effect of reducing family size in Yugoslavia. Small apartments plus industrialization and the availability of consumer goods seem to have produced more effective and widespread birth control than the publicity and polemics employed by other countries.

The elite that emerged from the Yugoslav civil war and revolution was as war torn as the countryside; of the approximately 12,000 Communist Party members who went into the civil war, 3,000 survived. A disproportionately large number of women cadre members survived the war because they were serving in illegal political organizations rather than in combat units. Thus, close to 30 per cent of the postwar party cadre – the one that really had power – consisted of women who had been tested in a civil war and revolution, not people who had joined a victorious governing organization. That percentage, of course, began to drop as the party became more massive. Nevertheless, this meant that a core existed of powerful well-connected women who used the same partisan old-fighter network for career advancement that was used by their male counterparts. This generation is highly compact. These are people who were generally between the ages of 18 and 24 during the war, have stayed in power for an unusually long time, and will retire more or less at the same time. The central and most interesting question is to what extent has this generation of leaders been able to transform those attitudes and norms of the society and its political institutions which they have sought to change?

Institutionally, the story is very much the same as that of the rest of eastern Europe. Most of the progressive family and women's legislation traditionally demanded by labor and left-wing parties was passed very quickly immediately after the war. I do not think many deputies even read the proposed social legislation in the first few postwar years of Parliament; it wasn't polite or safe to question the new laws. But as time went on, Parliament had fewer and fewer women in it. As it became more important, it became less and less representative, not just of women but also of workers, peasants, and the young. Parliament became the place occupied by those who held power in the society, because it was the place where rewards were distributed.

However, there are still powerful women in the political life of the country. For example, two of the largest of the Communist Party (League) organizations – those of Serbia, which has 8 million of Yugoslavia's 20 million population, and of Croatia with 4½ million – were headed by women who were purged for political reasons only a few years ago. These were women whose power was far from symbolic. The Croatian party organization is still headed by a woman, and the last Croatian government was headed by a woman. Given the competitive, almost Balkan, character of Yugoslavia, it is certain that no one gets to such posts for decorative purposes. One is there because one has the requisite political power to be there.

Wartime heroism, officially recognized, was an important factor in some women's rise to positions of importance in postwar Yugoslavia. Of the holders of the National Hero Medal, given only for extraordinary bravery in combat, 12 per cent are women. Also, 10 per cent of all combatants were women, most of whom still hold officer's rank in the reserve army and maintain links with the powerful military establishment. This is a very peculiar situation, made more peculiar by the fact that many of these women are from mountain areas – precisely the regions where female military prowess is most shocking to the local norms and values. The results were predictable. After the war such women did not go back to the mountains; they went to the cities and on to the important careers that were the cornerstones of their extraordinary social mobility after the war. Once liberated personally from the constraints of a traditional patriarchal peasant society, they generally had to leave it. Happily, in the period of mobilization of the five or six years following the revolution there was a rapid development of new social places, and opportunities opened when the old middle class was wiped out and a whole new state *apparat* had to be staffed. The people in line to fill these positions were the holders of the National Hero Medal and the partisan veterans; among them a large number of women took positions of real power.

Today, examining some institutional factors, a few figures are illustrative of the new situation. There is a very large number of university students in Yugoslavia – 129 per 10,000 (this can be compared to Britain's 72 per 10,000) – and 42 per cent of the Yugoslav students are women, broadly distributed among the faculties. In the agricultural sciences (the lowest in prestige in Yugoslavia because the countryside still represents all that is backward), comprising veterinary science, forestry, and agriculture, 15 per cent of the students are women; in technology, 19–20 per cent are women; in the high-prestige natural sciences and mathematics, 40 per cent; in economics, 36 per cent; in architecture (the highest-paid profession in Yugoslavia), 22 per cent; in the political faculties (the one forming cadres), 35 per cent. Further, women are well represented in the traditional middle-class faculties: 44 per cent in medicine; 57 per cent in arts and letters (the training ground of the intelligentsia); 52 per cent in dentistry; and finally, 77 per cent in pharmacy (a relatively low-prestige faculty). Thus, high concentrations of women students *do not* coincide with low prestige faculties; their representation is scattered. What is interesting about the distribution is that it tells a story about the current society; the further it is from the countryside, the more women are evident.

This is true in the occupations as well; the further away they are from associations with the countryside, the more women are represented. For example, *25 per cent* of all persons sitting on worker's councils (comparable to boards of directors) of large enterprises are women. These are, of course, the leadership group for large industrial organizations. Only *5 per cent* of the co-operative members sitting on rural workers' councils are women, although there are proportionally more women in the rural co-operatives and in small enterprises than in large enterprises. The same problem mentioned earlier in the case of Poland exists in Yugoslavia – the feminization of agriculture and the aging of agricultural populations. It is also a fact that the pool of new contingents coming into the cities today no longer has the ascriptive qualities that went with the partisan generation, and there is no equivalent way of earning it. There is no drastic social or political rupture going on, so today proper entry is by the routinized way through higher education, Communist Party (League) service, and the bureaucracies themselves.[2]

What is most remarkable about the statistics for women's participation in leadership roles in Yugoslavia today, however, is that they do not coincide with the social indicators that we should expect to find. The *lowest* percentage of women in leadership positions is found in the *most* developed republic, namely, Slovenia; the highest percentages of women in positions of power occur in Serbia and Bosnia, which are relatively low in development. The highest percentages of women students come similarly from the least developed areas. These data may mean that there are no alternative career slots for an ambitious person in a backward area and that the way up is through the higher education system and the political organizations. The occupation structure has too limited a range of opportunities in such areas.

In the more recent period – roughly during the last decade – the arm of the party has begun to be felt less heavily in the less directly political arenas. An aversion to some norms and values of the party on the part of a population subjected to years of rapid transformation has begun to re-emerge. The regimes in eastern Europe have not been willing substantially to liberalize the political power structure. Instead, they have liberalized, in eastern Europe and Yugoslavia, the pressures on spheres of private life. That has been the *quid pro quo*. Therefore, there is today more tolerance for the churches, more tolerance of consumerism, and more tolerance of relatively good living on the part of the higher income persons; there is less puritanism; and there are more patriarchal values reasserting themselves in the small towns in the countryside.

For the countryside there is yet another explanation for the 'backsliding' that is occurring. Given a very high mobility rate, who is left in the countryside? Only the less intelligent, the less ambitious, the more conservative, and the more religious individuals remain. The countryside is in effect more reactionary than it has ever been before, because those persons who can fit in with the values of the new modernizing communist system have gone to the towns. The more intelligent persons have moved up in the new hierarchies, which are continually expanding.

Another aspect of the problems encountered in changing the role of women in a formerly very backward society arises from the process of decentralization. In today's Yugoslavia the power pyramid, as far as women are concerned, is inverse. The higher the level in the party or government, the more women there are; the lower is the level, the fewer women there are. Why? It is because high positions within the party and state hierarchies are more subject to ideological pressures from the center, and their gatekeepers cannot dodge the party's norms so easily. The local party cell in a village or a neighborhood can nearly always get away with what it wants to in personnel policy. Institutions and persons in positions of importance, however, are subject to external pressures. From the point of view of feminists and others concerned with the problems of social justice, this may pose a moral dilemma; perhaps a little authoritarianism is needed in order to change deep-seated values and behavior patterns. I do not know, but it makes me uneasy.

There is a missing generation of women today in Yugoslav politics. The women who participated in the revolutionary period are generally high up and do fairly well, and the women who have been coming out of the university system since the mid-1960s face relatively egalitarian career patterns. (Women's wage patterns, by the way, do not deviate significantly from those of men, except for persons with college educations; 84 per cent of working women earn the equivalent of male wages in positions requiring elementary education, 82 per cent earn similar wages in jobs requiring secondary education, but only 70 per cent earn similar wages in positions requiring college education.) What has happened is that a middle generation of women, emerging roughly from the early 1950s to the early 1970s, is missing in the Yugoslav power structure. This was the period in which the party demobilized and became more decentralized and Western consumer goods entered the country on a large scale. There were alternate ways to seek prestige and acceptance: a villa at the seashore, modern and often ugly furniture, a car, a refrigerator, and other seductive things. A whole section of a new middle class was able to develop in Yugoslavia, and a division developed between the political elite and this middle class. It was no longer necessary to be a party member to have a decent career and life style. There were and are other options.

The democratization of the party, by increasingly turning its functions over to voluntary unpaid members, has meant that an increasing number of party jobs are now held by people who do something else for a living, and this has placed a special burden on women. As Cynthia Fuchs Epstein has pointed out, this means endless meetings and major sacrifices in the standard of living of the family, and it is increasingly unattractive to the modern young people, who have Western models of consumption. A Mercedes may not be proper for a party secretary, but it is perfectly permissible for a doctor or a psychiatrist. Therefore, there is a reassertion of middle class values in an increasingly professionalized society with a large proportion of university graduates. The only role model that they have for middle class behavior is the prewar one. There is no previous radical elite that possessed status of a type that can serve as an alternate model.

Today, in Yugoslavia a rebellion is developing against bourgeoisification of the party, and it tends to join the themes raised by feminists: egalitarianism and social change. Thus, in Yugoslavia – I do not think that it has yet developed in the rest of eastern Europe – there are left-wing feminist currents that express themselves in the phraseology and within the ideological framework of the party, in journals, and at the party congresses. The party ideology is thus used to attack questions of equality and participation, demonstrating that the room for maneuvering within the system is quite large. Activist women are *not* counterposing feminism to Marxism. Those who have done so – there have been a few authors influenced to do so by Western feminist literature – have immediately become marginal. Those working within the ideological values of the system, much as civil rights advocates did within the framework of the American Constitution, have said 'These are our claims; this is what we fought for, this is what has happened, and why isn't it what we want?'

A new development has complicated the eastern European situation as far as women's role in the society is concerned: a general and increasing surplus of labor. It must be noted that one of the major drives toward equality for women was not the ideological predilection of the party but the major necessity to rebuild a war-torn country and use every hand available. There was an extremely labor-intensive system of production in those early years of postwar construction, with all the implicit social consequences.

As a society automates, as industry is modernized, and as the population empties the countryside, a situation develops in which jobs become a scarce good for which there is increasing competition. This is a factor that has been holding back further advances for women. This is the economic basis for the ideological statement that perhaps a woman's more natural role is at home raising the family. This is what gives such attitudes some weight today. Previously, in the immediate postwar years it would have been an absurd statement; for one thing a family could not live on a single salary. Higher salaries, combined with a growing scarcity of urban jobs, in effect have once again created the desirable model of the classic Western middle-class family in which one breadwinner – a male – should be enough to support it. Thus, the growth rate of the economy and the expansion of the job market are intimately connected with the program of women's rights under socialism as well as under capitalism.

A further element exists: the openness of Yugoslavia, which raises pressing questions. What are the limits of social change in a single socialist country? Without oppression? With oppression, we know more or less what the limits are; they are almost infinite. But with open frontiers, with Italy right over the border, with Western movies and Western consumer goods, and with the ability simply to pack up and take a job in West

Germany, only a finite amount of pressure can be put on the population to conform to norms that may or may not reflect the values of people who were peasants within their own memory.

My conclusion is that what the Yugoslavs have done, by achieving figures for women's participation in the economy and in the professions that are superior to those of historically highly-advanced European countries, represents a great leap that is only explainable by conscientious and persistent efforts from the center. This effort has not been accepted by a substantial part of the population, especially the male population. It has been no more accepted than collectivization of agriculture by the peasant, or than the campaign against the churches, or than the voluntary work brigades, repeatedly formed despite their lack of success. The new values have not been internalized.

At the same time the economic base for women has shifted drastically in Yugoslavia. Women are now approximately 40 per cent of the workforce in a system that requires a high level of local worker participation and management. This means that an increasing number of management posts are being filled by women who have power bases and constitute a reasonable proportion of the professional–technical apparatus. Where they are most scarce, interestingly enough – I don't know why, but it duplicates the Polish data – is in the media. For some reason more women are Central Committee members than editors of newspapers. Since Central Committee members are more powerful than editors of newspapers, I am not sure why this should be so. The answer probably requires a cross-national study.

The other field in which women are scarce, oddly enough, is the most humanist field of all: the university faculties and the academies. The grossest discrimination found by the International Study of Opinion Makers,[3] which studied 600 elite respondents from the Central Committee through the occupants of high academic posts, was apparent in the universities, and the grossest discrimination within the universities was to be found precisely in the faculties of philosophy, social sciences, arts, and letters. There are more women in the faculties of medicine and engineering than in the faculties of philosophy and sociology.

This last fact is one indicator that Yugoslavia has become a relatively liberal country and that the party has not been twisting many arms in the matter of women's equality. Perhaps it should.

NOTES

(1) The distinction lies in the fact that the Catholic hierarchy welcomed, by and large, the German and Italian occupation and backed the formation of the fascist Croat *Ustasa* state, giving it legitimacy. The Orthodox leaders were far more ambivalent, generally backing the London government in exile; but for obvious reasons both they and their Moslem colleagues opposed the Communist-led partisans and tended to back various 'whites,' such as the Chetniks and other nationalists. The extent to which these in turn collaborated with the occupier is a complex question, but the effect of their collaboration is generally accepted in Yugoslavia.

(2) Considerable sophisticated research on the position of women in postwar Yugoslav society has been carried out in Yugoslavia. The most recent and accessible data are to be found in Meznaric (1974). The more striking of the findings is the increased similarity of the statistics between the less and the more developed republics in the recent period

in the socialist sector. For example, although the percentage of women university graduates in the workforce for Yugoslavia as a whole is 3·1 per cent, it is 4·8 per cent in underdeveloped Macedonia and 2·5 per cent in Slovenia – the reverse of what one would expect. Macedonia also has *higher* percentage of women in high-level white-collar positions than Slovenia and Yugoslavia as a whole for that matter, and a higher percentage of skilled workers than the Yugoslav norm. In 1970, according to the Federal Bureau of Statistics in Yugoslavia, women accounted for 41 per cent of all persons employed in jobs that required a high school education or more, 50 per cent of all white collar employees, and approximately 37 per cent of all persons employed in the economy as a whole. To be sure, they are grossly under-represented among students on the Ph.D. level, amounting to approximately 14 per cent in the behavioral sciences, 20 per cent in medical sciences, and 6 per cent in engineering, for example. What is striking about the more recent statistics is the increased and substantial numbers of women employees in industry in the skilled and semiskilled categories, from which previously they were almost totally excluded. For women as a percentage of all skilled workers the Yugoslav average is now 17 per cent, ranging from a low of 15 per cent in the less developed to a high of 24 per cent in the more developed republics. Although that is still under-representation, it is evident that sharp advances are currently being made.

(3) The international Study of Opinion Makers (ISOM) was a project conducted by Bogdan Denitch and Charles Kadushin at the Bureau of Applied Social Research at Columbia University of eleven national elites during the period 1968–75.

REFERENCES

Meznaric, Silva (1974) 'Social change and intergenerational mobility of women: the case of a post-revolutionary equality-oriented society,' in *Some Yugoslav Papers Presented to the Eighth ISA Congress, Toronto, 1974* (University of Ljubljana).

Schumpeter, Joseph (1942, 1947) *Capitalism, Socialism and Democracy* (New York: Harper & Bros).

8

Women and Power:

The Roles of Women in Politics in the United States*

CYNTHIA FUCHS EPSTEIN

In the United States, as in other countries, women rarely govern. They have not been regarded as part of the political arena, and until recent times this was considered to be normal. Politics at every level of participation was considered to be the province of men. The reasons offered for this phenomenon were: women's disinterest in politics, originating in their early socialization; their incapacity to assume political leadership roles; and their family responsibilities, which precluded political activity. These views have been held both by the popular culture and by social scientists,[1] although millions of women have participated as voters and as workers in political campaigns and although women formed and led one of the most effective political mobilizations in American history – the women's suffrage movement.[2] Perceiving women as 'outside' politics is as curious a matter of 'pluralistic ignorance'[3] or 'selective inattention' as can be found in history.

The reality of women's poor representation as political leaders and the fiction that they are not political actors are related issues. This paper will show how cultural myths and the ways in which women are located in the social structure interact to underplay and undermine women's access to and participation in, politics, particularly in decision-making roles. The paper will indicate that, although on the whole women participate less than men in political life, there is probably a far greater pool of interested and qualified women who would take on more political responsibility if they could than is commonly believed. It will show how a combination of prejudices against women's leadership roles and their differential placement in the tracking system makes it difficult for them to have political 'careers.' It will also examine how women who do have political careers achieve them

* I am grateful to M. Kent Jennings and Seymour Martin Lipset, whose comments and suggestions generated many ideas in the course of revision of this paper, to Howard M. Epstein for his patience and skill in helping to sort it out, and to Marilyn Johnson for corrective comments as it went to press. A number of other colleagues, at the Center for Advanced Study in the Behavioral Sciences at Stanford, California, and at various seminars in Europe and the United States, were helpful as this paper went through various revisions. None is responsible for the final outcome.

The research on which this paper is based was supported and facilitated by the Guggenheim Foundation, the Center for Advanced Study in the Behavioral Sciences, and the Ford Foundation.

by routes that are alternative to those followed by men – routes that are more limited and more difficult for a political aspirant to follow and situated to minimize competition with men. Finally, it will explore indicators of changes in American society that suggest the opening of opportunities to women to participate more freely and more 'normally' in political life.

MYTHS ABOUT WOMEN AND POLITICS

Myths about women and political activity abound at both factual and interpretive levels. They especially center on women's supposed political disinterest, ignorance, and inattention.

Myths About Socialization

Some political scientists who have sought to explain the participation of men and women in politics have suggested that political habits are formed early (Githens and Prestage, 1977); further, boys are socialized to believe that they should be interested in political affairs, and girls are socialized to believe that they should not. These conclusions have been reached by Herbert Hyman (1959), by Fred Greenstein (1961), and more recently by Dean Jaros (1973), who found boys to be invariably more 'political' than girls. The documentation of differences between male and female youngsters was considered evidence of different male and female tracks of development in political interest. The findings of these social scientists have recently been challenged both methodologically and theoretically by a group of sociologists at the University of Illinois. There, Orum and his associates (1974) found no sex differences among boys and girls in a large sample of Illinois schoolchildren, probing their views on a number of political dimensions. The discrepancy between earlier studies and the 1974 study, even considering the possible effects of social change in the society, raised questions about the limits of method in the earlier studies and led to challenge of the assumption that differences between the sexes in adult life are explained by childhood socialization. Orum *et al.* have suggested that a better explanation of male–female differences in adult political participation is a structural or situational view, explaining, for example, that fewer women than men go into public life because they are confined to their homes, whereas men are more active because of the demands of their jobs' ancillary activities. This latter view was offered earlier by Lipset (1960) and other political scientists who considered women's roles as wives and mothers to have a priority precluding the assumption of other roles. Lipset has written that 'the position of the married woman illustrates the problem of available time or dispensability as a determinant of political activity. The sheer demands on a housewife and mother mean that she has little opportunity or need to gain politically relevant experiences' (p. 204).

Although I agree with Lipset that housewives with young children may have difficulty replacing themselves in the home, 'having time' for politics is clearly related to cultural views about how people *should* spend their time. This leads directly to the other myths that explain that women are 'outside politics' because political behavior demands time that they must spend in performing family roles.

The myth of role conflict and the myth of political participation
Probably the most frequently offered explanation for the absence of women
from high office, as well as their lack of political participation, is the one
holding that women's roles as wives and mothers conflict with political
roles in the same ways as they do with work roles. As Lipset (1963) has
noted, meeting the demands of child care, when fathers do not share these
tasks, often makes political activity impossible and may even depress levels
of interest and self-confidence. From the local to the national level politics
includes evening and weekend activities. The woman whose family claims
her time may not be free to attend the meetings and social and other events
that are necessary to make contacts and build a power base. Many people
feel that motherhood precludes activity outside the home, where continuous time commitment is involved, and mothers of small children seem to
share this view. A study by Lynn and Flora (1973) of women's attitudes and
activities in the 1968 US elections has shown that mothers feel less politically effective than non-mothers.

Obviously, many women interested in politics face role conflict. But the
problem stems not only from actual time pressures on women but also from
the normative realm – from beliefs about how women *should* spend their
time. Thus, it is commonly expected, not only that women *will* feel role
conflict in such cases, but also that they *ought* to and that this should deter
them from political activity that is more than intermittent and casual. The
electorate may deny that a woman candidate for office has found personal
solutions to role demands or that political activity is her first choice, with
priority above family demands. Women who do manage to marshall their
energies and support from their families often face hostile and condescend-
ing attitudes from voters because they must withdraw from family responsibilities, as men do, during a campaign.

Although male candidates usually try to show that they have strong
family ties and the support of wives and children, they seldom face questioning from the electorate as to the quality or extent of the care that they
give their children or the affection that they give their wives.[4] A woman is
caught in what has been described as a 'double bind:' if she campaigns
vigorously, she is apt to be criticized as a neglectful wife and mother; if she
claims to be an attentive mother, her ability to devote time and energy to
public office is questioned.

This confluence of factors may account for the fact that in the United
States few women in top public office have family responsibilities, because
they are either single, widowed, or old enough to have grown-up children.
Of the eighteen women representatives in the Congress elected in 1976, ten
were married and eight were single, divorced, or widowed. At state and
local levels of government women tend to conform to the profile of the
average American woman; that is, more are married, and a greater proportion are widowed than divorced (Johnson and Stanwick, 1976, p. xxx).

Although few women officeholders have young children, it is interesting
to note that those who do are as active, if not more active, in outside organizations than those who do not have young children. There also appears to
be little relationship between motherhood and the amount of time that
women officeholders report they devote to their office (Johnson and

Stanwick, 1976, p. xliv). Those with children seem to work as hard as those without children.

That women's political activities are subject to cultural imperatives and mechanisms of exclusion is demonstrated by a case deviant from the general pattern – that of women who are active in school district politics. Although the presence of young children in the home does seem to affect women's political activity at a national level, even as voters, research by Kent Jennings (1977) has indicated that young mothers are more active in local school politics than young fathers in their age cohort and more active than young non-mothers. These women attend late night meetings and raise money to campaign and run for office. They do all the things that it once was believed mothers of young children couldn't do and didn't want to do and that were thought to be the reasons why they did not participate in politics.

It is not difficult to account for this. School board elections are considered legitimate activities for women, and men don't stand in the way of their participation; nor are school boards tied into networks of political patronage and economic benefit, as are other political offices. There is less at stake here in terms of power that men may wish to hold exclusively.

The fact of women's extensive activity in voluntary organizations, whether political, educational, or social contradicts the explanation that role conflict is at the root of their non-participation in public life.

Women have long been active participants in political campaigns. An estimated 6 million women did some sort of volunteer work in the Kennedy –Nixon presidential campaign of 1960 (Gruberg, 1968). In fact the percentages of women engaging in these activities are generally close to those of men.[5] Of course, much of this work was ringing doorbells, stuffing envelopes, and phoning. Yet, women's work as political 'footsoldiers' has also been explained by the fact that 'women have more time to give' (Gruberg, 1968, p. 52).[6] Of course, most women work within the boundaries of community, travelling little. But many have gone on the campaign trail as paid staff and volunteer workers.

Women have also been important disseminators of political information as members of the League of Women Voters and have engaged in lobbying efforts on matters of social legislation through such 'non-politically' oriented organizations as the National Council of Women, the American Association of University Women, the National Federation of Business and Professional Women's Clubs, and, more recently, the National Organization of Women – organizations whose memberships each run to the hundreds of thousands. Not all members of these clubs are active or interested in politics, but until recently most women who sought political office came from the ranks of voluntary workers in non-partisan or non-political organizations.

A study conducted by the Center for American Women and Politics at Rutgers University established a profile of the typical woman who runs for and wins public office in the United States. She is married, has two or more children, and holds a job in addition to running her home. She is a joiner; she belongs to more organizations than male officials on average (Johnson and Carroll, 1978). She is also politically ambitious, aspiring to one or more other offices in the future.

Clearly, not all women have time for politics, nor the inclination. But there appear to be sizable numbers of women who can circumvent those obstacles and wish to do so.

The myths about voting behavior

It has been documented that women voted less than men in the past (Lane, 1959, p. 209; Lipset, 1960). Their proportionately poorer turnout at the polls has precipitated the indictment that women are not responsible citizens. In the past some political scientists have attributed their behavior to cultural views of voting as unladylike, undesirable, or not permitted in their families (Lane, 1959, p. 211; Gruberg, 1968). But it has been noted that women voted less than men only among certain groups (e.g. in poor and rural areas and among recent immigrants), with male–female differences diminishing as social class, education, and occupational rank increased (Lane, 1959; Lipset, 1960). However, Shanley and Schuck (1974) have pointed out that over the broad spectrum women always voted *nearly* as often as men and that the differences have diminished with time. These political scientists have also stressed that women have expressed the same degree of party loyalty, shared men's sense of civil responsibility, and discussed politics in the home as much as men (citing the studies of Campbell *et al.*, 1964).

There is another aspect to myths about women's voting behavior – the differing interpretations of the reasons why women vote as they do.

We know that family members vote alike. The influence of male members of the family is assumed to be dominant, and it is believed that women vote for candidates favored by their husbands and fathers.

However, similar husband–wife voting patterns may come from the fact that most people marry homogamously. Most spouses come from similar backgrounds, and their common values bring them together in the first place. Where there are differences between spouses it has been assumed that women change and adopt men's opinions. But at various times proportions of men and women's votes differ, and political scientists have explained that husbands and wives are voting differently, along sex-linked lines rather than family lines.

Do the men (i.e. fathers) always influence children politically? Several studies have found that children of both sexes more often model or agree with the mother in political behavior and attitudes, when mother and father differ (Nogee and Levin, 1958; Jennings and Langton, 1969; Thomas, 1971). One study cited by Goot and Reid (1975) has shown that, where there is disagreement in the family between mother and father, some children vote the mother's preference. This is one of many studies that they have referred to in a monograph that disputes many popular and 'scientific' assumptions about male influence over women by taking a critical look at the classic studies of voting and political participation.

Critical analysis of the 'reasoning' offered by political scientists to indicate women's derivative decisions about voting has also been made by McCormack (1975). She has noted that when women vote as their husbands do it is assumed that their husbands are influencing them, but that when they vote differently, which occurs with some frequency, they are often damned as parochial, conservative, or politically unimaginative. McCormack has cited the findings of Lipset (1960) and Tingsten (1963), which show (1) that women do not always vote as their husbands do and (2) that when they do not their political sentiments are sometimes more conservative and sometimes less authoritarian: 'Among working class voters in Italy, wives do not share their husbands' pro-Communist sympathies; in France, they did not share their husbands' Poujadist support; and in Germany, they did not initially support National Socialism' (p. 21).

The studies cited provide sufficient contradictory evidence to make us wary about the ways in which causality is inferred in looking at men's and women's voting behavior and political participation.

Myths are created and perpetuated by the aggregation of all women or all men. It is misleading to aggregate all women in posing gender differences on such mass phenomena as voting behavior. For example, M. Kent Jennings (1977) has pointed out that whether women work or not affects their political participation; those who work full time participate more actively. He has also suggested that a staging process may exist, whereby higher-status working women become more politically active and are followed later by lower-status women. There are the impacts of education and age as well. Youth and higher education increase the political participation of women (Jennings, 1977; Lipset, 1960) and cancel out the effect of sex status.

Yet, sex status is often theoretically linked to women's access to, and participation in, leadership roles. This is also questionable.

Politics and the personality myth
Many political studies have led us to believe that women do not possess the needs and other traits of the males who opt for political careers and succeed in them. One school of literature has reasoned that people with certain kinds of personalities choose occupations and careers that are consonant with their emotional make-up. Costantini and Craik (1972), for example, 'found' women not to have male traits and took this to explain (1) their poor representation in political life and (2) the failure of those who do participate. Yet, later evidence (Kohn, 1977; Kanter, 1977) suggests that personality is often flexible and situational and is likely to change in the direction evoked by the role demands of social structures. Hence, *exclusion* from certain social structures may explain the differences in 'traits' found by personality studies.

Interpretations, perceptions, and judgements of motivating factors may be affected by cultural bias. For example, Costantini and Craik (1972), from their analysis of political activists in California, have reported that 'If the male leader appears to be motivated by self-serving considerations, the female leader appears to be motivated by public-serving considerations' (p. 235). Further, female leaders tend to express a 'forceful, effective and socially ascendant style in an earnest, sobersided and ambivalent manner', whereas male leaders tend to express the same personal style in a more 'easy-going, direct and uncomplicated way' (p. 217).

SOCIAL STRUCTURE: STATUSES AND SITUATIONS

The previous section of this paper has questioned the notions that women are not socialized to be interested in politics, that they lack the time to engage in politics, and that too few women play roles as political actors to constitute a pool of candidates for political office.

This section will explore how women's position in the social structure creates conditions that make it difficult for them to ascend political hierarchies. It will look at the ways in which women's status sets tend to exclude the acquisition of political statuses and at how the status sequences that lead to political office follow tracks from which women are excluded.[7]

Status sets and role integration

Although 'role conflict' may be challenged as a major explanation for women's poor representation in political roles, it is a fact that some combinations of statuses (i.e. status sets) are integrative and that others tend to create conflict.

Meeting the norms attached to one status can be facilitated by holding another status with complementary role expectations. For example, Max Weber in 1919 (in Gerth and Mills, 1946) pointed out that proportionately more lawyers than other professional men went into politics because their law careers would be enhanced by political connections. Politics makes lawyers more visible to potential clients and gives them knowledge that they can use in their legal practices. Physicians, on the other hand, would suffer professionally from political activity that prevented them from keeping up with developments in their fields.

Thus, in the course of their occupational activity men may find not only that it serves them to be political but also that they *must* be political. Many need to be aware of the politics of the community in which they work, to calculate what to do about tax policy or legislation that will affect their businesses. They need information about how contracts are given out by municipal agencies, they have to be aware of new regulations, and they need to know those administering them.

Because women are not working in positions that demand such knowledge, they are not propelled toward attaining certain kinds of political knowledge or becoming political themselves. Not all women have occupational roles, and rarely do they have decision-making roles that put them into community politics integrated with work. But when it is necessary for them to be political to carry out their roles, they are political, as has been shown by M. Kent Jennings's (1977) observations on women's activity in school board politics. Involvement in political life is usually situational and role specific.

Status sequences and background: tracking and political leadership roles

Although cultural norms support women's behavior as voters and their contribution as political workers during campaigns, it is far more difficult for women to win cultural approval as candidates for office or for serious political ambitions. The society's norms support women as political amateurs but not as 'professionals.' This means that women do not choose to run for office and that party leaders do not choose them to be candidates.

Women face difficulties wherever they are clearly in competition with men. In addition to the general cultural view that women ought not to win, they are handicapped because they cannot travel the same routes as men to legitimacy and competency. If they do, they have a chance. Johnson's studies have shown that, once women become candidates, they win in about the same proportion as men (1978, pp. 311–12; and note 13). The problems of women entering politics can best be conceptualized by examining whether and how they can acquire the same status sequences and the same status sets as males and can deal with the problems caused when their sex status is inappropriately focused upon in political and professional settings.

Passage through certain status sequences is characteristic of men in political life. Attending certain schools and having careers as lawyers or businessmen are important preparations for political activity. Women, under-represented in business and especially in the practice of law,[8] have been unable to develop networks and accumulate the resources that are necessary for building careers in politics.

Education Women holding political office have tended to have both less education than their male counterparts (Jennings and Thomas, 1968; Costantini and Craik, 1972) and a different kind of education. Even now, women in public office include fewer graduates than men in public office.

In the past even women who had elite educations experienced segregated schooling. Until recently they were barred from attending Harvard, Columbia, Yale, and Princeton, especially their schools of law and business, and they were thus seriously limited in access to the 'eastern establishment' and the political jobs that drew from those networks (Putnam, 1976). Attending the 'sister' institutions of Wellesley, Barnard, or Vassar was a separate and unequal experience that did not prepare women for later careers as the male colleges did. Of course, elite education was not typical for men elsewhere in the country, and the opportunity structure differed for them too.

To the extent that they were differently or less educated than men, women could not make friendships that would become politically useful and did not have colleagues who could be drawn on as a political constituency. This means that women rarely could travel the status sequence that led to careers, except at the lowest levels. Channels to political opportunity were usually closed to women. Jennings and Thomas (1968) have pointed out how discouraged women were in seeking a range of political offices when they were viewed as clearly unattainable.

Further, women often view their current political careers not as steps up the ladder but as completed achievements (Costantini and Craik, 1972). Kirkpatrick (1974, p. 73) has also shown that most women think of election to a state legislature as a last rather than a first step of a political career. This is true for most men (Wahlke *et al.*, 1972), but many more men than women consider it as only a first step. However, Marilyn Johnson (private communication) has pointed out that these studies are not of matched samples and that, when men and women holding the same public office are compared, patterns of gender differences are often mitigated or reversed regarding political ambitions.

Widow's succession and voluntary associations. Women who go into politics at most levels necessarily come by different routes from men. The most important of these leading to high office has often been characterized as 'widow's succession.'

Such women usually have come to office as appointed replacements on the death of a prominent husband or father with whom they served the functional equivalent of apprenticeship. Although these are idiosyncratic events, in sum they constitute a pattern, because a large proportion of women have followed this path. Werner (1966, 1968) found that, of the seventy women who served in Congress between 1917 and 1964, about one-half had relatives in Congress and more than one-half were either appointed or elected to fill a vacancy, often one caused by the death of a husband. This is still a pattern. The two women senators serving in the 95th Congress were filling seats vacated by the deaths of their husbands. The first two (of five) women governors came to office this way.[9] The third woman elected as a governor was widely acknowledged to be a figurehead for her husband, and it wasn't until 1974 that a woman governor – Ella Grasso of Connecticut – was elected in her own right. She was followed by Dixie Lee Ray in the state of Washington. All women in the US Senate were widows of senators or succeeded their still living husbands until Nancy Landon Kassebaum was elected in 1978, and even she too was related to a prominent political figure, Alf Landon – a presidential candidate in 1936.

It is probable that most of these 'successors' were supported because they were viewed as compliant persons causing no threat to the men in the political cliques created by the deceased male incumbents. In spite of this some of these women showed or are showing skill in wielding power for a time.

Another route to elective office is by way of participation in voluntary organizations – a path that is largely unique to the United States. Women in state legislatures and other elective bodies below the level of Congress have tended to come from the ranks of voluntary organizations. Jeane Kirkpatrick (1974) – author of the first in-depth study of women in state office – found that until recently the typical female officeholder came from a background of voluntary service, chiefly in church and school organizations. The women surveyed were older on average than their male counterparts and usually had first run for office after the age of 40; women in office through widow's succession are also on average older than their male colleagues. In contrast, 90 per cent of a matching group of male legislators had made their first attempt at public office before the age of 40.

Consequences of conforming to status set typing[10]
We have seen that most women come to political office by routes that disadvantage their long term careers. Yet, some women do follow more traditional routes, matching male patterns more closely, to the benefit of their future careers.

The salience of the lawyer status. The most useful route to political office for women, although not the most typical, seems to be through law, and their growing participation in the legal profession appears to be women's best hope for more political involvement in the future.

Kirkpatrick's (1974) study of women state legislators, for example, found distinct differences between lawyers and non-lawyers. Women lawyers were definitely younger than the median for non-lawyers who were candidates; four of the six studies were under 40 when they first ran for the legislature, and the only one under 30 was a lawyer. Kirkpatrick has noted that a woman who is a lawyer can win nomination and be elected to a legislature without the years of party or community service that characterize most other women's careers. 'If you are a woman and a lawyer,' one state legislator pointed out, 'you have an instant credibility that most women do not have.' This legitimacy created by the status of lawyer operates throughout the political hierarchy.

Women who are lawyers can more legitimately 'hang out' as men do at local political clubs. 'Clubhouse lawyers' are regarded as present for the purpose of doing business, and women's lawyer status helps to define their presence in these terms. In this context particularly, following the prescribed status sequences en route to political office serves to legitimate a candidate not only by providing the appropriate credentials but also by permitting the playing out of a set of dynamics associated with political roles.

All five of the new congresswomen elected in 1972 were lawyers (Diamond, 1977).[11] In spite of the fact that women constituted only 1–3 per cent of the legal profession during 1917–70 – the period studied by Bullock and Heys (1972) – 20 per cent of the regularly elected women congresswomen were lawyers.

Characteristics of women officeholders.   Status sequences that conform to the 'preferred' and 'ideal' are extremely important for women, even when most men fall short of the ideal. During the fifty-three-year period studied by Bullock and Heys (1972) 69 per cent of the regularly elected women but only 10 per cent of the widows had held public office before entering Congress; 57 per cent of the regularly elected women but only 20 per cent of all freshmen listed party activities. These data suggest that certain kinds of political experience are more crucial for women than for men who wish to be elected to Congress.

Ideology and opportunity structure.   Status sequences and opportunity structure can also explain patterns in women's ideology and partisanship as political actors.

As mentioned earlier, studies in the United States and western Europe have provided data said to show that women tend to vote more conservatively than men (Jacquette, 1974). This may be explained by their lesser education and workforce participation. Seymour Martin Lipset (personal communication, 1978) has pointed out that:

... women's conservative voting (by large margins) in much of Europe is related to the fact that women are more religious than men, and that in many countries religious people are more conservative than irreligious ones. Hence, in France, Italy, etc., women vote much more for right parties, while men vote left. In the U.S., religion versus irreligion does not exist as a factor related to voting. The more religious (females) are, however, more moralistic here. Hence women do show up as more anti-gambling, more anti-corruption, more opposed to liberal divorce laws, more favorable to prohibition in the past, less liberal with respect to homosexual rights, more peace oriented.

Here we see that the variables that explain voting behavior are not necessarily sex role linked, except in so far as what women do is interpreted differently from what men do. In American society women are not religious to a greater extent than men. But in the United States the assumption is made that women are more moralistic than men (Lipset, 1960; Gruberg, 1968). I suggest that women are as rational or irrational as men in voting their self-interest as well as their ideologies. For example, many women voted for prohibition because drunken husbands were poor providers and physically abused women and children in the home. Thus, it was not 'moralism' but self-interest that determined their decision in some cases, and social awareness in others. This same reasoning may be applied to their opposition to more liberal divorce laws, which have been seen a threatening to women's economic interests. Furthermore, the 'moral' positions said to be taken by women (e.g. being peace oriented) are often conceptualized as 'liberal' when applied to men's political behavior.

We must be wary in accepting the view that women are more conservative than men even by a 'male standard.' As mentioned earlier, women in Europe have been less favorable to authoritarian candidates than men at various times.

It has also been pointed out that the proportion of women voting conservatively, by classic measures, varies and is often very close to the figure for men. In the United States Campbell *et al.* (1964, p. 641) have reported that in 1948 and 1952 somewhat fewer women than men (2 per cent and 4 per cent respectively) supported the Republicans, and this again seemed to be the case in 1958 (Steinem, 1972, p. 51). And, in 1964, 1968, and 1972 more women voted Democratic. The proposition has been offered that women are more 'right wing than men' by a 'small but sizable proportion' (Blondel, 1965, p. 60). But counterindications have been cited by Goot and Reid (1975), notably from later studies, which show that more women than men opposed conscription, the Vietnam war, nuclear weapons, racial discrimination, and capital punishment and that more women than men were sympathetic to a wide range of social welfare programs (pp. 20–1). American women's acquisition of other statuses may account for this change, or their growing sense of political efficacy because of the women's movement. Historically, American women involved in politics have supported reform movements and voted liberally.[12] As indicated by Table 8.1, women Democrats outnumbered women Republicans at every level of public office in 1977.

Note that the proportion of women Democrats rose as the level of office rose, from 51 per cent among municipal councilors to 73 per cent among state executive officeholders and to an overwhelming 73 per cent (thirteen out of eighteen) in the US Congress.

When women party leaders[13] were compared to male party leaders by

Table 8.1 *Party affiliation of women officeholders, 1977.*

Party	US House (no.)	State Executive (%)	State Senate (%)	State House (%)	County Commission (%)	Mayor (%)	Municipal Council (%)
Democratic	(13)	73	71	60	59	50	51
Republican	(5)	16	26	36	30	33	33
Independent	(0)	11	3	4	10	17	15
Other	(0)	0	0	0	1	–	1
Total	(18)	(56)	(68)	(281)	(281)	(290)	(2,172)

Source: Johnson and Carroll (1978), p. 21A.

Costantini and Craik (1972), Republican women were not different from men with regard to public policy issues, but among the Democrats women were considerably more liberal. A 1976 analysis of the voting records of women members of Congress indicated that women officeholders of both parties tended more than men to oppose increased military spending and a hard-line foreign policy (*New York Times*, April 11, 1976).

Women officeholders also consider themselves more liberal than their male counterparts. In a study by the Center for the American Woman and Politics (Johnson and Carroll, 1978), among the women 30 per cent considered themselves to be liberal, 36 per cent middle of the road, and 35 per cent conservative. Among the men 22 per cent considered themselves to be liberal, 33 per cent middle of the road, and 45 per cent conservative.

The fact that women in politics tend to be more liberal than men, assuming that these findings hold, may be due to women's greater opportunity to be elected by parties that are more committed to ideologies of elite turnover and equality and whose appeal is to the underprivileged and to minority groups. However, in those parties they must also face the resistance of working class men, who tend to be conservative on issues of sex role equality.

Reform movements as a track for women.   Some women have been able to gain footholds in political life because their involvement in social or political protest movements and as members of reform political insurgent groups — these activities often overlap — has helped them to accumulate political and organizational expertise. But this pattern has had its negative as well as its positive consequences for women's attainment of political office. Reform movements often develop as a response to crisis on a temporary basis; they may not always become institutionalized. Therefore, reform activity has been only an occasional means of entry for women into mainstream politics. It should be noted, however, that women seem to have more chance to be elected in times of social crisis (Lipman-Blumen, 1973) and that many prominent women in leadership positions today have come from insurgent political clubs. Bella Abzug is one of the latter.

Reform and insurgent political groups may become a more important road for women into political life. In the early 1970s women moved into law in increasing numbers, and a good proportion of them were interested in, and confident about, assuming political roles. Many of them chose law careers because of their backgrounds in recent social-protest movements and their feeling that men could not and would not represent women effectively on such issues as abortion, sex discrimination in employment, and rape. They were politicized and eager to learn, to gain the political credentials conferred by the law, and to grasp the levers of power.

Women pursuing political office in the 1970s have been somewhat more likely to come from the left than from the right. Many have developed political ties with men through activities in the antiwar movement. For example, Carol Bellamy, who won the city council presidency in New York in 1977, went to work for one of the largest Wall Street law firms — Cravath, Swaine, and Moore — and was a principal organizer of Wall Street Lawyers Against the Vietnam war; Patricia Schroeder, Congresswoman from

Colorado, ran on a campaign stressing opposition to the Vietnam war and other social issues (Schroeder, 1977).

A matter of integrity.   Of the various attributes that women are expected to bring to office, integrity is one of the most curiously double edged. On the one hand, Americans like their political leaders to be honest. On the other hand, within the structure of the political system, where norms permit and encourage political actors to bargain and deal, people of too resolute integrity are suspect. Their role partners may believe that they are poor members of the 'club' and not amenable to trading.

Are women so pure? Are they pure 'naturally'? To some extent women's integrity has been demonstrated. They played no decision-making roles in the Watergate scandals, for example. However, their relative purity may stem only from the fact that they have not been part of the party machines or of the established political order. If they have played cleaner politics than men, it may relate less to their superior morality than to the structure of their political positions. Where women hold public office, it appears that they are concentrated in positions not on the route to the top leadership and that they experience less pressure toward corruption. Whether in the legislative or the executive branch, women tend to receive assignments in the fields of health, education, and welfare. In other countries the division of labor is similar, with the addition of the 'cultural' ministries. In the past they have been virtually absent from departments or committees dealing with business regulation, public utilities, economic and industrial development, public safety, and public works, although there is some change in this pattern. They are found only marginally in positions dealing with natural resources, transportation, labor and manpower, justice, foreign policy, and environmental protection.

To some extent women's political assignments reflect a society-wide division of labor along sex status lines; except for those in national or state political office their work is low paid and low in prestige and power. They are *expected* to be pure and not self-serving. But in countries where women have held high executive office, they have engaged in the same machinations, legal or extralegal, that men have. This has been true of Indira Gandhi in India, Golda Meir in Israel, Sirimavo Bandaranaike in Sri Lanka, and both Eva Peron and Isabel Peron in Argentina.

The dynamics of sexual status.   The processes that result in women's focus on moral issues and their relative success as reform candidates makes them vulnerable to some structural constraints on career. Furthermore, a cultural view that defines 'good women' as being pure, both ideologically and sexually, is a constraint on their access to the political opportunity structure.

One of the problems that women faced in the past came with the end of each political campaign. When the campaign crisis ended, it was difficult for women to maintain political relationships by 'hanging out' in the clubhouse as male party members did.

Regular party activity flourishes and expands during political campaigns in election years. But in interim periods – this is particularly true in city politics – clubs manage to attract a corps of workers chiefly by offering services to constituents and social activities. But the clubhouse atmosphere often discourages women's participation except as spouses or companions. The woman political aspirant is often isolated from the club's social life – a problem for those attempting to travel either the 'regular' or the 'reform' road to political power.

Allegations of sexual impropriety are a continuing problem for women who seek entry to a political leadershp. When women are sponsored by male leaders – an important way to advancement for both men and women – others may assume that a sexual relationship exists. There is also a great deal of sexual joking and innuendo in the political clubhouse.[14] Women who find such behavior embarrassing or offensive often stay away, unless there are specific tasks to be done or they are specially protected. Embarrassment and sexual harrassment reduce or channel women's political participation, so that it is available when needed but structured so that it will not become a political threat.

A presumption of sexual availability undermines the legitimacy of the woman's status and makes for discomfort. Sexual liaisons by women with members of political leaderships can have varied results. The sexually connected woman may gain an insider's access to contacts and information, but she may be considered as merely an appendage, without autonomy or political importance. On balance, sexual liaisons have not politically benefited women.

The effect of numbers of eligibles on the political opportunity structure[15]
The number of women engaging in political activities above the local level has been relatively small. This has had consequences both for the cultural view of the appropriateness of women's quest for political office and for the resultant stereotype of the 'proper' candidate and officeholder. The women's movement, however, has encouraged women to think of themselves as appropriate candidates. As a result, in the 1970s more women have presented themselves for party positions in a serious way, and more hav been qualified (e.g. as lawyers). Party leaders now feel it important to consider women as nominees and to consider their candidacies, even if they do not give them full support.

It seems to be true now, as studies have shown in the past, that parties tend to put up women candidates in districts where they have little chance of winning (Hightower, 1974; Diamond, 1977). In a study of all women candidates running for office in 1976, Carroll (1977) found that, in approximately half of the cases in which party leaders sought out and encouraged women to run for office, it appeared that they were recruiting candidates as 'sacrificial lambs.' Yet, even if most of these races were lost, both the parties and the electorate were getting used to the idea of women candidates, and the women were gaining campaign experience. Again, proper credentials were important to winning. In Hightower's sample (1974, p. 21) there were seven lawyers and one third-year law student among the forty-six women candidates running for office in New York; five of the seven elected were lawyers.

The number of women candidates for federal office increased by 38 per cent between 1972 and 1974. During this same period similar increases occurred at the state level, where the number of women candidates increased by 71·4 per cent and the number elected rose by 35 per cent (US Department of Commerce, 1976).

Campaigning
American political campaigning, grueling for anyone, requires days and nights of meetings and speeches. Usually, male politicians have the support of their political club, family, and friends. Wives of politicians are expected to meet the public and often give speeches for their husbands. Judith Stiehm (1977) has suggested that a two-person investment in a political career is typical in American politics. Women candidates, however, usually cannot depend on active support from the party organization. Therefore, they tend to rely on a personal rather than an organizational following for fund raising, publicity, and telephone and door-to-door canvassing.

Funding
Financial backing is unusually difficult to obtain for aspiring female office-holders, and every study of women candidates attests to this.[16] Women do not ordinarily have access to large sums for campaigning, even if they are from wealthy families—Judith Stiehm (1977) has estimated that it costs $400,000 to win a $40,000-a-year job in her study of state elections in California – nor do they have the contacts to tap outside financial resources, lacking access to the 'old-boy' networks that donate a great deal of primary campaign money. Since they are not able to make the kinds of contributions that men make, women do not get political backing in return. Backing a woman for election to even a moderately important office is usually considered a poor investment. Party leaders raise funds and acquire power by supporting winning candidates and then brokering their obligations through patronage. Since women have not been viewed as winners who are capable of producing a return on a backer's investment, few political bosses have been willing to sponsor them, except where they can make a gesture of support without fear that it will be costly. Women also do not get corporate contributions as do male candidates. But this may change; as women make more money in professional and business careers, they may feel free to contribute to causes and candidates who will advance their interests and careers.

Discrimination
Women officeholders reported in a 1977 study (Johnson and Carroll, 1978) that their access to political leadership was hindered by discrimination and prejudice, especially from party leaders. Between 68 and 86 per cent of women in every office polled agreed that men in party organizations tried to keep women out of leadership roles. In contrast, male officeholders identified the sources of women's difficulties as stemming from their own problems as family members or from their deficiencies of background or training.

The opposition of men and their view that they are not in opposition remain difficult constraints on women's political careers.

SOCIAL CHANGE AND ACCESS OF WOMEN TO THE
POLITICAL OPPORTUNITY STRUCTURE

Women's political and legal networks
One of the most serious problems that women faced in developing political
careers was the refusal of support by political groups with male leaderships,
coupled with the fact that there were no comparable women's political
groups with which they might seek alliance. But the activities of the
women's movement and of women lawyers both in the law schools and in
the political sphere (Epstein, forthcoming) have been important in moving
women into politics in greater numbers.

In 1971 women activists formed the National Women's Political Caucus
(NWPC) to promote the development of women's political potential and to
generate political action on the issues raised by the women's movement.

The NPWC is active in nearly every state in the union, raising campaign
funds for aspiring women candidates. It has become powerful enough
symbolically for women candidates to seek NWPC endorsement, but the
amounts of money that it has been able to raise are small. Since its founding
it has played a significant role in the presidential nominating process. It was
instrumental in bringing about rules changes to allow the seating of large
numbers of women delegates at the party conventions. In 1972, 40 per cent
of the Democratic National Convention delegates were women, compared
with 13 per cent in 1968; and women comprised 30 per cent of the Republican delegates in 1972, compared with 17 per cent in 1968. In 1976,
however, these figures declined somewhat.

Although it is not as strong and pervasive as major party organizations,
the NWPC has been important as a symbol of women's growing political
consciousness and frustration and represents a new source of political
pressure. Not since the suffrage movement have women's political associations acted so cohesively to lobby Congress and the Executive on 'women's
issues.'

Women also are uniting as officeholders to press for issues concerning
them that often cut across party lines. Caucuses promoting the interests of
special groups arose in the late 1960s and 1970s within many organizations,
and now in the Congress there is a Congresswoman's Caucus, as there are
Black and Hispanic Caucuses. The Congresswoman's Caucus, for
example, in 1977 exacted a promise from the Secretary of Health, Education, and Welfare that he would conduct a thorough study of social security
to identify any discrimination against women that could be corrected
through legislation (*New York Times*, November 27, 1977, p. 65).

The mutual support of women candidates has been striking. In particular, there is a group of women politicians who are lawyers and Democrats
that travels widely and has women's movement connections. They have
formed a professional and personal network and assist each other with
funds, endorsements, and planning. They also assist women who are newcomers to politics. In this way women running for local political office
often achieve national visibility because the media tend to focus on women
candidates because they are uncommon.

There is also anecdotal evidence to indicate that women politicians defer to their female colleagues' rights and status. It is now a commonly told tale that, when Bella Abzug was offered the post of chair of the Equal Economic Opportunities Commission (EEOC) by President Carter, she informed him that the EEOC rightfully belonged to the New York City Human Rights Commissioner, Eleanor Holmes Norton. Norton got the appointment. On the other hand, when Abzug sought the US Senate nomination in New York, although she lost the primary, she had national visibility and a great deal of support from women far from her state (Stein, 1978).

Women officeholders: an accounting
It will be remembered that until about 1972 most women who attained high political posts were usually appointed to fill vacancies left by husbands or fathers. Some of these women then sought election. By 1974, however, women were beginning to be elected to important posts in their own right, although their numbers remained small. In the 95th Congress, elected in 1976, only three of the eighteen Congresswomen held the seats of their late husbands; before 1949, 45 per cent of the women in Congress had succeeded their husbands; and in 1949–71, 29 per cent had (*New York Times*, January 30, 1978). All the women who have served in the US Senate until 1978 came to it by the route of widowhood or family affiliation.[17] As already noted, Ella Grasso was the first woman to 'make it on her own' to any governorship, and she was followed shortly by Dixie Lee Ray of Washington state. Two women were named to the Carter Cabinet, and women held 12 per cent of all presidential appointments in 1978 (Stein, 1978). Johnson (personal communication) has said that estimates ran as high as 18 per cent in 1979. There were six women lieutenant governors in the USA in 1979. The year 1979 showed no great increase of women in Congress (seventeen). In fact this was less than in 1978, when there were eighteen, or in the 'record' year 1962, when there were twenty. Women constituted 9·3 per cent of state legislators in October 1978 – 702 out of 7,561 members (*Wall Street Journal*, October 11, 1978). After the November 1978 elections women were 10·2 per cent of state legislators (National Women's Education Fund, 1979). In 1970 they numbered 334 or 4·4 per cent of the total. Irene Diamond (1977) has reported that, following the 1974 elections, women constituted 9·1 per cent of the state legislators in the lower houses and 5 per cent of the legislators in the upper houses. She has further reported that, except for the election year immediately following the winning of women's suffrage, no change of this magnitude has ever occurred in such a short time (p. 26).

Outlook for women in politics. It is difficult to envisage that sex status will ever become irrelevant to politics. Since government is the arena of highest power in society, it is guarded closely, and the interlocking networks of economic position, political patronage, informal associations, and entrenched party machinery all act as barriers to outsiders. For women to become insiders they will have to progress in political careers by all the routes that men take and by some new routes of their own in concert with all women.

NOTES

(1) This view has been noted by a number of political scientists in recent times. But Martin Gruberg (1968) has noted in his preface to *Women in American Politics*:

> In politics, American women have been virtually invisible. Political scientists, mostly male, have tended to overlook this major group. For example, the standard work on party and pressure politics, V. O. Key's *Politics, Parties and Pressure Groups*, ignores women completely except for a few pages about suffragettes. A basic book on pressure groups, Harmon Zeigler's *Interest Groups in American Society*, also omits mention of women; and most textbooks about American government make no reference to female political activity. The same is true of books on state and local government. (p. v)

(2) Although the suffrage movement has been characterized as an isolated phenomenon, not predictive of women's future political behavior.

(3) The term 'pluralistic ignorance' is used here to characterize collective misperception of actual facts, whether by genuine ignorance or by failure to 'register' what has been seen to occur. An extreme example of this phenomenon was the ignorance or inattention of Germans to the Nazi extermination camps. This is a somewhat different way of using the term than that of Robert K. Merton (1968), who, summarizing the work of Floyd Allport and others on 'pluralistic ignorance,' has offered his own interpretation that the phenomenon occurs when one's own attitudes and expectations are not shared and one nevertheless assumes that they are uniformly shared (p. 431).

(4) The memoirs of prominent national political figures show that, whatever their public stance as family men, as a rule they have rarely permitted their families to interfere with their work or careers. See Myra MacPherson (1975).

(5) Marilyn Johnson (private communication) has reported that the Michigan election studies show this.

(6) Shanley and Schuck (1974) have observed that, because *what men do* is used as a standard for political behavior, female political activities are often regarded as non-political. For instance, when a woman hosts a party for a candidate, she is said to be engaging in a social activity; but when men socialize at the clubhouse, they are said to be engaging in political behavior. Women workers are also seen as 'contributors' by their husbands. In research on New York City political clubs Moran (1978) has noted that male leaders often thank the unpolitically involved husbands of women political workers for contributing their wives' time and energy to the campaign. These 'redefinition' procedures are functional for underplaying women's political efforts and acquisition of expertise. I have discussed elsewhere (Epstein, 1970b) how the 'mechanism of redefinition' is used by a person to redefine a role to make it more compatible with cultural views of what a person of that status – age, sex, etc. – should be doing. For example, my study of women lawyers in practice with their husbands has shown that they say not that they are engaging in legal work but that they are 'helping their husbands' (Epstein, 1971). Thus, they shift focus from doing a socially disapproved activity (i.e. engaging in a male occupational activity) to a socially approved activity (i.e. engaging in the approved female role of being a good wife).

(7) I rely now, as I have before (Epstein, 1970a, 1970b), on the theoretical framework devised by Robert K. Merton's (1957, 1968) theoretical framework for the dynamics of status sets as enunciated in *Social Theory and Social Structure* and by 'oral publication' (again his concept) in lectures at Columbia University.

(8) The salience of a career in law as a characteristic background of political leaders has been pointed out by many prominent social scientists, among them Eulau and Sprague (1964), Schlesinger (1957), and Putnam (1976).

(9) They were Nellie Taylor Ross, elected in 1924 in Wyoming – the first state to give women the vote and the first to elect a woman to Congress. The second was Miriam Ferguson, elected in Texas in the same year but inaugurated sixteen days after Ross. Lurleen Wallace of Alabama served as governor in 1967–8, succeeding her husband George Wallace, who was prohibited by law from running for office for the third consecutive time.

(10) As defined before (Epstein, 1970a, p. 166), status set typing refers to the phenomenon

that exists when a class of persons who share a key status (e.g. lawyer) also share other matching statuses (e.g. white, Protestant) and it is considered appropriate that this be so.

(11) Unfortunately for my theory, new Congresswomen elected in 1974 and 1976 were not lawyers, but one of three new Congresswomen elected in 1978 was an attorney. However, I still predict a mounting trend as the numbers of women lawyers increase in the pool of eligibles.

(12) Women's special participation in reform politics, noted by Leon Epstein (1967), has been referred to in the study by Kirkpatrick (1976, p. 9) of the presidential election of 1972. She has reported that 'the new political breed of the 1970's' was said to contain large numbers of women who differed from traditional women even more sharply than the men differed from their traditional male counterparts. The new woman was said to be distinguished especially by her demand for a more equal share of power and by willingness to compete with men for it. See also Wilson (1962), Leader (1977), Diamond (1977), Frankovic (1977), and Mezey (1977).

(13) Party leaders studied include: Congress members and state legislators holding office in 1965; members of the state delegations (i.e. delegates and alternates) to the Republican and Democratic National Conventions of 1960 and 1964; members of the delegation slate pledged to Nelson Rockefeller, which lost to the Goldwater slate in California's 1964 presidential primary; and 1964 county committee chairs of the two major parties.

(14) I am indebted for this material to the preliminary report of her research on political clubs by Eileen Moran of the Graduate Center, City University of New York.

(15) I am indebted to the work of Robert Merton on the social consequences of relative and absolute numbers. See also Rosabeth Moss Kantner's (1977) discussion on the impact of numbers for women managers. See also Blau (1977).

(16) The most recent was done by an organization called the Center for the Study of Congress (reported through the Associated Press in the *New York Times*, March 4, 1978.)

(17) Maurine Neuberger was not appointed to fill the seat left vacant by her husband Richard Neuberger, but she ran for his seat and won.

REFERENCES

Alexander, Dolores (1978) 'It's November: why are these women running?,' *Working Woman* (November), pp. 65–6.

Blau, Peter (1977) *Inequality and Heterogeneity* (New York: Free Press).

Blondel, J. (1965) *Voters, Parties and Leaders*, rev. edn (Harmondsworth: Penguin books).

Bullock III, Charles S. and Heys, Patricia Lee Lindley (1972) 'Recruitment of women for Congress: a research note,' *The Western Political Quarterly*, vol. 25, no. 3 (September), pp. 416–23.

Campbell, Angus, Converse, Philip E., Miller, Warren E. and Stokes, Donald E. (1964) *The American Voter* (New York: Wiley).

Carroll, Susan (1977) 'Women candidates and state legislative elections, 1976: limitations in the political opportunity structure and their effects on electoral participation and success,' unpublished paper presented at the American Political Science Association, Annual Meeting, Washington, DC.

Citizens' Advisory Council on the Status of Women (1976) *Women in 1975* (Washington, DC: US Government Printing Office).

Costantini, Edmond and Craik, Kenneth H. (1972) 'Women as politicians: the social background, personality, and political careers of female party leaders,' *Journal of Social Issues*, vol. 28, no. 2, pp. 217–36.

Diamond, Irene (1977) *Sex Roles in the State House* (New Haven and London: Yale University Press).

Epstein, Cynthia Fuchs (1970a) 'Encountering the male establishment: sex-status limits on women's careers in the professions,' *American Journal of Sociology*, vol. 75, no. 6, pp. 965–82.

Epstein, Cynthia Fuchs (1970b) *Woman's Place: Options and Limits in Professional Careers* (Berkeley: University of California Press).

Epstein, Cynthia Fuchs (1971) 'Law partners and marital partners: strains and solutions in the dual-career family enterprise,' *Human Relations*, vol. 24, no. 6, pp. 549–64.

Epstein, Cynthia Fuchs (1975) 'Positive effects of the double negative,' *American Journal of Sociology*, vol. 78, no. 4, pp. 912–35.

Epstein, Cynthia Fuchs (forthcoming) *Women Lawyers* (New York: Basic Books).

Epstein, Leon D. (1967) *Political Parties in Western Democracies* (New York: Praeger).

Eulau, Heinz and Sprague, John D. (1964) *Lawyers and Politics* (Indianapolis and New York: Bobbs-Merrill).

Fichter, Joseph H. (1964) *Graduates of Predominantly Negro Colleges: Class of 1964*, Public Health Services Publication No. 1571 (Washington, DC: US Government Printing Office).

Fichter, Joseph H. (1971) 'Career expectations of Negro women graduates,' in Athena Theodore (ed.), *The Professional Woman* (Cambridge, Mass.: Schenkmann), pp. 429–48. Originally in *Monthly Labor Review*, vol. 90, no. 11 (1967), pp. 36–42.

Frankovic, Kathleen A. (1977) 'Sex and voting in the US House of Representatives: 1961–1975,' *American Politics Quarterly*, vol. 5, no. 3, pp. 315–30.

Gerth, Hans H. and Mills, C. Wright (1946) *From Max Weber: Essays in Sociology* (New York: Oxford University Press).

Githens, Marianne and Prestage, Jewel L. (1977) *A Portrait of Marginality: The Political Behavior of the American Woman* (New York: David McKay Co.).

Goot, Murray and Reid, Elizabeth (1975) *Women and Voting Studies: Mindless Matrons or Sexist Scientism?* (London and Beverly Hills: Sage Publications).

Greenstein, Fred I. (1961) 'Sex-related political differences in childhood,' *Journal of Politics*, vol. 23, no. 2, pp. 353–71.

Gruberg, Martin (1968) *Women in American Politics* (Oshkosh, Wisc.: Academia).

Hightower, Nikki Van (1974) 'The politics of female socialization,' unpublished Ph.D. dissertation (New York: New York University, Department of Political Science).

Hyman, Herbert (1959) *Political Socialization* (Glencoe, Ill.: Free Press).

Jacquette, Jane (ed.) (1974) *Women in Politics* (New York: Wiley-Interscience).

Jaros, Dean (1973) *Socialization to Politics* (New York: Praeger).

Jennings, M. Kent (1977) *Another Look at the Life Cycle and Political Participation* (Ann Arbor: University of Michigan).

Jennings, M. Kent and Langton, K. P. (1969) 'Mothers versus fathers: the formation of political orientations among young Americans,' *Journal of Politics*, vol. 31, no. 2, pp. 329–58.'

Jennings, M. Kent and Thomas, Norman (1968) 'Men and women in the party elites: social roles and political resources,' *The Midwest Journal of Political Science*, vol. 12, no. 4 (November), pp. 469–93.

Johnson, Marilyn (1978) 'Broadening elective and appointive political participation,' in Ann Foote Cahn (ed.), *Women in Midlife: Security and Fulfillment, Part I*, a compendium of papers submitted to the Select Committee on Aging and the Subcommittee on Retirement Income and Employment, US House of Representatives, Ninety-Fifth Congress, Second Session (Washington, DC: US Government Printing Office), pp. 299–319.

Johnson, Marilyn and Stanwick, Kathy (1976) *Profile of Women Holding Office* (New Brunswick, NJ: Center for the American Woman and Politics, Eagleton Institute of Politics, Rutgers – The State University).

Johnson, Marilyn and Carroll, Susan (1978), in association with Kathy Stanwick and Lynn Korenblit *Profile of Women Holding Office, II* (New Brunswick, NJ: Center for the American Woman and Politics, Eagleton Institute of Politics, Rutgers – The State University). Originally published in Center for the American Woman and Politics, *Women in Public Office: A Biographical Directory and Statistical Analysis*, 2nd edn (Metuchen, NJ: Scarecrow Press, 1978).

Kanter, Rosabeth Moss (1977) *Men and Women of the Corporation* (New York: Basic Books).

Kirkpatrick, Jeane (1974) *Political Woman* (New York: Basic Books).

Kirkpatrick, Jeane (1976) *The New Presidential Elite* (New York: Russell Sage Foundation and the Twentieth Century Fund).

Kohn, Melvin L. (1977) *Class and Conformity: A Study in Values*, 2nd edn (Chicago: University of Chicago Press).

Lane, Robert E. (1959) *Political Life: Why People Get Involved in Politics* (Glencoe, Ill.: Free Press).

Leader, Shelah Gilbert (1977) 'The policy impact of elected women officials,' in *The Impact* of the Electoral Process, Sage Electoral Studies Yearbook, Vol. III, ed. Louis Maisel and Joseph Cooper (Beverly Hills, Calif.: Sage Publications, 1977).

Lipman-Blumen, Jean (1973) 'Role de-differentiations as a system response to crisis: occupational and political roles of women,' Sociological Inquiry, vol. 43, no. 2, pp. 105–29.

Lipset, Seymour M. (1963) Political Man (New York: Doubleday; London: Heinemann).

Lynn, Naomi B. and Flora, Cornelia Butler (1973) 'Motherhood and political participation: a changing sense of self,' Journal of Political and Military Sociology, vol. 1 (March), pp. 91–103.

MacPherson, Myra (1975) The Power Lovers: An Intimate Look at Politicians and their Marriages (New York: G. P. Putnam's Sons).

McCormack, Thelma (1975) 'Toward a nonsexist perspective on social and political change,' in Marcia Millman and Rosabeth Moss Kanter (eds), Another Voice: Feminist Perspectives on Social Life and Social Science (Garden City, NY: Anchor Books), pp. 1–33.

Merton, Robert K. (1957, 1968) Social Theory and Social Structure (New York: Free Press).

Merton, Robert K. and Nisbet, Robert (1976) Contemporary Social Problems, 4th edn (New York: Harcourt Brace Jovanovich), pp. 432–40.

Mezey, Susan Gluck (1977) 'Local representatives in Connecticut: sex differences in attitudes towards women's rights policy,' unpublished paper presented at the Annual Meeting of the American Political Science Association.

Moran, Eileen (1978) 'The sexual division of labor in American political parties,' unpublished paper presented at the New York Women's Anthropological Conference.

National Women's Education Fund (1979) Roster of Women State Legislators as of January 1979 (Washington, DC: US Government Printing Office).

New York Times (New York, 1976–8).

Nogee, Philip and Levin, Murray B. (1958) 'Some determinants of political attitudes among college voters,' Public Opinion Quarterly, vol. 22, no. 4, pp. 449–63.

Orum, Anthony M., Cohen, Roberta S., Grasmuck, Sherri and Orum, Amy W. (1977) 'Sex, socialization and politics,' in Marianne Githens and Jewel L. Prestage (eds), A Portrait of Marginality: The Political Behavior of the American Woman (New York: David McKay Co.), pp. 17–37.

Putnam, Robert D. (1976) The Comparative Study of Political Elites (Englewood Cliffs, NJ: Prentice-Hall).

Sanders, Marion K. (1956) The Lady and the Vote (Boston, Mass.: Houghton Mifflin).

Schlesinger, Joseph A. (1957) 'Lawyers and American politics: a clarified view,' Midwest Journal of Political Science, vol. 1, no. 1 (May), pp. 26–39.

Schroeder, Patricia (1977) 'Explorations of external barriers to women's happiness and success,' unpublished paper presented at the Conference on Mental Health for Women: Challenges and Choices, Rochester, New York, November 12.

Schwindt, Helen Demos (1978) 'All the President's women,' Ms, vol. 6, no. 7 (January), pp. 51–4 and 91–2.

Seligman, Lester (1971) Recruiting Political Elites (New York: General Learning Press).

Shanley, Mary L. and Schuck, Victoria (1974) 'In search of political women,' Social Science Quarterly, vol. 55, no. 3, pp. 632–44.

Stiehm, Judith (1977) 'Ideology and participation: the first will remain last,' (unpublished paper presented to the Western Political Science Association, March 31).

Stein, Nancy (1978) 'Uphill all the way,' Newsbrief (New York: Women's Center for Community Leadership, Hunter College), p. 4.

Steinem, Gloria (1972) 'Women voters can't be trusted,' Ms, vol. 1, no. 1 (July), pp. 47–51 and 131.

Thomas, L. Eugene (1971) 'Political attitude congruence between politically active parents and college-age children: an inquiry into family political socialization,' Journal of Marriage and the Family, vol. 33, no. 2, pp. 375–86.

Tingsten, Herbert (1963) Political Behavior (Totowa, NJ: Bedminster Press).

US Department of Commerce, Bureau of the Census (1976) A Statistical Portrait of Women in the US, Current Population Reports, Special Studies Series P-23, No. 58 (Washington, DC: US Government Printing Office), pp. 55–6.

Wahlke, John C., Eulau, Heinz, Buchanan, William and Ferguson, Leroy C. (1962) The Legislative System: Explorations in Legislative Behavior (New York: Wiley).

Wall Street Journal (New York, 1978).

Werner, Emmy E. (1966) 'Women in Congress, 1917–1964,' *Western Political Quarterly*, vol. 19, no. 1 (March), pp. 16–30.

Werner, Emmy E. (1968) 'Women in the state legislatures,' *Western Political Quarterly*, vol. 21, no. 1 (March), pp. 40–50.

Wilson, James Q. (1962) *The Amateur Democrat: Club Politics in Three Cities* (Chicago: University of Chicago Press).

9

Women in Public Life in Austria

HELGA NOWOTNY

Women are still an exception in public life today and even a greater exception in elite positions. The dominant image of political and business elites, of trade union leaders, and of others in positions of control is male, and male is the world that they inhabit. Women, by contrast, populate the sphere of private life: family, home, children. This distinction between the private and the public is pervasive – a rift separating two domains of social existence, only partially mediated by the relative freedom that women have gained in moving between them while continuing to live predominantly in one.

For centuries women have been excluded from public power; they could, however, hope to achieve considerable power in the private sphere, especially in societies where public life was male dominated. Yet, however powerful they may have been in the private sphere, that arena continues to be subordinate to public power.

My underlying assumption is that the public and private spheres are two separate and distinct modes of existence, although the boundaries drawn between the two tend to vary according to the specific nature of the society being examined. Invariably, however, the public sphere contains the institutions in which are concentrated political, military, and economic power. The private sphere is clearly subordinate to the public one, and yet it supports it and assures its continuance in many ways.[1] 'Where power is, women are not' is how the historical record reads. In order to understand the difficulties that women face in gaining access to elite positions, which are invariably located in the public sphere, we have to understand why this distinction works to women's disadvantage.

This paper examines some tentative answers to questions arising from data collected in Austria.[2]

THE PUBLIC AND THE PRIVATE

It is a striking observation that women's activities are confined to activities that society regards as peripheral, whereas men are to be found at the centre of society's activities – those representing its value system. Why is it that public power and women do not coincide? Although it is true that women possess power in the private sphere, usually tied to their reproductive qualities, the crucial fact remains that no mechanisms seem to exist that allow women to transform this 'private power' into some kind of 'public power.'

In this connection it may be useful to turn to the concept of *social capital* as it was first employed in the work of Bourdieu (1971; and Bourdieu, Boltanski, and de Saint-Martin, 1973). By this term Bourdieu meant social knowledge, contacts, privileged access to culturally valued qualifications, and social skills as embodied in the various strategies employed by competitors in what he has called a *social field* – a network of power relations characterized by its own rules of competition, conflicts and strategies, and interests and profits. Social capital is a necessary ingredient in the continuous struggle for success, rewards, recognition, and power that characterizes a field. Although this picture, especially the assumption of a monistic form of continuous struggle, is probably too simple, social capital is a useful concept, for it covers especially the informal aspects of access to power, the mechanisms through which power is further accumulated by investing it in different ways, and the mechanisms by which power is reproduced. It determined social relationships to a significant degree. Status, authority, power of various kinds – whatever ultimate recognition a field has to offer – can be obtained through social capital, which in principle is therefore both expandible and convertible.

Following my distinction between the public and the private sphere, and noting women's difficulties in gaining access to the public sphere, I wonder whether there do not exist different rules of conversion of capital for men and women. Two of the outstanding questions to be answered in this connection are why women have been able to accumulate only certain kinds of capital, and why they have been equally limited in converting the capital that they have gained into certain other types. More specifically, my hypothesis is that women, by their overwhelming concentration in the private sphere, have been able to accumulate a kind of capital that differs from the kind to which men usually have access. What the private sphere has to offer can perhaps best be termed *emotional capital*.

This is knowledge, contacts, and relations as well as access to emotionally valued skills and assets, which hold within any social network characterized at least partly by affective ties. As long as women were confined to the private sphere, this was the only capital that they could acquire. Like other forms of capital, they could accumulate it and build up positions of dominance, but their reach extended only as far as the validity of this currency; it was limited to the private sphere. The rules of the labor market are such that emotional capital gained in the private sphere is not convertible into *economic capital*, for this exchange relationship has long been depersonalized, and private capital is of little value in the outside world.[3] This means that emotional capital, which is valueless in the public sphere, is largely used for further family investments in children and (especially upwardly mobile) husbands.

This is especially noticeable with regard to aspirations for, and investment strategies in, children. This is also the reason why women's access to education, taken in itself, can be meaningless as an indicator of women's emancipation. In several countries of the Third World women are now gaining access to universities, only to re-enter the private sphere again when their studies are completed, justifying this step with added educational qualifications that will benefit their children.

Thus, women work for their families by converting the economic capital that they gain in the labor market into emotional capital. Men also work for their families; but having less need for emotional capital, as they have an independent social standing outside the family, they use their economic capital to generate more or to convert it into 'higher' forms of social capital.

To a limited degree women can also acquire social capital, especially as members of the upper class, where they have always been instrumental in securing cultural assets and in supporting their husbands' strategies. This social capital, however, is reinvested by men, who are in a publicly recognized position to do so. If women lack such position, they will channel whatever social capital they may have gained through their husbands or other family members, which will leave them with only emotional capital at their disposal.

Thus, it seems that women are faced with an unsurmountable dilemma; their social location puts them at a disadvantage in the public sphere and bars their access to it. Even if they are in a position to accumulate social capital, it is used for their families rather than for themselves, as they lack the position that is necessary for further successful investment strategies. When entering a career in the public sphere, even with seemingly equal initial conditions, women are tempted to drop out again and objectively risk doing so. Public careers demand not only wholehearted allegiance and a clear subordination of private life to public exigencies, but also compliance to a mapped-out career structure.

THE CASE OF AUSTRIA: WOMEN IN TRANSITION

Whatever inroads women have been able to make into the public sphere have been facilitated by the 'publicization' of the private sphere (i.e. the transfer of more and more functions to public institutions and to professionals or others holding a job in them). Moving with this trend, women as a group have carried with them norms and values as well as behavioral patterns of the private sphere (Millgårdh, 1977). Women have retained, at least in principle, the voluntariness of moving between the two spheres – a convenient device to keep the private sphere at the disposal of the public and to use it as a reserve labor force. Women have earned a foothold in the public sphere, but the majority live and work only on its edge.

Since the First World War Austria has maintained a traditionally high percentage of women in the labor force, amounting in 1971 to 38·7 per cent of the total. Before the Second World War only unmarried middle-class women worked, mainly in jobs regarded as 'suitable' for female employment – extensions of familiar female activities. However, married and unmarried working-class women labored all their lives at menial factory jobs. Only at the turn of the century were women granted access to universities, and for some time afterwards girls' education remained officially different from, and inferior to, boys'. In their efforts to gain the right to education and a place in the labor market women encountered three arguments still heard today: biological 'weakness', destruction of the family (resulting from women's employment), and increased competition (endangering men's jobs).

Differences remain marked. Three-quarters of all women in Austria today have no education beyond the legal minimum, compared to only half of the male population. Among university graduates there are three times as many men as women. Although 21·8 per cent of Austrian men who prepare for a university education by passing their 'Matura' (i.e. the school leaving examination) achieve a top occupation later in life, only 2·9 per cent of the women do so. Also, 50 per cent of male university graduates succeed in obtaining leading positions, compared to only 17 per cent of females.

This situation is mirrored in a survey of opinions on equality in marriage. It has been found that 60 per cent of men and women believe that it is very bad for a marriage if a wife earns more than her husband, and that 65 per cent of men and 70 per cent of women think it equally bad if a wife is better educated than her husband.

This upholding of the traditional relationship between the sexes, which is especially strong among well-educated men in leading positions, is only partially offset by the trend towards what has been labelled 'partnership' in marriage (i.e. the readiness of men to share household chores and help in rearing the children); 53 per cent of women and 64 per cent of men still hold that women are better suited for bringing up children. Most mothers still reinforce their daughters' aspirations for a typically 'female' occupation and for marriage and children as the primary goals of their lives. Although government policies have succeeded in recent years in increasing the percentage of women at universities from 25 to 40 per cent, and although the percentage of girls in secondary schools leading to university has for the first time exceeded 50 per cent, choices of study and occupation remain overwhelmingly limited to traditional female fields.

Against this sober background of facts and figures, an analysis of women in elite positions is even more sobering. Within the national legislative body women do not exceed 6 per cent of Members of Parliament, but they do form 20 per cent of the politically less important second chamber. In the provincial governments the percentage of women members ranges from none at all (Tyrol) and 2·4 (Vorarlberg) to 19·4 in Vienna, with 5·4 (Lower Austria) and 9·4 (Burgenland) in between, which makes a clear west–east difference. Women's chances of entering a legislative chamber vary with party affiliation; they are double for Social Democrats (11·3 per cent) compared with Conservatives (5·5 per cent). Leftist parties have traditionally been more open to women's claims for advancement and egalitarianism.

Although, as we have seen, the pool of eligibility from which Austrian women can be drawn into elite positions remains significantly smaller than that for men, the severe under-representation of women at higher levels remains with discouraging persistence.

A few figures will suffice here. In teaching – a traditional women's occupation – which boasts 60 per cent women, only 13·4 per cent are to be found among directors of schools. In the highest political circles women are clearly under-represented. In the central committee of the Social Democrats 12·8 per cent are women, with a mere 5 per cent in the Conservative Party. In the majority of legislative interest groups – the various 'chambers,'[4] which play an important part in Austrian political life – women are virtually absent. Although women represent 30 per cent of all doctors, no woman is represented in the doctors' political pressure group. In the chamber of workers and employees there are 5·7 per cent women; in the chamber of commerce there are none. Among pharmacists, the majority of whom are female, women are 11·8 per cent of the professional organization.

Neither is the representation of women in the Austrian Trade Unions more encouraging. Although 28 per cent of all unionized employees are women, only 4·8 per cent of women are to be found in the highest decision-making body (the Bundesvorstand). The 'downward flow' of women when moving up the career ladder of institutions can be neatly observed in other figures on various unions.

CURRENT PUBLIC OPINION TOWARDS WORKING WOMEN

Men in positions of power may be expected to oppose intruders regardless of who they are or where they come from. The dominant group in any society defines both success and legitimate strategies for obtaining it in terms that are most beneficial to the maintenance of the *status quo*. Part of the resistance encountered by women who attempt to move into elite positions is therefore to be explained in terms of the reluctance of any dominant group to share power with a challenger. Strategies of defense vary in accordance with the principles and legitimation strategies used by the challengers. The question remains, however, whether male resistance to what is seen as female intrusion into an exclusive domain is limited to this phenomenon alone or whether more is involved.

Austrian public opinion, with a characteristic split between attitude and behavior, accepts the existence of working women and working mothers[5] but envisages different stereotypes regarding working women and men. Compared to men, women are said to be more diligent and more ambitious than men, but less solidary, less objective, less independent, and less enterprising. Especially among more educated persons, women as superiors encounter considerable resistance; this is hardly based on experience, for only 2 per cent of all men and 19 per cent of all women have ever had a female boss. There is an overall impression of strong male resistance, especially where more educated women have started to move into formerly exclusive male domains. More real is the opinion that women with the same qualifications receive lower pay than men and have fewer chances for promotion. This is not surprising, given the often negative attitudes of men in gatekeeping positions who have to decide on a woman's advancement or pay rise.

If women were to move massively into the public sphere, if they were more successful as a pressure group in winning power, if they were to achieve solidarity to help themselves and to prefer other women, the consequences would be far reaching indeed. It would upset the delicate balance between public and private spheres and leave the latter in chaos, at least initially. The whole reproduction mechanisms of the class and status systems of a society would become unpredictable and need restructuring. Finally, the private lives of the present power holders would undergo drastic changes. Most of them would lose the support of wives upon whom they now count to aid their public careers, and they would have to compete with women who felt no more responsibility for their families than men.

THE POLITICAL FAMILY: THE VIEWS OF MALE POLITICIANS

However unlikely such a scenario may be, conscious and unconscious fears of this kind seem to color men's perceptions when confronted with the problem of women's under-representation in public life. A sample of male politicians – a total of 105 individuals – was interviewed in 1973 with respect to women's political activities and careers, women's place in society, attitudes towards women's traditional roles, and, finally, consequences that they were likely to draw for their own behavior.

Not surprisingly, the attitudes of these male politicians towards the social position of women in general varied with party affiliation and more or less reflected official ideological positions. Concerning women's political activities, the following picture emerged:

(1) 78 per cent agreed that women were as qualified as men for leading political positions;
(2) only 11 per cent thought that the number of women now in politics was sufficient;
(3) 93 per cent agreed that women encountered more difficulties in becoming actively involved in politics;
(4) 92 per cent conceded that women experienced more difficulties than men in obtaining leading political positions; and
(5) 70 per cent could imagine a woman as leader of their party.

In contrast:

(6) 83 per cent believed that women were especially suited for certain areas of political life, which with few exceptions were those traditionally associated with 'women's affairs'; such central political concerns as economics were hardly ever mentioned.

Contrasts were even more pronounced when touching on the attitudes of these leading male politicians. Only 48 per cent agreed that women should be represented in the central policy-making bodies of their parties in proportion to female membership in the party. There was an outspoken reluctance to admit women to these bodies, although in general female participation was (seemingly) encouraged. Most sobering were the respondents' replies to how they would actually vote on changes in party statutes allowing female representation in the highest party bodies in accordance with female membership; 67 per cent of the Communists, 48 per cent of the Conservatives, 41 per cent of the National-Liberals, and only 31 per cent of the Social Democrats were ready to vote for such a change.

Male resistance to female participation in public life is real, whether or not women who have moved into elite positions report that they have encountered it in their careers. In the Austrian context highly educated men in top jobs tend also to be among the most conservative regarding female public participation. The attitudes of leading male politicians are hardly more encouraging. These men seem to aim for what can at best be called a compromise, fitting well into the dominant family ideology of the country. Although professing equality at the ideological level and making a realistic appraisal of the objective situation as women encounter it, they resist strongly when demands for public participation are pressed. They are ready to admit women into politics, provided that they concern themselves with women's affairs. What this amounts to is a re-enactment in the public sphere of the family situation typically found in the private sphere. It amounts to the creation of a 'political family' situation in which women re-enact their traditional roles, charged with peripheral concerns, leaving men free to devote themselves to the 'more central' matters.[6]

In a 'political family' situation women would be allowed to transfer emotional capital from the private sphere to the public sphere, where it would be officially recognized as valid through an act of political legitimation. The extension of the private into the public, or the publicization of private, would perhaps be the next logical step. Women's capital would still remain a secondary currency, however, reflecting the secondary positions that women could hope to obtain in the public sphere. Secondary currencies when officially recognized are still to be preferred to non-convertible currencies, however small the advantage may seem.

WOMEN'S VIEW: FEMALE POLITICIANS IN AUSTRIA

In the Austrian survey a small number of female politicians was interviewed in depth. Because of the small sample size and some distortions – of the twenty-seven interviewed, Social Democrats were over-represented with nineteen women, six belonged to the Conservatives, and one each belonged to the Communist Party and the National-Liberal Party – their answers are not to be taken as representative in the strict sense. Nevertheless, the career patterns that they exhibited and the difficulties that they reported are those which any female politician in Austria is still likely to encounter, although most of the female politicians themselves belonged to an older generation, the majority being between 45 and 55 years of age. Their career patterns typically differed with party affiliation. Female politicians of the Conservative Party began their political lives in their early forties, thus conforming in practice to the ideal that their party holds out for women in general, namely, to encourage them to re-enter public life only after the children have left home. Social Democratic women, by contrast, began their political careers much younger. Most of them started in youth organizations, and the rest began active political life at an average age of 25. Further, Social Democratic women and one Communist were introduced into politics by politically active parents, youth organizations, and their own professional lives. Early socialization into the public sphere through politically active parents endowed these women with a certain amount of social capital, in the form of political family ties and access to a political world that is quite small in a country like Austria. For the Conservative women, entry into political life was stimulated by joint political interest of husband and wife and partly facilitated through such non-professional activity as charity work.

For half of the Conservative women entry into politics in their own right (i.e. the acquisition of a formal public position) came as a surprise.

Although they had been interested in politics before and active in an informal capacity, it was 'by chance' that they obtained a formal position. The social capital gained earlier facilitated their switch to an official position, but undoubtedly it would not have been sufficient to create one for them.

Although the modes of entry into political (public) life differed widely with party affiliation, and the women encountered the same obstacles and attitudes that anyone is likely to meet when an attempt is made to cross the boundary into the public sphere, they did in fact fit into an existing career structure, and the paths that they took were similar to those which male politicians also take. Social Democrat men also tend to start political life in youth organizations, whereas Conservative men usually switch to politics from a business or other career in mid-life.

However, for these women family ties remained strong. Of all the female politicians, seventeen were married, five widowed, two divorced, and the rest single; and twenty-one had children. All married women emphasized the positive attitudes of their husbands as a precondition for their political activity, and the majority felt that the responsibility for organizing the household and care of the children was largely their own. Their dual positions, in public life and the family, continued to pose the greatest burden. This double–bind situation was frequently cited (charges of neglecting children on the one hand, or of being overly ambitious on the other). Also frequently mentioned were the additional difficulties encountered at the beginning of their political careers, where they had to make greater efforts in order to prove themselves: the women's own inhibitions; a lack of organizing experience and self-confidence; difficulties in combining family duties with political meetings, usually held in the evenings; and the fact that their own political interests often had to be subordinated to their husbands'. These women perceived clearly the legacy that a traditional education bequeathed on women and the difficulties that had to be surmounted until a woman was able to cope with contradictory demands. Women in the Conservative Party and National-Liberal Party reported strong pressure to be active in 'female fields'; and women in the Social Democratic Party, although commenting that they were welcome at lower levels, increasingly met male resistance when moving up the party ladder. All these women supported the necessity of maintaining a separate women's organization within their parties, although they hoped that this was merely a temporary measure until women had gained true equality both inside and outside the party. Questions regarding their attitude toward the women's movement drew mostly negative and strongly emotional reactions from them. They regarded the movement as inappropriate for Austria, exaggerated, and not helpful to women. Strategies advocated for women differed according to political party; Conservative Party women advocated that women should concentrate on women's affairs, whereas Social Democratic women thought that various legal activities (e.g. pressing for a general thirty-hour week or trade union activities) would be more productive.

Austrian women do not show much interest in politics. Of the women surveyed, 43 per cent were not at all interested, 14 per cent could not find time although they would have liked to, 36 per cent reported occasional interest, and only 7 per cent were actively interested. Other findings underlined their conservative attitude toward political involvement. This is reinforced by the attitudes of Austrian men, who still regard politics as a male province and doubt that women can be successful in politics because they are not tough enough to get things done. Yet, these same men believe that women basically have the same capabilities as men. They also hold that more women should be in politics but that they should concern themselves with women's affairs.

The handful of Austrian women who have obtained a top position in political life were able to overcome some handicaps and had to adjust to others as part of their personal and political reality. By entering public life through the accepted channels in the terms of reference set up for men, or by being able to convert their previously accumulated social capital into a formal public position, these women have concentrated on obtaining and reinvesting, via their own formal public position, social capital rather than emotional capital. Although their roots in the private sphere are still very visible and strong, they have been able to invest in their own public activities instead of in their husbands and children.

WHAT LESSONS CAN BE DRAWN FROM THE AUSTRIAN CASE?

Elite positions by definition are reserved for a minority. The crucial questions are what selection procedures are used, formally as well as informally, to filter out those whom a society and its gatekeepers of power will or will not admit, and what strategies are at the disposal of those who aspire to these positions. In the case of Austrian women one official selection criterion – qualification – clearly has not worked as it was supposed to, and others have been used elusively. Among the strategies and means that are open to women who aspire to elite positions, the crucial step seems to lie in the transition from the private into the public sphere and in their acquisition of the kind of capital needed there. Women's march from the periphery to the center is a long one indeed.

NOTES

(1) The anthropological literature on this theme is vast. See, for instance, Lewis (1976), ch. 8.

(2) If not otherwise indicated, all data presented in this paper have been extracted from *Bundeskanzleramt (1975)*, especially from Vol. 7, *Die Frau im öffentlichen Leben* (project leader, Paul Blau), and Vol. 1, *Das Rollenbild der Frau* (project leader, Helga Nowotny).

(3) One of the reasons for the relatively very low representation of women in public life in the Soviet Union seems to lie in the peculiar relationship between the public and the private sphere in that country. Although the Soviet Union has not succeeded in creating an alternative to the private sphere (which has been more or less left intact, including some very conservative features of family life), its standing in the public value system is very low. Ideologically, the private sphere should not exist at all; yet, it persists with very little public recognition. Women therefore suffer a double disadvantage: from the usual difficulties *qua* women in gaining access to the public sphere, and from the fact that they are located in a section of society that has lower public standing than in the West.

(4) Chambers are created by federal law and represent the interests of most professional

fields. Their representatives have a right to be consulted on laws falling within their fields.

(5) In Austria, 51 per cent of all men and 44 per cent of all women believe that children of working mothers will experience disadvantages in later life; 35 per cent of men and 41 per cent of women believe that these children will have the same chances for success as those of non-working mothers. In those strata which have relatively high aspirations for their children, more men than women believe that children can suffer from their mother's absence. Lower strata responses are more pessimistic throughout.

Opposition against working women is pronounced in the white collar occupations. In a sample of white collar employees in Upper Austria, 60 per cent of the men questioned opposed their wives' taking up outside employment after marriage (see Scharmann and Neubauer, 1973).

(6) To what extent may this be a more general phenomenon? Jacqueline Feldman (1975), for instance, has reported similar tendencies for women in science. To what extent are women in business expected to look after the 'female sectors' of the consumer world? What about 'female quarters' in law and in state bureaucracies? Although individual women, by an unusual combination of qualifications, may escape this re-enactment of the family situation, concerted counterstrategies are obviously needed for women as a group.

REFERENCES

Bourdieu, Pierre (1971) 'Reproduction culturelle et reproduction sociale,' (Social Science Information), *Information sur les sciences sociales* vol. 10, no. 2, pp. 45–79.

Bourdieu, Pierre, Boltanski, L., and de Saint-Martin, M. (1973) 'Les stratégies de reconversion: les classes sociales et le système d'enseignement,' (Social Science Information), *Information sur les sciences sociales* vol. 12, no. 5, pp. 61–113.

Bundeskanzleramt (1975) *Bericht über die Situation der Frau in Österreich: Frauenbericht, 1975* (Vienna).

10

Political Attitudes of Women in High Status Occupations* in West Germany

SYLVIA STREEK, ERIKA BOCK-ROSENTHAL, AND CHRISTA HAASE

Because women in high status occupations have been so rare, only in recent years have they become a matter for scientific attention. Although women are still a very small minority in top jobs, current discussions about equal career opportunities for both sexes have heightened the interest of social scientists. However, their studies have tended to focus on such topics as the individual and social—structural preconditions of women's careers, consequences for the family life of the women under study, and the structural barriers encountered by high-achieving women.

We wish to explore the political and ideological outlook of the women who attain high positions in societal elites. The questions that we are raising are: Will these women become adapted integrated members of the elites that they join, assimilating their values as well? Or can they be expected to contribute to a change of traditional elite orientations in a less competitive, less authoritarian, and less hierarchy-minded (i.e. less 'male') direction? We are thus asking whether these women will be critical of a societal structure in which the central institutions are designed to protect existing prerogatives (e.g. by denying minorities equal chances and denying them access to positions of power and privilege). We wonder whether there is a liberalizing effect when a member of an elite group has encountered and successfully overcome discriminatory barriers to personal and occupational achievement. Specifically, we are interested in the extent to which successful women in elite positions can be counted upon by other women as potential allies in their strivings for social change in general and equal opportunity in particular.

Actually, there are two possible arguments. As members of social elites, enjoying power, income, and prestige, successful women may be expected to develop the same political orientations as their male peers. Like them they profit rather than suffer from a social structure in which rewards are distributed as unequally as opportunities. Thus, they have something to defend, and their vested interests may be the same as those of all members of elites, regardless of sex. In addition, successful women who have made their way into high status occupations may be subject to the same pressures and influences as, say, sons of workers rising into managerial positions.

* The underlying larger research project was financed by Deutsche Forschungsgemeinschaft (DFG).

Often, in cases of upward mobility 'risers' feel impelled to certify their newly acquired, and therefore insecure, status by 'overadapting' to the group that they have succeeding in joining. From the perspective of their personal experience they may also tend to believe that there is a system of equal opportunity. The claim that anybody can reach the top, if he or she only strives hard enough, will hardly appear false to those who come out on the winning side, even if they happen to be rare exceptions to the rule. By providing them with a 'fitting' explanation of their success – a very flattering one – it may seduce them into accepting an ideology that basically serves as an instrument of preserving existing inequalities of opportunities, protects the political homogeneity of the dominant group, and integrates the newcomers into its 'community of assumptions.'

On the other hand, women in high status positions can be expected to be subject to a fairly unique combination of social pressures that may lead to an alienated rather than integrated attitude toward existing social structures. If they reach a position at the top of the occupation system, women seem to occupy two 'inconsistent statuses:' an inferior one (their sex status) and a superior one (their occupational status). Status inconsistency may be a source of deviant, particularly of liberal–political, orientations (Lenski, 1954), if only because the structural tensions and contradictions working on status-inconsistent groups demand some relief. In addition, to the extent that female elite members are relegated to second-rank statuses as far as intraelite stratification is concerned, they will find it difficult to identify completely with their new environment. As discrimination continues to be a fact of life in spite of their relatively high overall status, their experience of the structural handicaps that they face will be reinforced.

Analogous hypotheses can be developed under a 'cultural' rather than a structural perspective. Indeed, there is some evidence that women tend to be more conservative politically than men. In all federal elections in West Germany after the Second World War the percentages of women voting for the conservative parties[1] – the Christian Democratic Union (CDU) and the Christian Social Union (CSU) – were consistently higher than the respective percentages among men. This may lead us to expect that women in high status occupations will be prone to conservative influence; in addition to having privileges to defend, their basic propensities will push them in more conservative directions. However, the difference between men and women in voting preference is shrinking.[2]

It has also been argued that the central norms and values governing social behavior in the political as well as in the economic and occupational spheres of modern societies are essentially male in character, at least in the sense that they are usually stressed less strongly in the socialization of girls than in that of boys. These values – individual success rather than collective solidarity, aggressive competitiveness instead of peaceful co-operation, hierarchical ranking according to 'contribution' and 'achievement' rather than egalitarianism – also happen to be at the core of the dominant conservative ideologies in capitalist societies. But women, who are differently socialized and therefore experience the consequences of the dominant ideologies as discriminatory, may find it harder than men to become convinced conservatives. If this were true, the rise of women into elite positions would infuse new and basically incompatible elements into the elite's ideological composition; lacking the appropriate motivational structure, women would to a certain degree be resistant to the culture of the male dominant classes and more inclined than their peers to support structural changes.

METHOD

This paper draws on data from an exploratory 1975 study on career patterns, life styles, and attitudes among women in top jobs. The study was one of the first of its kind in West Germany. Data were collected by intensive interviews with fifty-six women having university degrees and holding occupational positions usually held by men.

Respondents were selected by a two-step process. First, official job statistics were employed to isolate seven kinds of occupations that required academic training but whose ranks were composed of fewer than 10 per cent women. Second, through contacts with professional associations, government bureaucracies, and university administrations the names and addresses of 149 potential respondents were secured. Contacts were established by a letter asking for an interview. The response was unusually positive; only 15 per cent of the women contacted declined to participate. With the first letter respondents received a short standardized questionnaire asking for basic information on their educational, professional, and marital careers. During the subsequent interviews the questionnaires served as useful bases for intensive questioning. The interviews took between one and six hours and were conducted on the basis of a loosely structured list of topics, supplemented by a small number of standardized questions. All interviews were tape recorded. The data were analyzed both qualitatively and quantitatively. To facilitate the rapid exploration of variables the information was coded and analyzed statistically with the help of a prepackaged computer program.[3] Because of the small sample statistical associations were taken as guides for ordering the qualitative material rather than as results in their own right; they were taken at face value only when they were unusually strong and supported by plausible qualitative evidence. The following presentation has to be read with these reservations in mind.

SAMPLE

The sample consisted of members of seven occupations:

8	lawyers	(7 self-employed)
8	professors of the natural sciences	
9	leading physicians at hospitals	
9	architects	(7 self-employed)
6	certified public accountants	(4 self-employed)
11	senior civil servants	
5	managers in chemical industries	

In West Germany the percentages of women in these occupations were as follows: lawyers 5 per cent; teachers at colleges and universities 8 per cent; leading physicians at hospitals 2·5 per cent; architects 5 per cent; certified public accountants 6·4 per cent; civil servants 5·4 per cent; managers in the chemical industries 8 per cent. Thirty-eight of the respondents were employed, and eighteen were self-employed. Age varied from 31 to 72 years; eighteen women were aged 31–40; nineteen were aged 41–50, nineteen were aged 51–60, and five were 61 or older. Twenty-eight respondents were Protestants, nineteen were Roman Catholics, and nine had no religious affiliations. None of the women came from the working class; fifteen were from the lower middle class, twenty-one from the middle middle class, and fifteen from the upper middle class; five belonged to the upper class.[4] More than half of the sample (54 per cent) was not married at the time of the interview. In comparison, of the total female population in West Germany, about 9 per cent of the respective age groups was unmarried in 1975 (*Statistisches Jahrbuch*, 1975). Even considering the small size of the sample, this difference seems to indicate that women in top jobs are more likely than other women to be single. Seventeen of the twenty-two married women in the sample had at least one child, and twelve had more than one; only one woman had as many as four children.

In the absence of a control group of unsuccessful women for comparison an index was developed to distinguish between the relatively more and the relatively less successful women in the sample. The index combined a respondent's income, her rank if she was employed in an organization, the number of her subordinates with academic degrees, and the number of her subordinates without academic degrees. The values of the component variables were standardized within occupations in order to control for inter-occupational differences. Income and rank contributed one-third each to the final score, and the two categories of subordinates accounted for the additional third. To the degree that differences in occupational status (e.g. employed versus self-employed) or occupation (e.g. lawyers versus architects) produced missing values on one or the other component variable, scores were weighted accordingly.[5]

The usefulness of the success index was shown throughout the study, some of the most interesting results of which were related to the distinctions between less and more successful women. For example, it was found that the highly successful women in the sample were *either* married and self-employed, often working with their husbands in the same professional practice, *or* unmarried and salaried. Thus, it seems that the contradictory demands of work and traditional family life do not permit women to build successful careers unless they find a way of overcoming the functional differentiation between home and occupation. For example, there is the self-employed woman who does her work at home while looking after the house and the children. By choosing self-employment she is deciding for the chance of combining a successful career with the possibility of having children. Self-employment is the foundation on which a woman can perhaps have both career and family life. Otherwise, success seems to be attainable for women only under the condition that they concentrate their energies on occupational achievement to the exclusion of marriage and family life.

RESULTS

The first indicator of the political attitudes of the respondents related to the aspect of party preference (Table 10.1). Of the fifty-six respondents, five refused to answer. Respondents in the mixed categories did not have stable voting records. However, although some of the women had switched parties,[6] two blocs could clearly be distinguished. There was the more conservative group, consisting of those who either (1) voted always for the Christian Democratic Union (CDU) or Christian Social Union (CSU) or (2) voted sometimes for the CDU/CSU and sometimes for the Free Democratic Party (FDP). There was also the more liberal group, consisting of those who voted for the parties of the then ruling coalition – for the Social Democratic Party (SPD) or for the somewhat more conservative FDP. Of the forty-eight women reporting some kind of party preference, twenty-eight (59 per cent) belonged to the more conservative type, and twenty seem to have had more liberal party preferences. The following analysis will be based on these forty-eight cases only.

Table 10.1   *Party preference.*

Party	N	%
CDU/CSU	20	39
SPD	12	23
CDU–FDP	8	16
SPD–FDP	5	10
FDP	3	6
Undecided	3	6
Total	51	100

That party preferences are in fact measures of conservative or liberal attitudes has been validated by their correlation with opinions on issues. Respondents believing that West German society was a meritocracy (*Leistungsgesellschaft*) – a society in which rewards are distributed according to achievement, with everybody having an equal chance to get to the top – were much more likely to prefer the conservative parties than those believing otherwise (Table 10.2). The women who believed that not everyone had the same chance for success leaned toward the Social Democrats and the liberals. This is in accord with the fact that, of all relevant West German parties, the Social Democrats are supported mostly by those who feel that they do not get an equal chance and believe that this should be changed.

A similar tendency can be found in the respondents' attitudes toward a second issue, namely, whether or not such organizations as universities,

Table 10.2   *Belief in West German society as a meritocracy and party preference.*

Meritocracy	Conservative		Liberal[a]		Total	
	(%)	(N)	(%)	(N)	(%)	(N)
No	35	(7)	65	(13)	100	(20)
Yes	80	(16)	20	(4)	100	(20)

$\gamma = -0.76$

[a] Social Democrats and liberals.

hospitals, and enterprises should provide their members with better chances to participate in decision-making processes. A more detailed analysis of this attitude appears below. At this point it is only necessary to know that those disagreeing with more participation tended to vote for the conservatives, whereas those supporting more democratic decision-making preferred the Social Democrats or liberals (Table 10.3).

Table 10.3   *Participatory decision-making and party preference.*

Participation	Conservative		Liberal		Total	
	(%)	(N)	(%)	(N)	(%)	(N)
No	84	(16)	16	(3)	100	(19)
Yes	32	(7)	68	(15)	100	(22)

$\gamma = 0.84$

A further issue related to party affiliation is the reform of the abortion laws. This heatedly discussed problem, which is of immediate interest to women, is at the same time one of the favorite topics raised by the conservative opposition against the liberal government coalition. The liberal respondents supported reforms of the abortion laws much more strongly than did the conservatives (Table 10.4). Nevertheless, 50 per cent of the conservative respondents deviated from the party line on this issue, on which a considerable number of conservatives are opposed to the party view.

Table 10.4   *Party affiliations and reforms of the abortion laws.*

Party	Against reform		For reform		Total	
	(%)	(N)	(%)	(N)	(%)	(N)
Conservative	50	(13)	50	(13)	100	(26)
Liberal	16	(3)	84	(16)	100	(19)

$\gamma = 0.68$

By now it was established that the sample consisted of two types of respondents: a more conservative one and a more liberal one. Looking for the reasons for this variance, we found that the more successful women tended to prefer the conservative parties ($\gamma = 0.31$). It was possible to be more precise by controlling for age and employment status (Tables 10.5 and 10.6). Most of the older and the self-employed women were affiliated with the conservatives, whereas among the younger and the employed the percentage of the CDU/CSU votes varied with success. The successful younger and the successful employed women clearly preferred the conservatives, but only a minority of the less successful women in these categories (42 and 43 per cent respectively) voted conservative.

Table 10.5 *Respondents preferring the conservatives, by age and success.*

Age	Less successful		Very successful	
	(%)	*(N)*	*(%)*	*(N)*
Younger	42	(12)	67	(12)
Older	67	(9)	69	(13)

Table 10.6 *Respondents preferring the conservatives, by type of employment and success.*

Employment	Less successful		Very successful	
	(%)	*(N)*	*(%)*	*(N)*
Self-employed	71	(7)	60	(10)
Employed	43	(14)	73	(25)

Liberal orientations are most likely to predominate among relatively less successful women, who stand to gain from liberal reforms – the younger ones, who would personally be able to benefit from the removal of discriminatory structures, and the employed, whose career chances are dependent on more liberal hiring and promotion practices within organizations. Successful professional women prefer the conservatives; their political preferences are basically the same as those of other elite members. Having worked their way up into positions usually dominated by men, they seem to have adapted without difficulty to the interests and attitudes usually associated with high social status.

One more hint at the sources of conservative party preferences among women in high status occupations can be gained from the individualistic interpretation of occupational success. Women who had been, at least once during their careers, the first woman on their job or the only woman among men – 'pioneers,' as we called them – showed a more conservative tendency than the 'non-pioneers' (Table 10.7). Even more than other high achievers, pioneers may be inclined to interpret their success as the result of personal talent and as an appropriate reward for hard work and enduring ambition.

Table 10.7   *'Pioneers' and party preference.*

'Pioneers'	Conservative		Liberal		Total	
	(%)	(N)	(%)	(N)	(%)	(N)
'Non-pioneer'	47	(7)	53	(8)	100	(15)
'Pioneer'	69	(18)	31	(8)	100	(26)

γ = −0·44

Although most of the women in the sample attributed their success exclusively to their personal skills and efforts, the particularly strong evidence of individually accountable accomplishments that was inherent in the 'pioneer' situation was related to politically conservative attitudes.

Table 10.8   *Participatory democracy in organizations.*

Question: Would you support more democratic participation in decision-making processes, as it happened at the universities during the student movement?

Answer:	N	%
No, one person has to bear the responsibility	14	29
No, quick decisions are necessary	3	6
No, members are not qualified	7	15
Yes, partially	20	42
Yes, participation	4	8
Total	48	100

Only half of the sample felt that an increase in intraorganizational democracy was desirable (Table 10.8). Those who preferred non-participatory structures tended to emphasize the need for clear allocation of responsibilities at the top of the hierarchy. This attitude was expressed in the following statement by a professor of chemistry:

> In most areas one person has to bear the responsibility. In collective bodies the sense of responsibility is often weakened. This does not mean that a leading doctor should not discuss the problems with his assistants; but it is he who has to decide and to bear the responsibility.

Or, as another professor put it:

> It is not possible that all people are on the same level. Concerning responsibilities and decisions, there has to be a difference. In the long run one would not be satisfied with groups without inner differentiation. We see that now in the university legislation. Everything stays in anonymity, every four weeks any decision can be reversed through some large commission. You rarely find a clear sense of direction any more.

Those who would have partly welcomed more democracy in organizations wished to limit the issues on which subordinates should have a say. For example, decisions on hiring and firing, promotion, and the intraorganizational reward structure should, according to these respondents, be excluded from participatory decision-making. As expected, the more successful women were likely to disagree with the necessity for more democracy (Table 10.9).

Table 10.9 *Success and attitude about participation in organizations.*

Success	No participation		More participation		Total	
	(%)	(N)	(%)	(N)	(%)	(N)
Less successful	37	(7)	63	(12)	100	(19)
Very successful	62	(16)	38	(10)	100	(26)

$\gamma = -0.47$

The less successful women – those who were more likely to feel disadvantaged through structural inequalities – were also more likely to agree to more participation. In contrast, the very successful professional women seemed to behave like any elite and resist more participation (Table 10.10). Less successful women are the ones who might benefit through changes in this direction. Very successful women, however, may fear the loss of some of the influence and power that they have had the opportunity to acquire. Obviously, this holds primarily for the employed and less so for the self-employed, because the latter do not work in large organizations and therefore would not have to bear the consequences of increased participation.

Table 10.10 *Advocates of more participation.*

Employment	Less successful		Very successful	
	(%)	(N)	(%)	(N)
Self-employed	40	(5)	56	(9)
Employed	71	(14)	29	(17)

$\gamma = -0.47$

Employed women confronted with the consequences of hierarchical and often authoritarian organizational structures in their daily work most clearly have an individual and material interest in introducing mechanisms for participation. The less successful, however, see better chances for themselves if participation is widened. On the other hand, the very successful are more resistant to sharing their privileges and powers.

The same contrast was obtained when the age of the respondents was considered. Older women (48–72 years of age) agreed less often with

Table 10.11 *Age and advocates of more participation.*

Age	No participation		More participation		Total	
	(%)	*(N)*	*(%)*	*(N)*	*(%)*	*(N)*
Younger	32	(8)	68	(17)	100	(25)
Older	70	(16)	30	(7)	100	(23)

γ = −0·66

participation than younger (31−47 years) (Table 10.11). One reason may be that older women either have already reached powerful and influential positions or have no further chance of reaching them. Thus, more of the younger women may have an interest in structural change in the direction of less hierarchical and more co-operative organization processes.

CONCLUSION

Among professional women as among men, conservatism correlates with success. Whether or not women in top jobs are inclined to support demands for social change seems to depend on their own possibilities for further attainment. Those who are relatively young and appear to feel that they can profit from liberal reforms (e.g. from less hierarchical and more participatory decision-making) support liberal parties and come out on the 'left' side of issues. However, those who have successfully worked their way into high status positions usually express the view that society is basically in order.

Status inconsistency does not seem to be a relevant factor, at least not with regard to political orientation. Once a woman has reached a high occupational status, the experience of being a woman does not seem to be important to her political interests. That successful women hold the dominant values of the male elite also indicates that, if there are different cultural orientations of men and women, they are completely submerged, at least as far as politics is concerned, by structural factors. Whether the tendency to accept 'male' values of success and competition is a consequence or a precondition of occupational success of women is, in the present context, of only secondary importance; the point is that successful women tend to defend these values in much the same way as successful men.

In conclusion, the majority of women who rise in the occupational structure seem relatively unlikely to cause changes in the outlook and ideological orientations of societal elites. To the extent that women in 'typically male' positions are successful, their attitudes toward the dominant values and institutions of contemporary society seem to be more often than not uncritical and affirmative. This may change to a certain degree if a new reference group other than their male colleagues comes into existence. In the long run the women's movement could produce a social climate that might allow for a somewhat different value orientation. Up to now, considering their strongly individualistic conception of achievement and success, women in top jobs seem to be adaptive to the value structure of the social class that they have joined by their occupational success.

NOTES

(1) The CDU (Christian Democratic Union) and CSU (Christian Social Union) are the two major conservative parties in West Germany. The SPD (Social Democratic Party of Germany) is a moderate left-of-the-centre party pursuing a policy of 'realistic reforms.' The FDP (Free Democratic Party) presents itself as a 'liberal' party in the tradition of European (not American) 'liberalism.'

(2) Difference between female and male preference of the CDU/CSU in percentage points: 1953 8·3 per cent; 1957, 8·9 per cent; 1961, 9·3 per cent; 1965, 9·7 per cent; 1969, 8·2 per cent; and 1972, 3·5 per cent.

(3) Computations were conducted at the Computer Center of the University of Münster, using SPSS H, version 6.

(4) Class was determined through intensive qualitative analysis. Major indicators were the education and occupation of father and mother as well as the living style of the family (e.g. servants).

(5) The final index correlated neither with occupational status nor with occupation.

(6) Those in the third and fourth categories voted for either of the named parties. How often they voted for the one or the other was not discovered.

REFERENCES

Berger, Joseph, Cohen, Bernard P. and Zelditch Jr, Morris (1972) 'Status characteristics and social interaction,' *American Sociological Review*, vol. 37, no. 3, pp. 241–55.

Bericht der Bundesregierung über die Massnahmen zur Verbesserung der Situation der Frau, BT Drucks. VI/4689. 1970.

Blalock Jr, H. M. (1967) 'Status inconsistency, social mobility, status interpretation and structural effects,' *American Sociological Review*, vol. 32, no. 5, pp. 790–801.

Chabaud, Jacqueline (1970) *The Education and Advancement of Women* (Paris: UNESCO).

Cornish, Mary Jean (1972) 'Die Entwicklung eines professionellen Selbstbildes,' in Th. Luckmann and W. Sprondel (eds), *Berufssoziologie* (Cologne: Kieperheuer & Witsch).

Epstein, Cynthia Fuchs (1971a) 'Encountering the male establishment: sex status limits on women's careers in the professions,' in Athena Theodore (ed.), *The Professional Woman* (Cambridge, Mass.: Schenkmann), pp. 52–74.

Epstein, Cynthia Fuchs (1971b) 'Women lawyers and their profession: inconsistency of social controls and their consequences for professional performance,' in Athena Theodore (ed.), *The Professional Woman* (Cambridge, Mass.: Schenkmann), pp. 669–85.

Epstein, Cynthia Fuchs (1973) *Woman's Place: Options and Limits in Professional Careers* (Berkeley and Los Angeles: University of California Press).

Ferber, Marianne A. and Loeb, Jane W. (1973) 'Performance, rewards, and perceptions of sex discrimination among male and female faculty,' *American Journal of Sociology*, vol. 78, no. 4, pp. 995–100s.

Fogarty, Michael, Rapoport, Rhona and Rapoport, Robert (1971) *Sex, Career and Family* (London: Allen & Unwin, in co-operation with Political and Economic Planning).

Fogarty, Michael, Rapoport, Rhona and Rapoport, Robert (1972) *Women and Top Jobs: The Next Move* (London: Political and Economic Planning).

Fogarty, Michael, Allen, M., Allen, A. and Walters, P. (1971) *Women in Top Jobs: Four Studies in Achievement* (London: Allen & Unwin, in co-operation with Political and Economic Planning).

Fuelles, Mechtile (1969) *Frauen in Partei und Parlament* (Cologne: Verlag fur Wissenschaft und Politik).

Goffman, Irwin W. (1957) 'Status consistency and preference for change in power distribution,' *American Sociological Review*, vol. 22, no. 3, pp. 275–81.

Hauschildt-Arndt, Sigrid (1965) *Berufsprobleme von Volks- und Betriebswirtinnen: Eine empirische Untersuchung in Hamburger Raum* (Tubingen).

Heinz, Margarete (1971) *Über das politische Bewusstsein von Frauen in der BRD* (Munich: Goldman).

Hochschild, Arlie Russell (1973) 'A review of sex role research,' *American Journal of Sociology*, vol. 78, no. 4, pp. 1011–29.

Hughes, E. S. (1976) 'Dilemmas and contradictions of status,' in L. Coser and B. Rosenberg (eds), *Sociological Theory: A Book of Readings*, 4th edn (New York: Macmillan), pp. 355–65.

Jackson, E. (1962) 'Status consistency and symptoms of stress,' *American Sociological Review*, vol. 27, no. 4, pp. 469–80.

Jackson, E. and Burke, P. (1965) 'Status and symptoms of stress; additive and interaction effects,' *American Sociological Review*, vol. 30, no. 4, pp. 556–64.

Kelly, K. Dennis and Chambliss, William J. (1966) 'Status consistency and political attitudes', *American Sociological Review*, vol. 31, no. 3, pp. 375–82.

Kemper, Th. D. (1968) 'Reference groups, socialization and achievement,' *American Sociological Review*, vol. 33, no. 1, pp. 31–45.

Komarovsky, M. (1950) 'Functional analysis of sex roles,' *American Sociological Review*, vol. 15, no. 4, pp. 508–16.

Lehr, Ursula (1964) *Die Frau im Beruf* (Frankfurt: Athenaum).

Lenski, Gerhard E. (1954) 'Status crystallization: a non-vertical dimension of social status,' *American Sociological Review*, vol. 19, no. 4, pp. 405–13.

Lenski, Gerhard E. (1956) 'Social participation and status crystallization,' *American Sociological Review*, vol. 21, no. 4, pp. 458–64.

Maccoby, Eleanore E. (ed) (1966) *The Development of Sex Differences* (Stanford: Tavistock Publications).

Meyer, John W. and Hammond, Phillip E. (1971) 'Forms of status inconsistency,' *Social Forces*, vol. 50, no. 1, pp. 91–101.

Riegel, M., Werle, Raymond and Wildermann, R. (1974) *Selbstverständnis und politisches Bewusstsein der Juristen, insbesondere der Richterschaft in der Bundesrepublik Deutschland* (Mannheim: Institut fur Sozialwissenschaften der Universität Mannheim).

Rossi, A. (1965) 'Barriers to the career choice of engineering, medicine or science among American women,' in J. A. Mattfeld and C. G. Van Aken (eds), *Women and the Scientific Professions* (Cambridge, Mass.: MIT Press), pp. 51–127.

Rossi, A. (1971) 'Women in science: why so few?,' in Athena Theodore (ed.), *The Professional Woman* (Cambridge, Mass.: Schenkmann), pp. 612–29.

Rossi, A. and Calderwood, A. (eds), (1973) *Academic Women on the Move* (New York: Russel Sage Foundation).

Suter, Larry E. and Miller, Herman P. (1973) 'Income differences between men and career women,' *American Sociological Review*, vol. 78, no. 4, pp. 962–74.

Theodore, Athena (ed.) (1971) *The Professional Woman* (Cambridge, Mass.: Schenkmann).

Treiman, Donald J. and Terrell, Kermit (1975) 'Sex and the process of status attainment: a comparison of working men and women,' *American Sociological Review*, vol. 40, no. 2, pp. 174–200.

Zapf, Wolfgang (ed.) (1965) *Beiträge zur Analyse der deutschen Oberschicht* (Munich).

11

Women in International Organizations: Room at the Top:

The Situation in Some United Nations Organizations

BETSY THOM

The position of women in international organizations is related to the situations that exist in various nations and to the link between international organizations and their member countries. As meeting places of different nations, international organizations must accommodate a range of cultures and, despite stated policies and ideologies, must often compromise and take a middle-of-the-road stance in regard to internal practice as well as external relationships with other bodies.

The problems encountered by women nationally in the occupational sphere with respect to available employment, training, and their chances of reaching top positions are similar in their basic aspects and differ only in their details. These problems arise from the nature of the overall occupational structure and how it affects the opportunities afforded to women (e.g. the cultural definition of male and female roles and appropriate behavior both within and outside the work situation; interaction between family and work, as well as between employees in the occupational hierarchy).[1]

An analysis of the barriers facing women must take into account both structural factors and *locational factors*. By structural factors I mean the broad make-up of society or of an institution and the laws, rules, and mores, both formal and informal, that limit movement across the strata. By locational factors I mean a person's exact location within the broader social or organizational structure and the effect of that location on the individual's chances for success.

The limitations imposed by the broader structural factors are clearly visible in European countries, where for both men and women the class barrier limits access to decision-making posts. *Social capital*[2] is acquired not only by meritocratic attainment; it is determined at least in part by one's location in the hierarchy and one's command over the relevant resources. In most western European countries the members of decision-making groups are drawn from the same social background, attend top schools and universities, and are linked not only through the 'old boy' network but often also through family and marriage ties (Ardagh, 1975; Wakeford, Wakeford, and Benson, 1974).[3] Thus, although the majority of men have access to *economic capital*, only those from a certain sector of society are able to convert it into sufficient social capital to become a member of a decision-making elite. It seems likely that the recruitment of women to elites will follow a similar pattern – that women in the elite sector of a society will find access easier and be more readily accepted by existing elites. This appears to be borne out by studies of women in some top jobs. In journalism, as Roger Smith points out in Chapter 16 below, and in politics, for example, top women have often come from families with a history of involvement in the field (Currell, 1974). However, what clues we have to the availability for recruitment of women in the elite sectors of society indicate that they are still less likely than men in the same situation to achieve elite status. There is usually no financial necessity to seek employment. They may find themselves involved in 'two-person' careers, in which they play the vicarious achievement role, or they may be subject to pressure toward the adoption of more traditional roles, as in France, where the tradition of the cultured intellectual woman of leisure appears to linger on and may even be considered more progressive and liberating than restricting (Hughes, 1973; Silver, 1973; Papanek, 1973).

In looking at locational factors, the case has been advanced that there are in fact no sex differences in work behavior that cannot be traced to the effects of one's precise location in the organizational structure. It is the already existing restrictions within the opportunity structure of an organization that result in behavior considered typically female. If women have lower aspirations and co-operative rather than competitive attitudes, it is because they are disadvantageously placed within the organizational structure. They're likely to limit their aspirations and to value solidarity with co – workers, making it more difficult to seek promotion out of the group and to be perceived by others as suitable for promotion. It has been shown that this is true of men similarly located (Kanter, 1976); and where women achieve top positions, because of their isolation within both the formal and the informal power networks they may feel less secure and less sure of continued upward mobility. This may lead them to adopt leadership styles that are considered peculiarly 'female' but that can once more be attributed to the effect of structural location and are common to both men and women. To apply such a structural analysis carries important implications for change strategies. The elimination of sex discrimination within an organization requires more than a simple revision of rules and policies granting official equality; it requires a radical revision of the opportunity structure (Kanter, 1976).

Women in international organizations are affected both by structural factors at the national level and by their locational position with the organization itself. Since many professional positions are filled by appointment from member countries, it is unlikely that women outside national elite sectors will ever reach positions where they become candidates for posts in an international organization. Internally, the location of the majority of women already working in these organizations and the nature of their opportunity and power structures bring the locational limiting factors into operation.

There are many international organizations, and they vary in size, function, structure, and relationship to member countries.[4] In size they range from the large United Nations 'family', consisting of a considerable number of sections, some of which are substantial bodies in their own right, to very small organizations with no permanent staff or secretariat. Taken as a whole, the function of these organizations is to promote peace, co-operation, and development in political, economic, social, and cultural spheres. Although some bodies (e.g. the Bank for International Settlements (BIS) and the North Atlantic Treaty Organization (NATO)) have narrowly defined aims in a very specific field, others (e.g. the United Nations Organization for Economic Co-operation and Development (OECD)) range over a number of areas – a situation that often leads to considerable overlap. A second functional distinction arises with respect to a body's capacity to pass binding decisions on its member countries. Many bodies function in a purely advisory capacity (e.g. the United Nations, the Council of Europe, and the Nordic Council). Others are advisory but have some powers of coercion and enforcement (e.g. NATO). Still others are decision-making bodies that are able to influence internal policies in member countries (e.g. the European Economic Community (EEC) and the Council for Mutual Economic Assistance (COMECON)).

The social fields covered by such international bodies follow the same patterns as in the national setting, forming an interlinking network along a center-to-periphery continuum, with the political and economic fields in the center. In addition, there is here a corresponding parallel continuum, running from policy decision-making to advisory functions only. As in the case of participation in national elites, women in higher positions are usually found on the periphery, in cultural and 'women's affairs' rather than in the center, and in the advisory rather than the decision-making spheres. This is the case in the United Nations, where 'women accounted for only 4·3 to 7·5 per cent of the total membership in six of the seven main committees, but 23 per cent in the third, the Social Humanitarian and Cultural Committee, which is the dumping ground for so-called "women's problems"' ('Women and the UN,' 1975).

Internal structures vary, but most international organizations consist of a ruling assembly or committee composed of representatives of member countries, delegations and permanent missions from member countries, and a secretariat. Internal policy and organization are strongly affected by member countries, including recruitment to professional positions. Candidates may be assigned by member countries, and sometimes recruitment is subject to a geographical quota system that ensures equality of representation. In the case of the United Nations it has been suggested that the subordination of equitable sex distribution to geographical representation is the major obstacle to increasing the number of professional women.

The composition of elite decision-making groups in international bodies therefore appears to be largely conditioned by the member states to reflect their attitudes and prejudices, as well as their opinions about the importance of the particular post. Thus, where assignment to an international post is regarded as important, it seems likely that a man who is already within or moving into the national elite will obtain the assignment. On the other hand, one suspects that in some cases the international organizations, particularly advisory ones, may be used as convenient 'dumping grounds' for members of national elite groups who become *persona non grata* but cannot easily be dismissed. These are also more likely to be men, since women, filling 'kitchen quarters' rather than 'engine room' elite posts,[5] are less likely to be regarded as a threat or nuisance if they become unwanted or ineffective at the national level.

Where a woman does obtain a post in an international organization, there may be additional difficulties to overcome. Top positions in such organizations may require frequent travel or movement of job location for promotion. It is still unusual for husband to follow wife; and although a top man is often supported by a wife's involvement in his career – entertaining, releasing him from home responsibilities, etc. – women are seldom free from their dual role of worker and wife–mother. Married women suffer a competitive disadvantage in a sphere that for some may prove incompatible with their own and others' expectations of the family role. Moreover, a top position in an international organization is in many ways similar to a diplomatic post, demanding contact with countries whose cultures still relegate women to comparatively low positions. Representatives from these countries may be unwilling or embarrassed to negotiate with a woman. Traditional diplomatic protocol may clash with traditional sexual courtesies. This raises the question of the saliency of sex over rank: Who stands up for whom? Within the organization the mixture of nationalities may cause women difficulties in dealing with colleagues at all levels. Where a man's own cultural heritage regards women as unequal, he may have problems in adjusting to a situation where he must work under, or on equal terms with, a woman and may be less ready to promote able women. Thus, in the international sphere women are likely to face a greater degree of inconsistency in male attitudes than is found within national organizations.

Yet, the fact that member countries affect the composition of elite decision-making bodies does not exonerate the international organizations from all responsibility for the lack of women in top positions. Until recently the international organizations have done little to review their internal policies toward women employees (Szalai, 1973; 'Women and the UN,' 1975; *Commission of the European Communities Staff Courier*, 1975), and this is not surprising while control rests in male hands both internally and externally.

The position of women in one particular organization and the attempts made to achieve greater equality provide a convenient illustration.

WOMEN IN THE UNITED NATIONS

In 1967 the United Nations finally became aware that, although equality regardless of sex was called for in the United Nations Charter of 1948, women in member countries were still discriminated against in terms of political and civil rights. A *Declaration on the Elimination of Discrimination against Women* (United Nations, 1973) was passed in November 1978, but it was not until several years later that any serious attempt was made to look at discrimination in staff rules and regulations inside the United Nations (Szalai, 1973). Attention was drawn to inequalities in such areas as appointments, assignments, promotions, and pension rights. A UNITAR

Colloquium of Senior United Nations Officials on the Situation of Women in the United Nations and the report that followed ('Women and the UN,' 1975) highlighted the extent of the discrimination. The appointment of the first woman assistant secretary general (for Social Development and Humanitarian Affairs) gained women a voice in the decision-making elite, and the designation of 1975 as International Women's Year led to active attempts on the part of United Nations women to end discrimination.

Table 11.1 *Attempts by the United Nations to end discrimination, 1974.*

Area of discrimination	Measures taken	Results
Financial		
Grants (e.g. repatriation, compensation in event of death, home leave travel).	Concept of male as bread-winner attacked. In staff regulations the word 'wife' is replaced by 'spouse.'	Minor discriminations remain.
Pension inequalities: mainly with respect to widow/widower rights. In this case applies to married women only.	Under attack from UN women.	No results as yet.
Welfare		
Paternity rights: do not exist in UN.	Women's groups in UN considering legislation nationally and pressing for implementation of paternity rights.	No results as yet.
Apointments		
By member countries: very few women nominated	Member governments urged to select more women. Vacancy notices carry specific invitation to qualified women.	The attitudes of member countries toward nominating women to official posts may be judged from the proportion of women delegations to the General Assembly and on the staff of permanent missions (see Tables 11.2 and 11.3). No significant changes as yet.
Within the UN.	Women's groups pressing for positive discrimina-tion and a target number of women in recruitment.	Table 11.4 shows some increase in women's senior positions, but this is a mere 'trickle.'

Table 11.1   *Continued.*

Area of discrimination	Measures taken	Results
Promotion Quicker for men than women. Discrimination arising from attitudes rather than policy.	Pressing to obtain a minimum number of female promotions from general to professional category each year, for positive discrimination.	'Numerically and percentage-wise women gained most (1972–1974) at the P-2 level, i.e. at the lowest level at which, for various reasons, the majority of new appointees enter the professional service ... the P-2 level has more and more women, not because the number of women entering the professional service is increasing so rapidly, but because women who have entered the professional service by this door stay so long at such a low level. Men have a better chance of promotion' ('Women and the UN,' 1975).

Sources: See note 6.

Table 11.2   *The proportion of women on the staff of the permanent missions, 1972–4.*

	1972	1973	1974
Total no. of permanent missions[a]	130	133	133
No. of permanent missions listing no woman staff member	79	80	80
Percentage of permanent missions listing no woman staff member	61%	60%	60%
Total no. of staff members[b]	1,130	1,199	1,242
No. of women staff members[b]	118	115	128
Percentage of women staff members	10.4%	9.6%	10.3%

[a]   The number of permanent missions is always somewhat smaller than the number of the member states, because a few member states do not maintain permanent missions at United Nations headquarters or had not established their missions at the time when the official list for the respective year was published.

[b]   A very small fraction of registered staff members do not bear diplomatic (i.e. professional) titles but belong to secretarial and other categories.

Table 11.2 *Continued.*

Comment: Permanent missions and their foreign ministries play a major and direct role in shaping personnel policies that determine the composition of the Secretariat. A considerable part of the United Nations's professional staff is appointed on the basis of candidatures put forward by governments through their missions.

The attitude of governments, as indicated in this table, showed no significant change toward the appointment of women during 1972–4.

There was some growth in the number of women in higher policy-making posts in permanent missions. Despite the possibility of tokenism and the small numbers involved, this may indicate some response to United Nations pressure.

Source of table and comment: 'Women and the UN' (1975).

Table 11.3 *The proportion of women in the delegations to the twenty-seventh and twenty-ninth sessions of the General Assembly, 1972 and 1974.*

	1972	1974
Total no. of delegations	132	138
No. of delegations listing no woman member	59	52
Percentage of delegations listing no woman member	45%	38%
Total no. of delegates	2,252	2,548
No. of women delegates	164	211
Percentage of women delegates	7·3%	8·3%

Source: 'Women and the UN' (1975).

Comment: The table shows that some progress was achieved between 1972 and 1974. It is, however, disappointing to observe that more than one third of the member states (38 per cent) did not see fit to include even one woman in their delegations to the twenty-ninth regular session of the General Assembly, although this was down from 45 per cent two years earlier. The percentage of women delegates rose from 7·3 to 8·3 per cent, but even the latter figure was very low.

Table 11.1 indicates areas of discrimination, measures taken for their relief, and the outcome of these measures.[6] So far, it seems, the measures taken have had little impact, although it is too soon to judge their real effect. But more active recruitment of women, a more equitable promotion policy, and revised staff regulations are a start in the structural barriers facing women.

Structural limitations are, however, only one of the barriers to be dealt with. In the United Nations, as elsewhere, the ideological factors form a major stumbling block; and although the replacement of 'wife' with 'spouse' in staff regulations may symbolize official recognition of this, it is not enough to overcome deep-seated traditional attitudes and beliefs. These take effect in two ways. First, since they are prevalent in society, or the organization in general, they color the expectations of others toward women at work and in positions of authority. Second, women have to some extent themselves internalized these ideologies and may have to overcome their tendency to confine themselves to non-leadership and complementary roles, which often makes them reluctant to aspire to policy-making

Table 11.4 The proportion of women on the professional staff of organizations in the United Nations system, 1971 and 1974.

Organization[a]	Year	No. of women at each professional level[b]								Total of women on professional staff	Total professional staff (both sexes)	% of women on total professional staff
		USG ASG DDG ADG	D-2	D-1	P-5	P-4	P-3	P-2	P-1			
United Nations	1971	—	3	5	28	105	189	144	43	517	2,374	21·7
	1974	1	2	7	41	103	216	200	35	605	3,093	19·6
UNDP	1971	—	—	2	3	4	13	17	8	47	493	9·5
	1974	—	2	1	6	15	18	27	7	76	623	12·2
UNICEF	1971	—	—	—	2	2	10	10	1	25	209	12·0
	1974	—	—	—	2	7	9	11	1	30	249	12·1
ILO	1971	—	—	2	2	10	63	4	40	121	640	18·9
	1974	—	—	2	3	19	49	25	17	115	776	14·8
FAO[c]	1971	—	—	—	3	41	48	60	35	189	4,073	4·6
	1974	—	—	—	6	24	40	64	33	167	1,278	13·1
UNESCO[c]	1971	—	—	1	20	99	50	66	23	267	1,795	14·8
	1974	—	—	3	17	48	48	62	7	185	851	21·7
WHO[c]	1971	—	—	2	9	64	189	90	33	387	1,794	21·5
	1974	—	—	4	11	25	45	62	12	159	845	18·8
IBRD	1971	No comparable professional levels[d]								103	1,483	6·9
	1974									172	1,652	10·4
IMF	1971	No comparable professional levels[d]								103	617	16·6

	1974	—	—	—	—	—	2	10	8	1	21	240	8·8
IUPU	1971	—	—	—	—	—	—	1	—	1	2	68	2·9
	1974	—	—	—	—	—	1	—	2	1	3	53	5·7
ITU	1971	—	—	—	—	—	1	8	5	3	17	143	11·8
	1974	—	—	—	—	—	1	6	9	3	19	187	10·2
WMO	1971	—	—	—	—	—	1	3	2	3	9	114	7·8
	1974	—	—	—	—	—	1	5	4	1	11	100	11·0
IMCO	1971	—	—	—	—	—	—	1	2	3	6	42	14·2
	1974	—	—	—	—	—	—	3	5	3	11	51	21·6
GATT	1971	—	—	—	—	2	1	7	9	5	24	88	27·2
	1974	—	—	—	—	—	4	6	12	2	24	103	23·3
IAEA	1971	—	—	—	—	1	3	12	12	12	40	344	11·6
	1974	—	—	—	—	1	8	11	16	11	47	350	13·4
Total[e, f]	1974	—	1	4	17	87	258	466	507	133	1,787	11,178	16·0

[a] For abbreviations, see note 7.
[b] The criteria for appointment to a given level differ somewhat from agency to agency.
[c] The basic populations used by the FAO, UNESCO, and WHO in 1971 were entirely different from the populations used in 1974.
[d] As the professional grades of IBRD and the IMF are different from those used in the rest of the United Nations system, only the total figures are given.
[e] IBRD and IMF are included only in the three final columns, not in the level-by-level totals for 1974.
[f] Totals for 1971 have been omitted from this table because the basic populations used in 1971 by three major agencies (FAO, UNESCO, and WHO) were entirely different from the populations used in 1974. Since such large groups are involved, no comparison of totals and percentages for 1971 and 1974 is therefore possible. There were no agreed system-wide definitions in the compilation of these figures and no agreed methods of data compilation prior to 1974.

Source: 'Women and the UN' (1975).

Table 11.4 *Continued*

Comment: It will be seen from the table that there were uneven trends with regard to the change in the proportion of women in various organizations; in some places there was a reduction and in some of the major agencies an apparent increase. However, it is necessary to warn against the overestimation of some of the 'jumps' in the percentage of women, since it can be observed for some agencies (e.g. the FAO) that they have made a radical difference in the basis of the calculation. Consequently, it cannot be concluded that there actually was any improvement in the position of women for these agencies or on an overall basis.

However, apart from this the table shows that women were beginning to infiltrate into highly senior and even policy-making levels in 1974. No real break-through had occurred. What we see was merely a trickle, but already a puddle had formed, which seemed to be spreading. From P-5 up to ASG-DDG the number of women officers had increased on each and every level:

(1) in 1971 there were 70 female P-5s, but in 1974 there were 87;
(2) in 1971 there were 12 female D-1s, in 1974 there were 17;
(3) in 1971 there were 3 female D-2s, but in 1974 there were 4; and
(4) in 1971 or before there never was a female assistant secretary general, but in 1974 there was one.

Admittedly, these were still very small numbers, but it should be remembered that this increase at the upper professional levels occurred during a period in which the absolute number of women in all the lower professional levels of the United Nations system, with the sole exception of the P-2 level, *decreased.* One should not, however, cherish any illusions. The table also bears witness to a number of unpleasant facts:

(1) Not a single woman headed an agency or was a deputy to the head of an agency (i.e. a USG or DDG) in the United Nations system. The first column of the table is *empty.*
(2) Of the sixteen agencies registered in the table, only *one* had a woman at the ASG–ADG level and only *two* had a couple of women at the D-2 level. The second and third columns of the table are *nearly empty.*
(3) The majority of the sixteen agencies were unable to find any woman professional who was worthy of the D-1 level. Astonishingly, UNICEF belonged to this category. It must be really hard to find a woman who has some expertise in matters of child care, health, education, and nutrition.

positions. Even then, especially in the international sphere, there may be direct conflict between family and career roles; in the United Nations Secretariat '86% of all male professionals but only 35% of all female professionals... are married' ('Women and the UN,' 1975).

Central to the problem of overcoming psychological and ideological barriers is an identity crisis facing women who are offered and who accept authority roles. Taking an authoritative decision-making role is not part of the traditional female identity. Women entering top echelons may first have the problem of establishing their identity and their right to authority. As one woman minister found, it may be necessary for a woman to point out that she is not a secretary, adviser, or somebody's wife ('Women and the UN,' 1975). Although adaptation to an authority role is generally made possible by others' recognition of that role and of the rights of the person occupying it (Berger, 1963), a woman may first have to establish the compatibility between female identity and her authority role in the eyes of others before she can begin the process of personal adjustment that lets her wear the decisionmaker's hat unselfconsciously.

In relationships with male colleagues a woman may have to overcome traditional 'gallantry,' a reluctance to discuss serious matters, or being considered window dressing at meetings – all of which reinforce her 'feminine' identity at the expense of her professional identity. Internal promotion may be hindered because of the clinging belief that men dislike working under a woman, and this may also diminish her chances of obtaining a post that demands contact with officials outside the United Nations (L'Emploi des femmes à l'office des Nations Unies à Genève,' 1975).

The belief has been found, not only that men dislike a woman boss, but also that women dislike other women in authority and find them less congenial to work for. It may be that, whereas a male boss obtains instant recognition of his authority, a woman in the process of distinguishing herself from her female staff may have to establish more social distance and adopt a firmer authoritative stance. In other words, a woman manager may be forced to adopt, more extremely than a man may, what are considered male attitudes, values, and methods. Those who argue that it should not be necessary for successful women to adopt so-called masculine attributes ignore the fact that, given social definitions of 'male' and 'female' identity traits, this may be the only possible strategy to gain acceptance as a woman in an authority role. There is some evidence that women in top positions are believed to identify themselves with male ideology.[8] If our role theory is correct, this can easily be accounted for by the fact that, in the process of adapting to the role, women internalize the values and attitudes that they have tactically employed in interaction with others.

In the United Nations, as elsewhere, until women in decision-making elites become less of a curiosity, until there is a wider recognition of 'parental' rather than 'maternal' rights and obligations, and until there is a less rigid distinction between 'male' and 'female' identity traits, absorption into the male *status quo* is perhaps the best for which women can hope. Whether this will prevent them from paving the way for further female entry and opening the door to change remains to be seen.

NOTES

(1) Some examples from different countries, all of which make reference to such factors as the compartmentalization of the labor force, the strength of the family role of women, the acceptance of traditional ideas on 'male' and 'female' traits, and the lack of women in decision-making positions, can be found in Bundeskanzleramt (1975), French Ministry of Labor (1974), Gaudart (1975), Gould and Kim (1976), Hebron (1974), Hunt (1975), and Pross (1975).

(2) Defined by Helga Nowotny in Chapter 9 above.

(3) Boyd (1974, p. 305). D. P. Boyd found an increase in the number of top people who had attended public schools and Oxbridge–judiciary, ambassadors, bankers, army and naval officers. There was a decrease for top civil servants, but the figure was still 68 per cent.

(4) *The Europa Yearbook, 1975* lists seventy-four 'major' international organizations as well as a large number of 'other international bodies.'

(5) The terminology is taken from Beckerus and Kälvemark (1975), where reference is made to the 'kitchen quarters' and the 'engine room' of the Swedish university system.

(6) Apart from the above-mentioned UNITAR publications, the following documents were useful in specifying the nature of discrimination and in compiling the table:

'Towards the elimination of discrimination based on sex: a big step forward,' *ILO Staff Union Bulletin*, no. 421 (June 14, 1974).

'Differential treatment based upon sex under the staff regulations and staff rules,' report to the Secretary General, UN General Assembly, A/C.5/1603 (September 12, 1974).

Draft resolution on International Women's Year by IAEA Staff Association (April 1975).

'Career development in the context of International Women's Year,' resolution by UNIDO staff (April 17, 1975).

'Integration of Women in Development,' resolution adopted by the Industrial Development Board, 9th session ID/B/RES.44(IX) (May 1975).

Report of the 28th session of the Council of FICSA (Geneva, May 1975).

'Composition of the Office of Personnel Services: UN headquarters, 1970–1974,' *Secretariat News* (New York, October 31, 1975).

Femmes fonctionnaires unissez-vous!, UN Special, no. 310 (Geneva: Revue mensuelle des fonctionnaires internationaux, 1975).

67th session report to the Administrative Committee on Co-ordination on the status of women (March 12, 1976).

(7) Abbreviations used in Table 11.4, Notes, and References:

UNDP	United Nations Development Program
UNICEF	United Nations Children's Fund
ILO	International Labour Organization
FAO	Food and Agricultural Organization
UNESCO	United Nations Educational, Scientific, and Cultural Organization
WHO	World Health Organization
IBRD	International Bank for Reconstruction and Development (World Bank)
IMF	International Monetary Fund
ICAO	International Civil Aviation Organization
UPU	Universal Postal Union
ITU	International Telecommunications Union
WMO	World Meteorological Organization
IMCO	Intergovernmental Maritime Consultative Organization
GATT	General Agreement on Tariffs and Trade
IAEA	International Atomic Energy Agency
UNITAR	United Nations Institute for Training and Research
UNIDO	United Nations Industrial Development Organization
FICSA	Federation of International Civil Servants' Associations

(8) 'Most of the delegates to the Mexico Conference – 891 women from 131 governments –

had already identified themselves with male ideology and had tacitly adopted the domi-nant socio-political structures and the "thinking" behind them' (UNITAR, 1975b).

REFERENCES

Ardagh, John (1975) 'The French corps d'elite,' *New Society*, vol. 31, no. 650 (March 20), pp. 711–14.

Beckerus, Göran and Kälvemark, Torsten (1975) 'Two Swedish men on the situation of women university graduates in Sweden,' *Current Sweden*, no. 67.

Berger, Peter (1963) *Invitation to Sociology* (Harmondsworth: Penguin Books).

Boyd, D. P. (1974) 'The educational background of a selected group of England's leaders,' *Sociology*, vol. 8, no. 2.

Bundeskanzleramt (1975) *Bericht über die Situation der Frau in Österreich: Frauenbericht, 1975* (Vienna).

Commission of European Communities Staff Courier, no. 365 (1975).

Currell, Melville (1974) *Political Woman* (London: Croom Helm).

French Ministry of Labor (1974) *L'Evolution de la situation des femmes dans la société française* (Paris, December).

Gaudart, Dorothea J. (1975) 'Women and social policy decision-making: the case of Austria,' unpublished paper for a research symposium on the occasion of the International Women's Year, Geneva.

Gould, Ketayun H. and Kim, Bok-Lim C. (1976) 'Salary inequities between men and women in schools of social work: myth or reality?,' *Journal of Education for Social Work*, vol. 12, no. 1 (Winter), pp. 50–5.

Hebron, C. C. de Winter (1974) 'Jobs for the girls?,' *New Society*, vol. 29, no. 617 (August 1), pp. 290–1.

Hughes, Helen Macgill (1973) 'Maid of all work or departmental sister-in-law? The faculty wife employed on campus,' *American Journal of Sociology*, vol. 78, no. 4, pp. 767–73.

Hunt, Audrey (1975) *Management Attitudes and Practices towards Women at Work* (London: Office of Population Censuses and Surveys, Social Survey Division, HMSO).

Kanter, Rosabeth Moss (1976) 'The impact of hierarchical structures on the work behavior of women and men,' *Social Problems*, vol. 23, no. 4 (April), pp. 415–30.

'L'Emploi des femmes à l'office des Nations Uniés à Génève,' *Action Geneva*, no. 22 (June 1975).

Papanek, Hanna (1973) 'Men, women and work: reflections on the two-person career,' *American Journal of Sociology*, vol. 78, no. 4, pp. 852–73.

Pross, Helge (1975) 'Aktuelle Probleme der Berufstätigkeit von Frauen in der Bundes-republik Deutschland,' in *Die Stellung der Frau in Gesellschaft und Recht* (Vienna: Institut fur Gesellschaftspolitik in Wien).

Silver, Catherine Bodard (1973) 'Salon, foyer, bureau: women and the professions in France', *American Journal of Sociology*, vol. 78, no. 4, pp. 836–51.

Szalai, Alexander (1973) *The Situation of Women in the United Nations*, UNITAR Research Report, No. 18 (New York: UNITAR).

The Europa Yearbook, 1975, Vol. 1 (London: Europa Publicaitons, 1976).

UNITAR (1973) *Equal Rights for Women: A Call for Action: The United Nations Declaration on the Elimination of Discrimination against Women* (New York. *Solidarité au féminin*, UN Special, No. 307 (Geneva: Revue mensuelle des fonctionnaires internationaux). *The Inter-national Women's Year is Drawing to a Close*, UN Special, No. 311 (Geneva).

Wakeford, J., Wakeford, F., and Benson, D. (1974) 'Some social and educational character-istics of selected elite groups in contemporary Britain: a research note based on a "K means" cluster analysis,' in the British Political Sociology Yearbook, 1974, *Elites in Western Democracy*, ed. Ivor Crewe (London: Croom Helm), pp. 172–98.

'Women in the UN,' *UNITAR News*, vol. 7, no. 1 (1975).

Part Two

Women and Economic Elites: Business and the Professions

12

Women, Business Schools, and the Social Reproduction of Business Elites:

Britain and France

RICHARD WHITLEY

The study of women in elites should be more than the listing of proportions of women in top jobs in various countries and in various activity systems. Their participation in elites should be considered within the framework of general processes of elite reproduction. These processes have changed in recent years. Adopting the conceptualization of Bourdieu (Stanworth and Giddens, 1974), it can be said that business has shifted its exclusive focus on the need for economic capital to a focus on the need for social and cultural capital. To the extent that this is the case, women's chances for participation will increase at least to some extent in the near future.

In examining these processes the impact of major changes in social institutions and economic structures on positions of control must be considered. Increased size of large firms and their concomitant changes in managerial structure, for example, can affect the processes by which traditional elites appropriate positions of privilege and control and maintain them.[1]

Changes outside the managerial system can also affect recruitment. For example, Bourdieu and his colleagues have shown how the educational system in France, although normatively egalitarian, ensures continued unequal access to privileged positions and how major changes in industrial structure have resulted in, or been associated with, altered relations between the higher education system and the 'elite labor market,' so that continued reproduction of traditional elites is assured (Bourdieu, Boltanski, and de Saint-Martin, 1973). The increasing numbers of managerial cadres required to co-ordinate multinational firms with geographically dispersed plants and markets have resulted in problems of managing the managers as well as increased division of labor and specialization among managerial employees. New forms of control and more sophisticated technical skills have been developed to deal with the emergence of multidivisional leviathans that both increase the demand for qualified 'professional' managers and result in more effective central control over diversified and decentralized activities. Traditional processes of maintaining access to central positions of control in these firms are no longer adequate, and so alternative 'strategies of reconversion' (Bourdieu, Boltanski, and de Saint-Martin, 1973) are developed. These imply changes in the educational system, such as the establishment of business schools.

Whether these changes serve to modify existing close connections between elite educational institutions and control positions, as in France (Bourdieu, Boltanski, and de Saint-Martin, 1973; Bourdieu and Passeron, 1970; Marceau, 1975), or attempt to establish new forms of educational organizations to create such connections, as in Great Britain, the main consequence has been to formalize and institutionalize relations between a small number of higher education institutions and elite labor markets. Consequently, an examination of how these educational institutions function as processors of aspirants to elite positions, in terms both of their 'publics' and of their connections to managerial structures, is valuable in tracing the impact of macro socioeconomic changes on the social reproduction of elites.

The situation in Great Britain and France, and the relative opportunities that business schools create for women in these countries, are here selected for discussion.

THE ROLE OF BUSINESS SCHOOLS IN THE REPRODUCTION OF BUSINESS ELITES

Relations between institutions of higher education and occupational structures can be expected to vary among nations, but a general demand for technically qualified managers has grown all over the world, and this has brought about an increasingly close relation between business and the educational system.

In spite of their viewing themselves as an open society with universalistic and meritocratic criteria for mobility, the French have largely perpetuated unequal patterns of access to privileged positions in business. Their educational system has been highly differentiated into the elite and non-elite institutions of the *grandes écoles*, which have traditionally fed the managerial elite, and such other institutions as the new schools of business management, which have yet to establish reputations as producers of an acceptable pool of recruits. This is not so much a matter of training as one of initial selection. The *grandes écoles* have educated the sons of the rich and powerful, whereas the newer schools have drawn from lower social strata.

Yet, there are pressures to change the former pattern of tracking to the top. There has been a decline of family-owned and controlled businesses in France[2] and a rise in large national and multinational enterprises. (In addition to work by Bourdieu already cited, see: Bourdieu and Passeron, 1964; Bourdieu, 1966, 1971.) This means that the economic capital that an individual brings into a business career is less important than it once was and also that the social skills inculcated by schooling in the *grandes écoles* are less relevant to top management positions.

Instead, new kinds of educational criteria have become important, which stress technical competence and the building of a different kind of cultural capital from that provided in the traditional schools. Yet, there seems to be integration of traditional institutional means with the new to meet the needs of changing business systems. Also, old elites have managed to establish footholds in the newer institutions and to use them in maintaining their advantage.

For example, the founding in 1958 of the Institut Européen d'Administration des Affaires (INSEAD) by the Paris Chamber of Commerce, with help from the Harvard Business School, provided a means for traditional elites with economic capital to become enculturated in the new modes. Jane Marceau's (1975) study has shown they have increasingly taken advantage of this opportunity. INSEAD is expensive, and a high proportion of its students come from the *patronat*, especially families in the textile industry, and from the liberal professions. Upon graduation they obtain large salaries and have clear expectations of achieving leading positions in large firms at a relatively early age. Most students, it should be noted, have already attended one of the *grandes écoles*, although not usually one of the 'top' three – Ecole Normale, Ecole Polytechnique, and L'Ecole Nationale d'Administration – before going to INSEAD. Given their family and educational backgrounds, these students already have substantial economic, social and cultural capital before entering INSEAD. Thus, INSEAD functions as a super *grande école* for a highly selective group, which thus seems assured of highly privileged positions in business. The business school provides new forms of cultural capital and extends the range of its students' social networks. Basically, it reinforces and extends the current reproduction mechanisms of French business elites.

Britain differs from France. Its top management has the least education and vocational training in Europe (Hall and Amado-Fischgrund, 1969; Hall, de Bettignies, and Amado-Fischgrund, 1969). Higher educational qualifications are not regarded as an essential 'cultural capital' for top management. Unlike the top business elites in France, who have had elite schooling, attendance at elite Oxford and Cambridge colleges is not vital for aspirants to elite positions in business, and certainly not in industry (Whitley, 1973, 1974), although the proportion attending Oxford or Cambridge of those attending universities is about two-thirds. Students at Oxbridge traditionally study subjects without vocational connections. The only technical training that seems relevant to becoming a director of a top British firm is accountancy – a skill usually obtained outside the university system.

However, there do seem to be some changing trends in Britain. The very largest firms, particularly nationalized industries, have recruited university graduates into junior management on a relatively large scale since 1960. This recruitment has already begun to affect the upward mobility of technicians without degrees, and a definite 'graduate barrier' (Roberts, Loveridge, and Gennard, 1972) has been discerned that reflects the stratifying consequences of linking the educational system to managerial labor markets.

Until recently the new business schools in Britain were regarded with some suspicion by both universities and business elites. But since the demand for 'professional' managers has increased and managerial strata have become more differentiated and specialized, the two major business schools at London and Manchester may attract those who cannot expect to obtain quasi-elite and administrative positions without further cultural capital. These recruits are likely to come from two main sources. First, recruits may come from those families which formerly relied upon private education and family contacts to find suitable middle-class occupations, particularly the military and colonial services and small and medium-sized businesses, which have now declined. Second, students can be recruited from comparatively disadvantaged backgrounds. These may have acquired technical competence that they realize is inadequate for access to senior positions without a broader expertise and more prestigious qualifications.

WOMEN IN MANAGEMENT IN GREAT BRITAIN

Where do women fit in this state of tension between the hold of old elites on recruitment to their ranks and the changes brought by new institutions?

A 1965 national survey of women's employment in England showed that 'only about one woman in twenty was employed in a managerial capacity' and that over 80 per cent of these women worked in establishments employing fewer than twenty-five persons (Hung, 1968, Vol. 1, pp. 30–1; Vol. 2, table A12). Furthermore, 64 per cent of women whose education continued to the age of 19 or over were categorized as working at the intermediate non-manual level (Hunt, 1968, Vol. 2, table A12) and so could scarcely be termed 'managerial.'

A more detailed study carried out for Political and Economic Planning (PEP) in the late 1960s indicated that in two large British corporations the proportion of women managers was about 3 per cent and that this figure decreased as one went up the hierarchy (I. Allen, 1971). Most of these women were employed as specialists, particularly in market research, advertising, personnel, and scientific research. The few who rose to senior management had developed great specialist expertise, which was highly valued but did not qualify them for top general-management posts. The areas in which women are specialists almost form 'female ghettos' in some companies. It is noticeable that marketing and production departments, which are more in the mainstream, had very few women managers in the surveyed corporations (I. Allen, 1971).

A study of women directors found that they were concentrated in small firms, received lower incomes than male equivalents (unless in their own companies), and were mostly (69 per cent) daughters of businessmen or professionals (A. J. Allen, 1971). They had become directors through family connections or by working as personal assistants to male directors. Nearly a quarter had started their own firms. Many had begun their managerial careers during the Second World War, when there was a shortage of male managers. Generally, women have needed substantial social capital to become directors, even of small firms, or considerable entrepreneurial capability and access to economic capital.

Finally, *Women's Who's Who* for 1975–6 reveals that, of sixty-seven women in 'management' (very broadly defined here), twenty-one were 'in business' – ten with personnel training and eight with market research or advertising backgrounds.[3] Three of these twenty-one seemed to run their own firms, all of which were service organizations. Of the remaining forty-five women managers, fifteen were health service administrators and seventeen were in education, thus demonstrating the importance of the public service for professional women. Almost all the women sent on middle management courses at business schools in Britain are employed in this sector.

Women have been a major disadvantaged social category in British society and are generally unlikely to rise to senior managerial posts (A. J. Allen, 1971, p. 133). Even when they do obtain university degrees, their chances of professional success have been generally limited. According to a study by Kelsall *et al.* in the 1960s, a higher proportion of men from manual working-class backgrounds obtained jobs in the professional category than did women whose fathers were themselves professionals (Kelsall, Poole, and Kuhn, 1974, table 25). In other words, despite having what is regarded as social capital, women graduates were highly discriminated against compared to male graduates.

BUSINESS SCHOOLS AND WOMEN IN MANAGEMENT

What will be the effect of business schools on women's potential in management? This question has two aspects: first, the general consequences of institutionalizing elite vocational-training courses in management for women as a whole; and second, the kind of women who will be attracted to business schools and their subsequent careers.

If the increasing integration of the educational system and labor markets does make existing occupational strata more formal, opportunities to achieve middle and senior management posts through internal promotion are likely to decrease, and the role of chance and personal acquaintance in the upward mobility of disadvantaged groups will be reduced.

It could be argued that the establishment of 'universalistically' based institutions should enable women to obtain additional cultural capital to overcome discrimination and so achieve senior management posts. This leads to the second aspect of the problem: the recruitment of women to business schools and subsequent careers.

First of all, it must be pointed out that business schools have not in the past sought female students. Harvard did not admit any until 1963. INSEAD had its first French woman student in 1968; a glance at its alumni roster indicates a total since then of under fifteen. The London Business School had fourteen female graduates from 1968 to 1975. At Manchester only twenty of the 525 (i.e. well under 5 per cent) graduate enrollees during 1965–75 were women. Although this may partly have been the choice of most female graduates, who believed that business schools were not for them, the schools did not until recently show themselves particularly determined to correct this impression. Because the public service sector is perceived as fairer to women, the small number attending business schools may not increase substantially for some time. At present, however, it may be useful to look at the characteristics of the small group of women who do go to business schools.

At the moment data on the background characteristics of female students at INSEAD, the London Business School, and the Manchester Business School are still being collected and analyzed. However, some preliminary findings can be given.[4] The most noticeable aspect of the French women students is the extent to which they have family or educational links with the United States and a high socioeconomic background. At Manchester all six women entering in 1975 had fathers in senior management positions, whereas 25 per cent of the male entrants came from workers' families. At London five of the fourteen female students came from families in business (two of these were US citizens), another seven came from professional backgrounds, and the remainder came from lower status families. Eight of the nine women whose families were not in business often had quite extensive previous business experience, and two of the three British women with business backgrounds came directly from university. Obviously, this evidence is too sketchy for substantial inferences, but at least it does not indicate any important differences from earlier evidence.

Information on the careers of women with business degrees is also inconclusive. Women tend to join management consultant firms more than men do and seem to be attractive recruits to American banks operating in Britain. Yet, no overall pattern of differences from male graduates has yet emerged. If they follow previous patterns, we should expect women graduates to remain in specialist areas outside mainstream managerial jobs and not to advance to top management unless they bring considerable economic and social capital or have worked in businesses that provide 'feminine' products and services.

Although the greater number of specialized management jobs that require technical knowledge may result in more women going to business school and then into management, this does not necessarily mean that they will obtain controlling positions. They are rather likely to remain in technical posts. In this they probably share the fate of many male business-school graduates from working class backgrounds. However, women may have an advantage in obtaining managerial jobs, because they have the advantage of the social capital arising from their tending to emerge from already professional families.

A further point here is that, as social skills become more important in managerial jobs, having the 'right background' to deal with other managers, clients, and other appropriate contacts will increase as relevant criteria for senior appointments. Although business schools may increasingly focus on providing social skills, a 'good' family and educational background will probably remain more influential than the acquisition of a Master of Business Administration degree. Thus, if women use the business schools as a credential-forming base, they will probably stand a better chance than they did before to gain a toehold in management. Because they seem to come from high socioeconomic backgrounds and can obtain technical training, and because there are increasing opportunities for them in multinational corporations, they may increase their proportion in managerial elites. Yet, it will probably be in the lower echelons of those elites, since at least up to now technical expertise alone has not seemed sufficient to provide entrance into top management, where a more generalized knowledge and set of attributes seem to be the criteria for success.

There have been other changes, including pressures on the business schools to increase their proportion of women students and the changes in women's own aspirations to rise through the managerial hierarchy. There also seems to be more general public awareness of women's problems and an attempt to redress them. In May 1977, for example, INSEAD sponsored a conference on 'Women in Management,' where strategies for moving women into managerial positions were discussed by representatives of major European corporations and industries.

CONCLUSIONS

In this short discussion I have tried to analyze the present situation and possibility for change of women in business elites within a broader framework that takes into account the processes of reproduction of elites in a changing industrial and economic structure. The framework has been presented in schematic fashion, and not all the logical connections have been fully detailed, but it does enable the study of women in elites to become more than the simple listing of percentages of women in 'top jobs' in various countries. By focusing on processes of elite reproduction, involving education and new occupational structures, the approach discussed here highlights some key issues in the study of elites and control structures. It also suggests a way of linking general analyses of class structure and economic change with data on a particular disadvantaged group.

NOTES

(1) Cf. Pondy (1969) and Starbuck (1965), as well as the 'strategy and structure' school of thought.
(2) Although the importance of these businesses is still considerable in France and certainly much more so than in the United Kingdom.
(3) I am grateful to Alan Thomas for these figures.
(4) I am indebted to Jane Marceau for comments on the INSEAD students, to Alan Thomas for the data on the 1975 entrants at the Manchester Business School, and to Janet Cabot for information on the London Business School students.

REFERENCES

Allen, A. J. (1971) 'The woman director,' in Michael Fogarty, A. J. Allen, I. Allen, and P. Walters, *Women in Top Jobs: Four Studies in Achievement* (London: Allen & Unwin, in co-operation with Political and Economic Planning), pp. 81–154.
Allen, I. (1971) 'Women in two large companies,' in Michael Fogarty, A. J. Allen, I. Allen, and P. Walters, *Women in Top Jobs: Four Studies in Achievement* (London: Allen & Unwin, in co-operation with Political and Economic Planning), pp. 23–77.
Bourdieu, Pierre (1966) 'L'école conservatrice: les inégalités devant l'école et devant la culture,' *Revue française de sociologie*, vol. 7, no. 3, pp. 325–47.
Bourdieu, Pierre (1971) 'Reproduction culturelle et reproduction sociale,' *Information sur les sciences sociales* (Social Science Information), vol. 10, no. 2, pp. 45–79.
Bourdieu, Pierre, Boltanski, L., and de Saint-Martin, M. (1973) 'Les stratégies de reconversion: les classes sociales et le système d'enseignement,' *Information sur les sciences sociales* (Social Science Information), vol. 12, no. 5, pp. 61–113.
Bourdieu, Pierre and Passeron, J.-C. (1964) *Les Héritier: Les Etudiantes et la culture* (Paris: Editions de Minuit).
Bourdieu, Pierre and Passeron, J.-C. (1970) *La Reproduction: Éléments pour une théorie du système d'enseignement* (Paris: Editions de Minuit).
Hall, D. and Amado-Fischgrund, G. (1969) 'Chief executives in Britain,' *European Business*, no. 20 (January), pp. 23–9.
Hall, D., de Bettignies, H.-Cl., and Amado-Fischgrund, G. (1969) 'The European business elite,' *European Business*, no. 23 (October), pp. 45–55.

Hunt, Audrey (1968) *A Survey of Women's Employment* (London: HMSO).

Kelsall, R. K., Poole, A., and Kuhn A. (1974) *Graduates: The Sociology of an Elite* (London: Tavistock).

Marceau, J. (1975) *The Social Origins, Educational Experience and Career Paths of a Young Business Elite: Final Report to the SSRC* (London: SSRC).

Pondy, L. R. (1969) 'Effects of size, complexity and ownership on administrative intensity,' *Administrative Science Quarterly*, vol. 14, no. 1, pp. 47–61.

Roberts, B. C., Loveridge, R., and Gennard, J. (1972) *Reluctant Militants* (London: Heinemann).

Stanworth, P. and Giddens, A. (eds) (1974) *Elites and Power in British Society* (Cambridge: Cambridge University Press).

Starbuck, William H. (1965) 'Organizational growth and development,' in J. G. March (ed.), *Handbook of Organizations* (Chicago: Rand McNally, pp. 451–533.

Whitley, R. (1973) 'Commonalities and connections among directors of large financial institutions,' *Sociological Review*, vol. 21, no. 4, pp. 613–32.

Whitley, R. (1974) 'The city and industry: the directors of large companies, their characteristics and connections,' in P. Stanworth and A. Giddens (eds), *Elites and Power in British Society* (Cambridge: Cambridge University Press), pp. 65–80.

13

Women Managers:

Career Patterns and Changes in the United States

CAROL ANN FINKELSTEIN

THE STUDY OF WOMEN IN BUSINESS ELITES AS A STRATEGIC SITE FOR SOCIOLOGICAL RESEARCH

The obstacles that women face in the business world have been well documented. We know that from their earliest socialization experiences women in American society are not prepared to assume positions of power and responsibility in the corporate world. We know too that, if they take on jobs in addition to their socially mandatory twin roles as wives and mothers, they are more often than not plagued by role conflict. Finally, we know that, if they enter the business arena, both the formal and informal structures will present barriers to their advancement.

US TRENDS IN THE POSITION OF WOMEN IN BUSINESS

Women in the Business Community
Until recently statistics on the progress of women in the business world indicated a pattern of stagnation or, at best, slow progress. Although the number of women in the work force has steadily increased, from 14 million in 1940 to 23·5 million in 1960 and over 40 million in 1977, the 1970 United States Census indicated that a mere 3 per cent of all working women were managers and administrators and that men in this category outnumbered women by five to one – a ratio that has improved only negligibly for women in the 1960s and 1970s.

According to *Fortune Magazine*, 'far rarer, even, than the male registered nurse is the woman who has made it to a very high position in a large American corporation' (Robertson, 1973, p. 81). At that level, according to a *Fortune* survey, men outnumbered women by about 600 to one. A check of the names of the three highest-paid officers and directors earning over $30,000 in each of the 1,000 largest industrial companies in *Fortune's Directory, 1972* and in each of the fifty largest companies in six non-industrial fields, comprising a total of 6,500 executives, revealed that only eleven were women, and one woman was actually a retired figurehead in a family organization. As Caroline Bird (1976) has put it, 'In business, at least, women are still where they've always been – at the bottom' (p. 231).

There is no precise information on the extent to which women have made recent strides in the business community, but various investigations of major companies throughout the United States have indicated that women are in fact getting more than just token positions. Moreover, according to *The New York Times*, they are moving into 'the professional and lower managerial jobs that feed into the pipeline [the key jobs from which candidates are chosen to run companies] such as corporate staff lawyer, auto factory foreman or computer marketing manager' (Bender, 1974, p. 1). Several large companies have added women to their boards of directors (e.g. Exxon – Martha Peterson, former President of Barnard College; Sears Roebuck – Norma T. Pace, economist; IBM – Patricia Harris, Washington lawyer; and Xerox – Joan Ganz Cooney, television executive). No doubt many of these companies are bowing to governmental and public pressures, and some are acting in anticipation of federal intervention. Yet, whatever the impetus, the significant facts are that women are gaining access to positions once completely blocked to them and that in these positions they have the potential to exert power in the direction of changing the male-dominated business world and 'bringing women in.'

It will be particularly interesting to look at that small group of women who have in fact 'made it' in the most masculine world of the corporate executive. Isolating some of the mechanisms that have enabled elite executive women to overcome the barriers should provide insight into the problem of bringing women into the corporate executive sphere and other positions of power. Finally, I hope to find clues to illuminate the more generic problem facing outgroups generally in gaining access to positions traditionally closed to them.

These questions motivated initial inquiries of women executives in a general investigation of women in business. The following is a report of the first findings from preliminary exploratory interviews with fifteen women in executive positions, in a variety of business enterprises ranging from banking and finance to cosmetics and fashion. No single area of enterprise was represented more than any other. In addition, the findings reported here and ideas for future inquiry are based on secondary data from both popular and academic publications.[1] The subjects for this pilot study were selected through personal contacts and a snowball technique.

Women's Role and Occupational Roles
Comparing women in male-dominated social spheres with other women in regard to their assumption of feminine roles and attributes, it appears that a disproportionate number of women executives have never been married or are divorced and that a few are lesbian. This may be strikingly different from 'most' women in one sense. Yet, there are indications that 'feminine' styles are pervasive even when women assume male statuses. For example, both a never-married 40-year-old executive woman and a 38-year-old lesbian assistant vice president expressed the 'fun of flirting' with their male colleagues, as well as the importance of using 'charm' in business transactions. Said the 40-year-old executive: 'Women have got to use whatever resources they have available to them.' This contrasts with Margaret Hennig's reports (Hennig, 1970; Hennig and Jardim, 1977) that most of the twenty-five top executive women whom she interviewed indicated that they attempted to achieve a male behavioral style at work and consciously eliminated a personal life in the early stages of their careers. I found that, on

the way to the top, women seemed to travel alone but did not affect a 'male' style as they did so.

Of course, there are many differences in what various people or groups characterize as male or female behavior. Because some of the women in the study were loners, they may not have fit the stereotyped view that women are typically warm and friendly. Although the older women in Hennig's sample may have assumed what they thought was a male executive style, hoping it would make them more acceptable to their male colleagues, it may be that the younger women in our study felt fewer resistances and could be more relaxed. As to other characteristics, *Business Week* (1976) reported that the top hundred corporate women in the United States whom they profiled were 'distinguishable for one thing: they are indistinguishable from their male counterparts in how they came to their present business eminence. More than a dozen founded their own businesses, a handful inherited a business. Some are highly educated . . . Some have a high school education' ('One hundred top corporate women', p. 56).

Caroline Bird, in her book about the lives and careers of over fifty American women who headed their own businesses from 1776 until 1976, observed that women in the past who engaged in business pursuits at a level of entrepreneurial behavior far beyond that of their contemporaries were often spurred by a family crisis, such as the death or absence of a husband, father, or brother. 'This not only made it essential that they earn their keep, but often it meant taking over the enterprise that had been run by the man of the family' (Bird, 1967, p. 233).

This historical trend has persisted, according to the British studies of Michael Fogarty and Rhona and Robert Rapoport (1971). They found that managerial women in government service, the British Broadcasting Corporation, and two large companies made use of opportunities that were created by luck, the wartime absence of men, or the death of a family member.

Women who got their start through a family business account for a substantial portion of every list of enterprising women in every historical period. Seven of the 'Ten most important women in big business' chosen by *Fortune Magazine* in April 1973 were in family businesses. Thirty-eight years earlier, in 1935, *Fortune* had looked for important women in business and located sixteen in that category, six of whom benefited from family connections (Bird, 1967, p. 233).

More significant than the statistics, however, is the change in *Fortune*'s tone. In the 1935 article, the patronizing suggestion was made that women could not succeed in business without 'help from home.' Commenting on the more recent *Fortune* article, Bird suggested that 'In 1973, chastened no doubt by some consciousness-raising from its predominantly female research staff, *Fortune* wondered how many potential women managers were being held back simply because they did *not* have a family connection behind them' (ibid.).

In the 1976 *Business Week* analysis of the top hundred corporate women in America who were 'indistinguishable from their male counterparts in how they came to their present business eminence,' almost no data were provided on the personal background of these top women executives.

Some studies (e.g. Cussler, 1958; Hennig, 1970; Hennig and Jardim, 1970) have indicated a disproportionately high number of single women in their samples of business women. This has also been my finding. Historically, women entrepreneurs seem to have been 'child- and/or husband-free during the years they began their careers' (Bird, 1967, p. 233). Executive men, in contrast, are much more likely to be married. In fact it is well known that corporations prefer their male managers to be married and to have children as well. They assume that a 'family man' will be more dependable or 'more manageable' (Uris, 1972).

Just the opposite appears to be the case for women executives. Marriage and children are seen as exerting a force so great that women will be pulled from the boardroom into the nursery to care for an ailing child. The male president of a New York consulting firm specializing in psychological services accused male executives of committing 'corporate bigamy' – of neglecting wife and children for the corporation. 'Corporate bigamy' is an offense for which male executives are not always apprehended, but for women executives the fear of committing this crime is so devastating that many have either chosen to remain single or have been seen as unmarriageable (see Coser and Rokoff, 1971). Carol Tatkon – a manager in the International Financial Planning Division of the Exxon Corporation – has commented thus on her role conflict as wife, mother, executive, and leader of various community organizations and professional associations: 'Role conflict perhaps should not be a pejorative term, but a positive one. There is a distinct possibility that having a set of very different roles results in synergism – the greater effectiveness in each role undertaken.' Among the various mechanisms for the reduction of role strain, according to William J. Goode (1960), is the taking on of many statuses, so that the overloaded status set serves as an excuse for failing to fulfill particular role obligations, for eliciting the aid of others in helping one to fulfill certain obligations, or for making role partners aware of the overload, so that they will hesitate to make added demands (see also Sieber, 1974; and Coser, 1975).

Role performance priorities may be situation specific rather than *status* specific:

> The net result of dividing various roles horizontally, and not vertically, is that no one role assumes top priority, nor is any major area of responsibility left at the bottom to receive short shrift, or perhaps not to be performed at all. Instead, the very *critical* elements of each role are in a category by themselves. ... The conflicts within a role are minimized, and if the top layer is kept lean, the competition in that category is less frequent, more isolated and therefore easier to handle. Priorities can be set by value, not role, in series of layers. The critical elements of each role are in the first layer, receiving highest degree of commitment. (Tatkon, 1976)

Thus, for example, caring for the needs of a sick child would receive more attention than mopping a floor, and formulating a critical policy recommendation more than writing a routine report. The serious problems occur, of course, when tasks come up with competing urgency.

Aspirations

When the ambitions of women as compared to those of men are explored, the evidence also contradicts stereotype. My interviews with women executives, married and single alike, and all studies as well as journalistic accounts of top women managers, indicated that they had tremendous drive and 'went for broke' in pursuit of the highest positions in the business world. Furthermore, their expectations continued to rise as they rose in the corporate structure. This continuous and often single-minded push toward the top distinguished them from men and particularly from other women, who accepted low level positions as both the most appropriate and the 'best that they could do.'

Such women are no longer unique. The ideology of the Women's Movement and governmental pressure have created an impetus to success on the part of many women. Executive-training organizations have reported a great demand for their new management-skills seminars for women. Former secretarial schools (e.g. the long-established Katherine Gibbs School) have begun offering management courses for women. The influx of women into management has also given rise to a new breed of consultants to train women executives.

In 1975 *Business Week* reported that some experts saw women as having made the greatest strides in middle management in the fields where they already had management experience (e.g. consumer goods) and in areas where considerable numbers of women professionals provided both the pressure and the talent (e.g. banking, data processing).

In 1976 *Business Week* identified the 100 top corporate women in America by industry. The largest number of these women (22) had achieved senior corporate posts in banking or financial services. The remainder were distributed as follows, in order of magnitude: manufacturing 14, cosmetics and fashion 11, publishing 9, food 7, public relations and advertising 7, services 7, broadcasting 6, electronics 5, petroleum 4, retailing 4, and utilities 4 ('One hundred top corporate women,' 1976).

The penetration of women into executive levels varied with the industry. Women have rarely had access to executive positions that required an extensive technical background. This is changing now, as women are training themselves for just such positions.[2] I attended several seminars in 1976 and 1977 devoted to helping women succeed in business and found that much stress was placed on the demand for women in technical industries, which are under pressure from the government to hire women.

The most promising projected trends seem to emerge from the fact that growing numbers of women are enrolling in business, management, and technical-training programs. *Business Week* reported in 1975 that, at the University of California at Los Angeles, women graduates with master's degrees in business administration 'get jobs months ahead of men and command salaries 5 percent higher' ('Up the ladder, finally,' 1975, p. 62).

Competition with Men for Limited Job Opportunities

'[T]he resentment of some men towards women managers is exacerbated by the shrunken job market. As some male executives see it, the influx of a large number of women into their ranks could not have come at a worse time' (Smith, 1975, p. 58). Many women readily admit that men do indeed have reason to be troubled. 'A knockout woman will move aside a mediocre man,' stated Madeline H. McWhinney – the first President of the First Women's Bank of New York. 'A man who in an earlier day might have moved ahead will be left behind, and he really has it rough. But no change comes easily' (Smith, 1975, p. 58). In addition, corporations are not charitable institutions. They want the best man for the job, even if he turns out to be a woman. Thus, many a mediocre male executive fears for his job. As Cynthia Fuchs Epstein (1975) has noted:

> These fears are not groundless; they stem from women's obvious potential. It is certainly true that women, who constitute such a large proportion of the educated, could take over quite a few men's jobs tomorrow if they were so inclined and if they were given the opportunity. Yet, it must be possible to devise work structures in which we can upgrade *all* jobs, provide reward incentives for all, and define competition from the bottom to the top in terms of sheer creative talent, ambition and drive. (pp. 18–19)

Pearl Meyer (1975) – financial analyst and vice president of an executive search firm – has noted a 'curious paradox' that confronts the US business establishment:

> Numerically, U.S. business is currently staffed with the smallest management generation in modern history; executives between the ages of 35 and 45 are Depression babies, born when the nation's birthrate fell to its lowest point before now. On the other hand, recessionary business conditions have made companies less tolerant of poor executive performance; managers who do not shape up are being shipped out. These new realities of executive recruitment – urgent need, rising standards and short supply – are working directly counter to each other in the managerial marketplace. (p. 47)

As a result, corporate recruiters are looking for talented women where these are most likely to be found (i.e. in the less visible positions – the supportive staff or subordinate roles – rather than in the highly visible executive positions):

> Knock on any company's door and you will find high-caliber female buyers but not merchandise managers, analysts but not research directors, tellers but not treasurers, assistants to presidents but not vice presidents – all positions of low visibility. (Meyer, 1975)

Striking Down Anti-nepotism Rules: The Issue of Being Both a Spouse and a Colleague
With more and more women working the chances increase for making the job sphere a readily available marriage market. In addition, with more and more women staying on at their jobs after marriage the problem of husband and wife being employed by the same organization becomes more

wide-spread. As women move up the occupational ladder, the chances of finding both husband and wife in high level positions increase, and the spectre of nepotism rears its ugly (or perhaps not-so-ugly) head in an environment supposedly based on universalistic standards.

Some companies are responding to these changes and are not only hiring married couples or tolerating the marriage of two employees, but also are actually beginning to see the advantages of this practice. Husbands and wives who received their graduate degrees in business administration together are beginning to job hunt together, so that they can be placed as a team with large companies. Management consultant Loring and Wells (1972) have noted that 'Executive couples are a new breed, acting in concert when it comes to hiring or relocation' (p. 119). It is well recognized that the practice of employing both husband and wife tends to increase company loyalty.

Of the 17,000 employees of the First National City Bank in New York, approximately 600 are related to another employee. When asked for the number of married couples among them, the Vice President for Staff Services explained: 'We don't know ... because we don't keep track of them. That means they aren't giving us any trouble; if they were we'd be counting them' (Warren, 1976, p. 56).

Educational Paths to Business Careers
The American Council on Education conducted a national survey in 1975 to determine the degree to which college women in the United States were aiming at careers in traditionally male-dominated fields. One in six female college freshmen (16·9 per cent of the total) entered college in the fall of 1975 with the goal of becoming a business executive, physician, lawyer, or engineer. Business was the choice for almost two-thirds of them. In a comparable survey administered in 1965 a considerably smaller proportion (5·9 per cent) planned for careers in these areas. The assumption can easily be made that, in the course of a college education and through the exposure to many professional women in academia, many more women college students may consider entering one of these fields by the time they have graduated.

In 1971 only 2·8 per cent of all women obtained undergraduate degrees in either accounting or business, compared with 22 per cent of all male graduates. Business has been the most popular single major for men. Education used to be the most popular area of concentration for women (36 per cent of all women graduates in 1971 (Robertson, 1973, p. 87), compared with less than 10 per cent of all male graduates). Given the dim employment prospects for new teachers today, the drop in elementary school enrollment, the various budget cuts, the number of women majoring in education will undoubtedly fall, and many of them may consider business.

Interestingly, at two recent New York University conferences on 'Women and Management' a striking number of women reported that they were unemployed teachers changing their careers. Some older women, who had taught for fifteen to twenty years, were also attending these conferences in order to find out about possibilities in the business world, because they were contemplating career changes. These women with training and experience in education represent a new pool of recruits.

At the graduate school level the greater interest of women in business is also obvious. The number of women who took the test of the Educational Testing Service for admission to graduate study in business increased from 3·3 per cent of the total in the 1966–7 academic year to approximately 8 per cent in 1971–2 (Robertson, 1973, p. 87). Actual female enrollment at the nation's thirteen leading graduate schools of business in 1973 was up by an impressive 400 per cent over 1970.

There has been a substantial increase in the percentage of women students in graduate schools of business. Of the first-year students at Harvard's Graduate School of Business, 7 per cent were women in 1972 compared to 4 per cent in 1970. Harvard only began to accept women into its two-year Master of Business Administration program in the fall of 1963 (Robertson, 1973, p. 87). The Wharton School of the University of Pennsylvania had a 25 per cent female enrollment in its entering class in the fall of 1975, which was up from an average of under 4 per cent between 1968 and 1970. At the Stanford University Business School the total student enrollment was less than 1 per cent female in 1969; in 1975 it was 20 per cent ('Up the ladder, finally', 1975, p. 62). The Columbia University Graduate School of Business, which has been open to women for many decades, increased female enrollment from 5 per cent in the fall of 1968 to 13 per cent in the fall of 1972 and then to 35 per cent in the fall of 1976 (phone communication). The trend is clear.

Few of the older women executives in my study had graduate training in business, as was true of the 100 top corporate women selected by *Business Week*. But graduate training is becoming more important for men in business, and it is likely that women will profit if they enter the corporate arena armed with graduate business training.

There are alternative and perhaps unanticipated educational paths to a business career. The women who have been choosing to study law, engineering, and other traditionally male and technically oriented subjects may also be paving their way into the business community. Many men have traveled this route. Although women with this training may not have a business career as a goal when they decide to enter law school, neither did many male law students who preceded them and who now find themselves in the upper echelons of large American corporations. About a dozen of the 100 top corporate women in the United States 'found a law degree either handy or the principal tool in their rise' ('One hundred top corporate women,' 1976).

A few women business executives whom I interviewed began their careers with training in computer science at a time when the field was just emerging. As one vice president explained: 'If you knew anything, you were an expert and very much in demand.' This may have encouraged many women's careers. Their sex status was less problematic because they had valuable skills. Perhaps, too, competent performance in a technical area is more difficult to undermine than it is in more 'human-relations-type' managerial positions. Having proved themselves in the technical areas, many women rise to line executive positions. Margaret Hennig's findings provide support for this hypothesis. Technical expertise may have been a valuable ticket of entry to success in the business world for many women in the past, and it may not have lost its value today.

Women as Owners of Businesses

Since Mary Goddard printed the Declaration of Independence in 1776, there have always been women who have owned their own businesses. Some have been enormously successful, heading multimillion-dollar companies (e.g. Mary Wells Lawrence in advertising, Estee Lauder in cosmetics, and Florence Eiseman in children's clothing). A *New York Times* article (Bender, 1976) has noted that these women were not 'feminist heroines,' in part because they shunned involvement in the Women's Movement, in part because some of them were in partnership with their husbands, but basically because their successes were so exceptional.

The impact of the Women's Movement is seen in the increased willingness of women to start their own businesses. Some women seem willing to take large risks rather than gamble on the possibility of advancement in the corporate hierarchy. A greater willingness by some banks to lend women money for capital, in addition to the availability of special loan funds, are encouraging female entrepreneurs. The proliferation of literature and training seminars urging women to 'start your own business' must also be mentioned as both responding to a need and perhaps creating one as well.

Many of the women in my pilot study who 'made it' in large corporations indicated a desire to run their own businesses and to reap the more immediate gratification lacking in decision-making processes in large scale organizations. Some of the younger women entertained the possibility of leaving the large corporation to open their own businesses.

Statistical information on women-owned businesses has been almost non-existent; however, the Office of Minority Business Enterprise of the Department of Commerce is now gathering such data. Tabulations based upon the Census Bureau data indicate that in 1972 there were 402,025 businesses owned by women in the United States. They grossed $8·1 billion − a mere 1 per cent of the total receipts.

SOME PROBLEM AREAS FOR WOMEN IN MANAGEMENT

The Lack of Role Models

In the sociological literature on socialization much has been written on the importance of the role model. For the female executive the lack of more experienced women to initiate her into the traditions and manners of the corporate world is often seen as her single greatest handicap. A female management consultant pointed out some of the issues: 'What does she wear at each level?[3] When does she start to call her boss by his first name? What's the right tone of voice? Men find out by looking around them. Women know it's important, know it's part of the process of moving up, but they've no one to copy' ('Up the ladder, finally,' 1975), p. 66).[4] With no peer group and no referent for her behavior the female executive is at a distinct disadvantage.

Some women executives insist that the lack of female role models is over-stated, and some older women executives believe that men can be role models for women. Indeed, many women identify their fathers, male bosses, and other businessmen as their own role models. It has also been suggested that women executives can become models for men as well.

Yet, although most women in this pilot study indicated that their paths to success might have been eased somewhat by the availability of a woman role model, many of them, particularly those in less high-level positions, expressed a fear of negative female role models – Queen Bees who have sacrificed their personal lives for occupational success and continue to resent female newcomers who 'have it too easy.'

The Queen Bee is Dead, but Sisterhood is Powerful

Although several of the women executives whom I interviewed expressed some exhilaration at being 'the only woman,' these same women felt the need for female colleagues with whom they could share common problems. They expressed a desire to help other women, and some referred to situations in which they had given 'extra' assistance and guidance to women seeking advancement within the organization.

One woman who was contemplating a move was grooming a female protégé for her position. Another woman vice president explained the little extra help she gave women: 'Well, you know how it is, Italians tend to be a little more helpful to Italians, Jews tend to help Jews...' These same women tended to speak very highly of other women in their organization. The stereotypical feminine cattiness was noticeably absent.

Interaction with Male and Female Subordinates

Despite the widespread belief among male managers that men will refuse to work for women, some top executive women dismiss this proposition with comments like those of a vice president of a multinational manufacturing corporation: 'I never made a man a job offer that was turned down' ('Up the ladder, finally,' 1975, p. 66). A corporate vice president of research for a multinational petroleum corporation explained: 'It is the power of my posi-tion, not whether I am a man or woman, that determines whether people will work for me. They know who I am and what I do' ('Up the ladder, finally,' 1975). The vice president for consumer and employee relations at a large department store approached the question rationally. She pointed out that few employees had many options regarding whom they worked for, and therefore they worked for whoever possessed the status of boss in their organization and adjusted to him or her as best they could ('Up the ladder, finally,' 1975).

The women executives whom I interviewed indicated varying degrees of openness in their interactions with male subordinates. Some, however, indicated a very marked openness. They reported situations in which they had confronted a male subordinate with the issue of 'working under a woman.' One of the top three women in a large communications corpor-ation told of offering a man a job that paid considerably more than his present position and corresponded perfectly to his area of expertise. Assuming that she was the 'personnel person' rather than his prospective supervisor, the applicant readily accepted the position. Aware that there might be some confusion, this woman executive felt compelled to eliminate possible misunderstandings and asked the man if he would object to working for a woman. Shocked, disappointed, and disturbed, he refused the position. 'Somehow he would be less of a man in the eyes of his friends if he were working for a woman,' she explained. Interestingly enough, this same female executive expressed some doubt as to whether or not she would feel totally comfortable working under a woman. She confided that in some ways she always seemed to view her job as a helpmate to some man, even though that was no longer the case.[5] The impact of the Women's Movement is evident here in this openness and willingness to confront issues that at one time were rarely articulated.

Some have maintained that female secretaries will not want to work for women executives and that harmonious interaction will be impossible.[6] It has been suggested that the strong relationship between the male executive and his female secretary is predicated on a flirting relationship that minimizes the tension that is inherent between superior and subordinate (Smith, 1975, pp. 58–9). This does not seem to be a very powerful argument against the existence of the female executive, for the relationship between superiors and subordinates certainly cannot be predicated on the possibilities for a flirting relationship. Male superiors and male subordinates – the statistically more common case – typically work together effectively without sexual byplay.

The Consequences of Being a Token

Women who enter large organizations on managerial levels are numerically rare, and rarer still are the women who have ascended to the upper executive echelons. Rosabeth Moss Kanter (1976) has defined a 'token' as anyone who is numerically rare. Being a token makes one more visible, and this creates special performance pressures on the token. Tokens must be twice as careful as others, for their performance is nearly always public. Therefore, it is difficult for them to share confidences with colleagues, for example.[7]

Many women have commented on the difficulties of the lone pioneer. In one woman's words: 'Being a pioneer woman is an exhausting task. I was hardly ever allowed to be tired. I was suspect when I was sick, I was generally expected to be perfect and was ready to defend myself at all times if I weren't' (Insel, 1975, pp. 135–6). However, it should be noted that a smaller number of women have indicated that they like being trailblazers. A manager at American Telephone and Telegraph said: 'I like the idea of being a pioneer...If few women have ever run a meeting at AT&T, that means I can be part of setting the precedent of how women do things here' (Smith, 1975, p. 61).

A male manager who performs less brilliantly is not unusual, but a mediocre woman manager is 'in management's eye, proof that she holds the job simply to satisfy the unreasonable demands of an interfering government, and in her own eyes, a disaster' ('Up the ladder, finally,' 1975, p. 68).

We are still in the first-woman syndrome at most companies,' a business school psychologist observed. 'And that puts a tremendous burden on the woman' ('Up the ladder, finally,' 1975, p. 67). One of the first female corporate lending officers at the United California Bank explained: 'If I were a male, I could probably make at least one small mistake without disrupting my career. As a woman, I know there's no room for even one. I exhaust every possibility before I make a loan because I'm putting my career on the line every time' ('Up the ladder, finally,' 1975). A male planning executive concurred with this observation: 'All it takes to convince both men and women that females don't make good bosses is for one woman to fail' ('Up the ladder, finally,' 1975). A recent management study found that top management accepted a certain male failure rate rather routinely but regarded female failure as an argument against further female promotions ('Up the ladder, finally,' 1975, p. 67–8). Most of the women whom I interviewed commented on their initial difficulties in their striving to be perfect. For some the difficulties persisted, but others – clearly the more highly placed – could relax once they had 'proven themselves' to their coworkers and themselves.

The consequences of being a token extend beyond the individual, for the token's performance stands as representative of all other members of the particular minority group to which he/she belongs (e.g. women, blacks, Jews). Tokens sometimes respond in ways that look like fear of success. Perhaps they hesitate in taking risks that could catapult them into higher level positions for fear of alienating those around them who have had difficulty enough in accepting them where they are. Fear of success has been considered a personality trait of women by some; however, Kanter (1976) has maintained that it is a social structural reaction to being a token.

In a study of a group of seventy-five women who worked in the technical, marketing, advertising, and community relations departments of eight large corporations, conducted at Marymount College, it was found that 50 per cent of the women managers or potential managers interviewed had turned down job promotions at one time. The women said that they had refused promotions *not* because they feared success or failure but because the promotions offered 'weren't real' or 'were created for women because they looked good.' 'There was no ambivalence about getting ahead,' said John Somerville – an anthropologist who conducted the study with five other Marymount faculty members. 'These women say they want to go all the way' ('Unequal rungs up the corporate ladder,' 1975). If women fear success, Loring and Wells (1972) have asked, 'why are the Equal Employment Opportunity Commission, the Office of Federal Contract Compliance, the Wage and Hours Division, and the courts being inundated with cases involving discrimination against women?' (p. 149).

It is hard to be an individual when you are, say, the only woman or black manager in the company. Stereotyping is more likely to occur. Absolute numbers do *indeed* make a difference, and the absolute number *one* is very significant (Kanter, 1976).

There are two divergent expectations for the rare case that is the executive woman. Either of these expectations can be activated at the appropriate time and result in undermining the achievement or emphasizing the failure of one who has a statistically infrequent status set. The first expectation is that the individual will be like all other members of his/her minority group be they women, blacks or the elderly. The second is that the individual is the rare exception, unlike all others who share the particularly problematic status. When a female executive is clearly doing a superior job, her performance is explained by the fact that she is unlike other women. Here, she is essentially defeminized. However, if she slips up in some way or loses her temper, she is seen as very much like all other women (i.e. highly emotional or hysterical). Thus, what we see is an effective means of maintaining stereotypes and fortifying the barriers that keep women out of the executive suite.

The token is also subject to status-leveling. This can be an upgrading of status (e.g. the male nurse addressed as 'Doctor') or a downgrading of status (e.g. the female executive referred to as a secretary). Being in a situation where one has consistently to define one's status for others may well have damaging psychological effects. The executive woman who is mistaken for the secretary must each time correct the error for the other, but in some measure of sense she must reidentify herself for *herself* as well. Feeling the pressure of this kind of interaction, one executive vice president reported not taking a notebook to meetings anymore. Another woman executive told of how she sometimes felt too exhausted, and perhaps too threatened, to correct the mistaken individual.

Turnover Rates Linked to Mobility

Women who have succeeded as managers and executives in the male bastion of the corporate world have often had to struggle through a considerable period of adjustment, both on their part and on the part of those around them. After 'proving their competence a little bit more than should be necessary; and after having set up effective personal relationships, which define them to their coworkers as individuals rather than as members of a sexual group,' (Alpert, 1976, p. 28), they are often wedded to the particular organization.

This extensive adjustment experience seems to be one of the reasons why women managers have tended to do considerably less job-hopping than their male counterparts. It takes a substantial investment in time and energies to establish these asexual relationships on the job. Therefore, job-hopping is clearly less attractive to women than it is to men, despite the fact that it is well recognized as a career pattern of many, if not most, successful male executives.

The vice president of an executive search firm noted that: 'In the past, women have been reluctant to change jobs. They were loyal and afraid to move.' However, '[this firm's] national mobility survey for the last six months of 1973 indicated that 4 percent of those seeking executive positions were women, the first time women counted for more than half of 1 percent' (Bender, 1974, p. 43). This may be a good indicator of changes to come.

Inhospitable Informal Structures

Sociologists have long recognized the importance of informal structures.

Epstein (1975) has pointed out that 'informal behavior is institutionalized at least as thoroughly as the formal modes of interaction depicted on organizational charts, and it is probably more important to analyze informal interaction' (p. 8). This is particularly essential in the upper echelons of any organization, where the decision-making process is often highly idiosyncratic. The decisions that top executives are often called upon to make deal with those problems that the rules and regulations of the bureaucracy have been unable to solve:

> The closer one gets to the top, the more commonly are decision-making judgments and rewards determined by subjective criteria; 'understandings' rather than rules govern behavior, and personal qualifications are judged against a range of attributes not immediately relevant functionally to the job at hand. (Epstein, 1975, p. 8)

A woman who operated a Los Angeles management consultant firm with her husband was made very much aware of the importance of the male 'club' when a vice president for finance at one of her client companies described the way in which he had selected a male assistant.' "[The candidate] told me that he used to play ice hockey," ' she said. 'The vice president said that was all he needed to know: the candidate must be a "team player." He therefore got the job. That one fact immediately set up a framework of understanding' (Smith, 1975, p. 60). A woman vice president of an executive search firm explained that: 'Most women don't realize the importance of sports talk ... That casual talk about yesterday's football game or the chat on the 19th hole on the golf course may give an executive the feel that, yes, this man will fit into our operation or, no, he won't' ('Up the ladder, finally,' 1975, p. 66).

Several of the women in business whom I studied expressed unease and boredom at being the only woman at a Monday morning meeting and having to tolerate an extended rehashing of Sunday's afternoon football game. Like war stories and sports analogies, this element of the informal structure serves to bind males together, and is often interpreted by women as a design to exclude them from full participation. Whether or not this is the intent of all or some of the lone female executive's male colleagues, or simply the continuation of an informal pattern of interaction established long before a woman ever sat at such a meeting in this capacity, its consequences are the same: the woman is made to feel like a spectator, when she should really be feeling like one of the team.

Yet, women see their participation in the informal structures of the business establishment as crucial for their career enhancement. Middle management women with their eyes on positions up the corporate ladder are often angered by the fact that they learn about new projects and even upcoming job openings weeks after such information has been discussed over lunch by their male colleagues.

Women executives indicate that they feel excluded from what they refer to as the 'old boy network' (i.e. the support system of the male executive). This support system is made up of old college friends, twice-daily interactions in smoking cars on the commuter lines from and to the suburbs, and memberships in clubs that have been 'for men only.' The information exchanged in this network is often unavailable in the nine-to-five office setting—information that alerts potential candidates to job openings, offers advice to new incumbents concerning the personal idiosyncracies of superiors, and generally eases the path toward the plushest of the executive suites. Epstein (1975) has summed it up well in the following passage:

> When women cannot mingle easily with men as colleagues in the informal settings where business gets done, they cannot become fully prepared to exercise influence. When women expect and are given full participation in the formal and informal structures of their occupations at every level, including the top one, they can be included as equals and be let in on the silent rules of the game along with the males. (p. 14)

'Sexual Politics' in Business

Sexuality has been described by Bradford, Sargent, and Sprague (1975) as part of the rationale for the exclusion of women executives from participation in the informal networks that are essential for advancement in the corporate structure. They have offered the hypothesis that male sexuality is enhanced not only by the power that the executive wields but also by the all male exclusivity of the executive world. Thus, the entrance of women into this male bastion is seen not only as an intrusion but also as an attack on males' precarious feelings of sexual strength.

There are other aspects of sexuality that create problems for women executives. Actual sexual attraction between colleagues or the fear of potential attraction can prove to be detrimental to a woman rather than catapult her to executive stardom.[8] Male senior executives may be hesitant to sponsor an attractive woman who shows great executive promise for fear of gossip or wifely objections. A woman executive of a well-known manufacturing company pointed to these problems while stressing the function of mingling socially with male executives: 'Wives get very nervous when you are around and don't have a husband ... And yet seeing top executives socially can be very important. In an executive environment, men can invite one another to their homes and clubs. A senior executive will promote a junior executive that way' (Smith, 1975, p. 60).

It has long been observed that the entrance of a female into an all male situation, or the opposite situation, tends to alter the behavior of the original same-sex group. Consider, for example, the fear on the part of some male executives that the presence of a woman at a planning meeting will activate competitive feelings among the men and undermine the 'team spirit,' mutual trust, and general cohesiveness upon which the group depends for successful decision-making. However, it must be remembered that women secretaries are often present at executive meetings, and yet no one feels inhibited by their presence. Furthermore, one-upmanship at meetings among colleagues, even single sex meetings, is surely not at all atypical.

CONCLUSION

I have attempted to sketch some of the recent trends and problems in the participation of women in the US business community. The evidence points to the continued greater involvement of women in this arena. However, barriers are still sizable against large numbers of women entering this male-dominated domain and, moreover, rising to positions of power and prestige.

Those who man the barricades against them are not only the men in high positions who fear the entry of women and thus act as sexist gatekeepers. They also include other men and women variously located in the occupational and personal worlds of these aspiring women. Barriers are erected by the structural organization of many business settings, both formal and informal, and by the early experiences of women, inadequately socialized and educated for business careers.

Some of these barriers will relax with the passage and enforcement of continued affirmative action legislation; others will fall away as business enterprises realize that women can be as competent and as ordinary as their male counterparts; but some will demand the radical resocialization of many men and women.

Clearly, then, the problem areas are numerous for executive women, especially for aspiring executive women, but the problems are not insurmountable. As more and more women move into such positions, there will be even greater changes, which will make the business world a more hospitable place in which talented women can realize their full potential, and the organization for which they work can reap the benefits of quality performance. Of course, while business organizations are always looking for talented people to fill their executive ranks, and while there has been an increased effort to recruit women for management-training programs, the gentle or not-so-gentle push of governmental pressure will also contribute to fundamental changes in the career patterns of women managers in the United States.

NOTES

(1) Rosabeth Moss Kanter (1977), in *Men and Women of the Corporation*, has dealt extensively with many of the issues raised in this paper. Her work corroborates a number of my preliminary findings. I have made only passing reference to Kanter's book in several additional notes, because this paper was completed prior to the publication of her book.

(2) The direct relationship between an increase in access to the opportunity structure and a rise in the level of aspiration has been dealt with in great depth by Kanter (1977, pp. 129–63).

(3) Various articles have appeared in newspapers and magazines offering fashion advice to the executive woman and the aspiring executive woman. One entire book, *The Woman's Dress for Success Book* – a best seller by 'wardrobe engineer' John Molloy (1977) – is devoted to this subject. In addition, considerable advertising of women's attaché cases has emphasized their value as symbols of executive status.

(4) The lack of role models with whom to identify, mentioned by some aspiring female executives, is echoed in a reciprocal way by some established male executives who have difficulty selecting a female protégé. The aspiring woman executive may have difficulty selecting a male role model with whom to identify, just as the male sponsor may have difficulty in selecting a female protégé with whom to identify. But in the aspiring male executive the sponsor can relive his past and see himself at a more youthful and earlier phase of his career. Moreover, whereas the population of female role models remains limited, there is surely no shortage of aspiring male executives. For more on the crucial

link between sponsorship and mobility and its relationship to women in business, see Epstein (1970, pp. 168–73), Epstein (1975, pp.7–21), and Kanter (1977 pp. 181–4).
(5) Several of the women in Kanter's (1977) study also expressed this psychological comfort with the role of helpmate.
(6) For an elaborate discussion of the relationship between the female secretary and the male executive, see Kanter (1977, pp. 69–103).
(7) For a well-developed chapter on the 'token issue,' see Kanter (1977, pp. 206–42).
(8) This is contrary to the strong popular belief in the 'casting couch' phenomenon (i.e. the young aspiring actress who sleeps with the director to win a starring role).

REFERENCES AND OTHER SOURCES

Alpert, Dee Estelle (1976) 'The struggle for status,' *MBA*, vol. 10, no. 2 (February), pp. 25–8.

Bender, Marilyn (1974) 'More women advancing into key business posts,' *The New York Times* (January 20) pp. 1 ff.

Bender, Marilyn (1976) 'More women are becoming owners of businesses,' *The New York Times* (April 25), pp. 1 ff.

Bird, Caroline (1976) *Enterprising Women* (New York: W. W. Norton).

Bradford, David L., Sargent, Alice G., and Sprague, Melinda S. (1975) 'The executive man and woman: the issue of sexuality,' in Francine E. Gordon and Myra H. Strober (eds), *Bringing Women into Management* (New York: McGraw-Hill), pp. 39–58.

Coser, Rose Laub (1975) 'The complexity of roles as a seedbed of individual autonomy,' in Lewis A. Coser (ed.), *The Idea of Social Structure: Papers in Honor of Robert K. Merton* (New York: Harcourt Brace Jovanovich), pp. 237–63.

Coser, Rose Laub and Rokoff, Gerald (1971) 'Women in the occupational world: social disruption and conflict,' *Social Problems*, vol. 18, no. 4, (Spring), pp. 535–54.

Cussler, Margaret (1958) *The Woman Executive* (New York: Harcourt, Brace).

Donnelly, Caroline (1976) 'Keys to the executive powder room,' *Money*, vol. 5, no. 8 (August), pp. 28–32.

Epstein, Cynthia Fuchs (1970) *Woman's Place: Options and Limits in Professional Careers* (Berkeley: University of California Press).

Epstein, Cynthia Fuchs (1975) 'Institutional barriers: what keeps women out of the executive suite?,' in Francine E. Gordon and Myra H. Stober (eds), *Bringing Women into Management* (New York: McGraw-Hill), pp. 7–21.

Fogarty, Michael, Allen, A. J., Allen, I., and Walters, P. (1971) *Women in Top Jobs: Four Studies in Achievement* (London: Allen & Unwin, in co-operation with Political and Economic Planning).

Fogarty, Michael, Rapoport, Rhona, and Rapoport, Robert (1971) *Sex, Career and Family* (London: Allen & Unwin, in co-operation with Political and Economic Planning).

Fowler, Elizabeth M. (1975) 'Wall St's unhappy women,' *The New York Times* (February 4).

Ginzberg, Eli and Yohalem, Alice (eds) (1973) *Corporate Lib: Women's Challenge to Management* (Baltimore: Johns Hopkins Press).

Goode, William J. (1960) 'A theory of role strain,' *American Sociological Review*, vol. 25, no. 4 (August), pp. 483–96.

Hennig, Margaret Marie (1970) 'Career development for women executives,' unpublished doctoral dissertation (Cambridge, Mass.: Harvard University).

Hennig, Margaret Marie and Jardim, Anne (1977) *The Managerial Woman* (New York: Anchor Press and Doubleday).

Insel, Barbara (1975) 'Women in management: vignettes,' in Francine E. Gordon and Myra H. Strober (eds), *Bringing Women into Management* (New York: McGraw-Hill), pp. 34–6.

Jabs, Cynthia (1976) 'Making management a neuter term,' *The New York Times* (May 2).

Kanter, Rosabeth Moss (1976) 'Women in organizations,' unpublished paper presented at Sociologists for Women in Society Conference on Women and Work, New York, February.

Kanter, Rosabeth Moss (1977) *Men and Women of the Corporation* (New York: Basic Books).

Klemesrud, Judy (1975) 'Feminist shareholders challenge the corporate structure,' *The New York Times* (May 15), p. 52.

Loring, Rosalind and Wells, Theodora (1972) *Breakthrough: Women into Management* (New York: Van Nostrand Reinhold).

Meyer, Pearl (1975) 'Women executives are different, *Dun's Review* vol. 105, no. 1, pp. 47–8.

Molloy, John (1977) *The Woman's Dress for Success Book* (Chicago: Follett).

'One hundred top corporate women,' *Business Week*, no. 2437 (June 21, 1976), pp. 56–68.

Robertson, Wyndham (1973) 'The ten highest-ranking women in big business,' *Fortune Magazine*, vol. 87, no. 4 (April), pp. 80–9.

Rosen, Benson and Jerdee, Thomas H. (1974) 'Sex stereotyping in the executive suite,' *Harvard Business Review*, vol. 52, no. 2 (March–April), pp. 45–58.

Schwartz, Eleanor Brantley (1971) *The Sex Barrier in Business* (Atlanta: Georgia State University Press).

Seidenberg, Robert (1975) *Corporate Wives: Corporate Casualties?* (New York: Anchor Books).

Sieber, Sam D. (1974) 'Toward a theory of role accumulation,' *American Sociological Review*, vol. 39, no. 4, pp. 567–78.

Smith, Lee (1975) 'What's it like for women executives?,' *Dun's Review*, vol. 106, no. 6, pp. 58–61.

Tatkon, Carol (1976) 'Role conflict and the woman manager,' unpublished paper presented at New York University Conference on Women and Management, February 7.

'The executive suite,' *Harper's Bazaar*, no. 3177 (August 1976), pp. 83 ff.

'Unequal rungs up the corporate ladder,' *The New York Times* (February 5, 1975), p. 23.

'Up the ladder, finally,' *Business Week* (November 24, 1975), pp. 58–68.

Warren, Virginia Lee (1976) 'When love blooms at the water cooler, fewer firms throw cold water on it,' *The New York Times* (February 11), p. 56.

14

Women in Management in West Germany

HELGE PROSS

The presence of women in economic elites in West Germany is rarer than in any other decision-making bodies in the society. This paper will explore this situation and the reasons for it.

Since the foundation of the Federal Republic of Germany in 1949 the general situation of women in West Germany has vastly improved. As regards their legal status, equality of the sexes is now complete. In addition there has been much progress as to woman's position in the family. The traditional pattern of male dominance has broken down and been replaced by a more, although certainly not yet fully, egalitarian one. Since the mid-1960s dramatic changes have taken place in the educational system. Whereas previously the majority of girls received little or no formal occupational training, nowadays it is only a tiny minority who leave school after the obligatory nine years and turn immediately to paid employment without any further formal education. The average educational standard of young women has certainly not yet reached the average for males. Women still prefer occupational and academic studies that are less demanding and of shorter duration. Nevertheless, the proportion of girls seeking higher education has risen almost from year to year. Today almost as many girls as boys graduate from the *Gymnasium* (i.e. after thirteen years of general education), and almost as many young women as young men enter an apprenticeship – one of the most highly esteemed ways of occupational training in the country. Female students in institutions of higher learning now make up slightly more than one-third of the student body, and this proportion is also rising.[1] Finally, women have made remarkable advances in the working world. At present there are some 10 million women in paid employment. The majority are working as employees; roughly one-third are laborers (Statisches Bundesamt, 1975).

Although progess is evident, it has, however, advanced only to the middle levels of the various occupational hierarchies. With regard to leadership or decision-making positions, the situation has improved only little or not at all. Virtually no changes have taken place in the economic power elite as far as sex composition is concerned. Before going into details it may be useful first to give a brief description of the general structure of that elite.

The economic power elite of West Germany is a heterogeneous body, including chief executives of large corporations, leading officials of business associations, and leading trade-union officers. None of these groups can by itself decide what course the West German economy should take, nor are the three of them the only economic decisionmakers of national importance. Both the federal government and the governments of the eleven states forming the Federal Republic are continuously involved in economic policy. Although they do not interfere directly with the decision-making process of corporations, they do so indirectly by elaborating and altering the sociopolitical framework within which economic activity takes place. To a lesser degree this is also the case for the supranational authorities of the European Economic Community (EEC or the Common Market) – an integral component of top business in West Germany and part of the nexus of corporate management.

The structure of the West German economic power elite is probably much like that of other advanced industrial countries that combine capitalist economics with democratic politics. There is a state of tension between top management and trade unions and between the capitalist economy and the welfare state, but this tension has not upset a relatively stable balance. The strife and mutual criticism that exist among management, labor, and the state have so far not threatened the functioning and the legitimacy of the country's present economic and political system.

The management sector on which I am focusing includes solely chief executives of top rank in large corporations (*Mitglieder des Vorstands* – the German equivalent to president and vice president). In the category 'large corporation' I include those considered the fifty largest in the country (1970).[2]

In West Germany the top management of large corporations is virtually an all male affair. There are almost no women in this stratum of the economic power elite. Women who head independent enterprises do not belong to this elite, since their firms are too small to wield influence on a national or even a regional level. In 1970 women made up some 15 per cent of independent 'entrepreneurs,' the vast majority of them being located in small businesses with ten employees or less (Hartmann, 1968; Roesch, 1970). There is thus a female profile that parallels that of other sections of the occupational world; the larger the firms, the less likely they are to have women at top levels.

The majority of large corporations are private in that their capital is held by private individuals or institutions. Most of these have sufficiently large numbers of shareholders to guarantee management control instead of owner control. In that sense, but in that sense only, they are 'public' corporations.[3]

Women do not fare better in other types of 'public' companies, as in those in which the capital is held by the federal government (*Bund*), a provincial state (*Länder*), or a local community (*Gemeinden*). On the whole the state at all levels – *Bund, Länder* and *Gemeinden* – is the largest owner and entrepreneur in the country, controlling a huge number of firms. The biggest of these are the railroads (*Bundesbahn*) and the postal services (*Bundespost*), including telephone and telegraph. Neither railroads nor postal services are part of the market economy system, decisions on investments and prices being made by political bodies. Both federal government and state governments are the sole or the major capital holders of large market-oriented corporations, the most famous being *Volkswagenwerk*. In none of these units, whether market oriented or not, does a woman serve on the executive committee. The state as capital owner and controlling body acts in the same way as private business in the appointment of women to high office.

There is only one exception to this general policy of total exclusion of women from government-controlled businesses – the appointment of a woman as president of a state reserve bank (*Landeszentralbank*). Ironically, the appointment was made by a conservative government – the Christian Democratic Union (CDU) government of Lower Saxony (*Niedersachsen*) early in 1976.

Trade unions should also be examined with regard to the entry of women. In West Germany trade unions act not only in their traditional social and political functions but also as entrepreneurs. They own and control one of the major banks (*Bank für Gemeinwirtschaft*), one of the largest housing companies, a major chain of food stores, and a vast number of printing firms, publishing houses, and newspapers. All these enterprises operate like those owned privately with the market system. None of them has had a woman among its top executives. Exclusion of women passes class boundaries and other antagonisms as well.

However, in their role as representatives of labor, trade unions do act somewhat differently from corporations. Practically each of them has at least one woman on its executive committee, and so has the German Federation of Trade Unions (*Deutscher Gewerkschaftsbund*). Furthermore, the German Federation of Trade Unions has elaborate programs for improving the situation of working women and in recent years has become more active in having these programs executed. Whatever initiative there has been in this area, credit for it goes almost exclusively to the activity of women within the unions. With few exceptions men of all ranks do not include women in their demands for more self-determination and codetermination (Lossef-Tillmanns, 1975).

A few decades ago the absence of women from top management in large corporations, whether private or under state or trade union control, might have been taken for granted. Today, however, it can no longer be thus regarded. In fact, aside from the Protestant and Roman Catholic Churches in West Germany, large corporations are the only occupational hierarchies with practically no women at their head. There are female minorities of varying size in top positions in academia (including an occasional university president), in the judiciary, and in the mass media. There is at least one woman on the executive committee of each major political party, and several serve in the federal and state governments as ministers and state secretaries. Women form a 6 per cent minority in the federal Parliament (*Deutscher Bundestag*). Thus, women in elite positions are not as unheard of as they used to be during the Nazi period (1933–45) or before that in the more equality-minded Weimar Republic (1919–33). Despite this, and despite the fact that most men have declared via a public opinion poll (Pross, 1978) that they would be willing to accept women in positions of economic leadership, very few women have so far been admitted to those ranks.

Why this is so is by no means clear. Undoubtedly, the unique situation of top management as compared to other elites cannot be attributed to just one cause. It is curious that not even social scientists in West Germany have so far analyzed this phenomenon.

The exclusion of women from economic elites seems to be consistent regardless of their role in different political systems and related standing in political elites. The comparison of women in East and West Germany is interesting, because there are almost no women in prominent economic leadership positions in socialist East Germany also. This is particularly notable, since the percentage of women in the highest echelons of East German government and the Communist Party is larger than it is in West German government and political parties (Herber and Kung, 1968, p. 267; Pross, 1973, pp. 137–63; Helwig, 1975). To a certain extent the picture seems similar in the Soviet Union. As far as figures are available there, they suggest that the percentage of female heads of large combines, and of various ministries of economics and industry, is much smaller than in other occupational and political sectors (Dodge, 1966; Ahlberg, 1969; Revesz, 1970). Poland and other countries of socialist eastern Europe follow the same pattern (Sokołowska, 1973). The representation of women in top management jobs has also been extremely small or non-existent in most, if not all, industrial countries of the West.[4]

Thus, it seems that two patterns dominate: the complete exclusion of women from the ranks of top management, and the discrepancy between their ability to penetrate other power elite positions and their actual presence in them.

The interesting question is not why there are fewer women in leading economic positions than in other professional elites. This difference can probably be explained by more women being attracted by the professions or finding opportunity to work in them because of a long tradition of their participation in them; in some instances their presence is linked to traditional views of feminine qualifications (e.g. medicine and education). The fascinating issue is the difference between female representation in positions of *political* power and that in positions of *economic* power.

In contrast to the normative structure of political organizations, values guiding West German corporations do not include the notion of equality between the sexes. There is no tradition demanding the representation of both men and women – much less their equality – in decision-making positions. Whereas political parties, parliaments, and governments are almost constantly under attack today for having too few women at top levels, corporations are not. These challenges may not be very successful for the moment; but if they continue, they are likely to have effects in the future. Political bodies are accountable to their operational political values, which include equal opportunities and participation for men and women. Economic elites, in contrast, are more likely to be judged in terms of production or goal values. As long as the general public perceives the national economy as achieving what it is meant to (i.e. growing standards of living, full employment, and decent work conditions, however the last may be defined), pressure on its leaders to comply with such moral or social values as equality of the sexes is likely to be weak or even absent. In fact there has been no such pressure up to the present time in West Germany. There has been some concentration on obtaining equal pay for men and women, on improving opportunities for women to enter the ranks of middle management, and on increasing options for further training on the job, but nobody has demanded that corporations, like political bodies, should bring more women into their highest ranks.

No known major organization, probably not even informal groups, are making such demands. Even outspoken critics of the capitalist economy in recent years have not pointed to the male monopoly on top management jobs. With the norms of equality not applied to corporation management there can be no discrepancy between norm and reality – no tensions promoting even a verbal protest that might bring about change.

It is difficult to explain this absence of norms of equality for the sexes within the corporate realm, and I know of no attempt to do so. As far as West Germany is concerned, I believe specific national traditions to be decisive. Democratic movements in modern West German history have had mainly three aims: political democracy as an aim of the state, human rights, and protection for the socially weak. From its very beginnings the major democratic political organization – the Social Democratic Party (SPD) – favored welfare programs more strongly and principles of philosophic individualism less strongly. Collective action and class solidarity ranked higher than ideas of individual mobility and individual self-realization. Thus, ideas of equal opportunity for all human beings, regardless of class, religion, or sex, were never very popular. They have become so only within the 1960s and 1970s but are as yet restricted to the sector of education. It may be a matter of time for the programs of equal opportunity to expand to other sectors and finally to find a place in the economic sphere. Up to now they have not done so.

To a certain extent it is also true that there is virtually no pool of women within large corporations who aspire to get to the top. This is probably because prevailing structures weigh so heavily on qualified women that they resign before even trying to get ahead. The facts of corporate life militate against the mere idea of opposing them.

Male chief executives do not possess attributes necessarily limited to one sex. Studies on managerial careers do not suggest that there are qualification demands that can be considered specifically male, like those of the military or the Roman Catholic Church.[5] Fragmentary as the data are, they leave little doubt that careers in industry, no matter what its type of ownership, have become semibureaucratized. Most chief executives get to the top the hard way, starting at the level of middle management in the same firm that they will eventually head after some twenty years. Most of them have academic degrees, mainly in law, engineering, or economics. Most were born to upper middle class or middle class families and almost none to working class families. Very few have been heirs to fortunes. Yet, many women share these backgrounds. The middle class and upper middle class also send their daughters to universities; and since many women have graduated from law and business schools in recent decades, questions of social origin or lack of academic qualifications cannot be a major explanation for this sex difference. It cannot be attributed to the peculiarities of the average female working career either. Most women quit their jobs after the birth of their first child and stay at home for ten to fifteen years. But there are also large numbers of women, now in the middle of their lives, who have never married and have no children. In fact this subset of the current generation of West German women can be considered a sort of control group. The women whom I have in mind are those whose husbands or fiancées were killed in war or in concentration camps. Many of them work as employees in large firms. Many of them are devoted to their jobs, not having families of their own to claim a share of their attention. Having been in gainful employment for some twenty or thirty years, it is likely that they will continue thus until retirement age. To be sure, many of these women had pursued a limited education while they were young. However, a substantial minority of this group did acquire training and the experience that could qualify them for managerial positions. Undoubtedly, it would have been easy to find among them highly competent persons who were no less qualified for top positions than were men. However, they were never encouraged to compete for such posts. During the years of postwar economic reconstruction in West Germany corporations were always looking for talented personnel, particularly to fill leadership roles. They had to do so in order to get the economy going again and to regain a strong position in the world market. However, this search was never extended to women. It simply did not occur to employers that it might be useful to have women in the upper ranks, and it did not occur to women either that they might assert themselves as candidates. Prevailing ideologies of the female nature and its inappropriateness for leadership activity were at work in women's exclusion from executive ranks. Although male top management was not completely responsible for barring women from like positions, its attitude produced a deleterious effect. When asked early in the 1960s if they believed that a woman could achieve as much as they did (*'Meinen Sie, dass an Ihrer Stelle eine Frau das gleiche leisten könnte?'*), 94 per cent of seventy-one corporate presidents and vice presidents replied in the negative (Pross and Boetticher, 1971, p. 104).

However, there have been some changes in norms in West German society. Although the underlying antifeminist convictions may remain unaltered, it is now out of fashion to express them verbally and frankly in public. It is still too early to tell whether behavioral changes will follow.

To summarize, there are explanations as to why only a handful of women have reached top management positions in large corporations. In my view these explanations are chiefly ideological. The ideologies are strong and constitute almost insurmountable barriers to women. To the extent that women share them with men they may constitute 'false consciousness.' These ideologies still strongly influence primary and secondary socialization, the life goals of men and women, and attitudes toward qualified women. They make for a kind of innocence on the part of employers in general and of top management in particular, granting them a clear conscience while they discourage women's attempts to advance themselves.

As yet this view is unshaken in West Germany as far as top management is concerned. However, as the political success of student movements of the 1960s has shown, power elites in West Germany have not proved to be as rigid in their outlooks and prejudices as their leftists critics believed. Once under heavy attack they conceded to programs of reform aimed at more equality of opportunities for all classes and at more equal distribution of decision-making power.

But comparable progress on the part of women's groups has been comparatively slow. There is no politically relevant feminist movement, and the few feminist groups that exist tend to isolate themselves from politics. Should this change, I am sure women would also improve their chances to reach the top of large corporations in West Germany. At present such changes are not in sight.

NOTES

(1) For exact figures, see *Zwischenbericht der Enquête-Kommission Frau und Gesellschaft des Deutschen Bundestags* (1976, pp. 36–8).
(2) For a list of the twenty-five largest West German industrial corporations, see Ermrich (1974, p. 158).
(3) For terminology I follow here the classic study of Berle and Means (1956). For estimates, see Pross (1965).
(4) See, for example, Shell Italiana (1973), Held and Levy (1974), and Bundeskanzleramt (1975).
(5) See Zapf (1965), especially the chapter on social profiles and career patterns of top West German managers; Hartmann and Wienold (1967); Pross and Boetticher (1971); Hartmann, Bock-Rosenthal, and Helmer (1973); Witte and Bronner (1974); and Pippke (1975).

REFERENCES

Ahlberg, René (1969) *Soziologie in der Sowjetunion: Ausgewählte sowjetische Abhandlungen zu Problemen der sozialistischen Gesellschaft* (Freiburg: Rombach Verlag).
Berle, Adolf and Means, Gardiner C. (1956) *The Modern Corporation and Private Property* (New York: Macmillan).
Bundeskanzleramt (1975) *Bericht über die Situation der Frau in Österreich: Frauenbericht, 1975* (Vienna: Österreichische Staatsdruckerei).
Dodge, Norton T. (1966) *Women in the Soviet Economy: Their Role in Economic, Scientific and Technical Development* (Baltimore: Johns Hopkins Press).
Ermrich, Roland (1974) *Basisdaten: Zahlen zur sozio-ökonomischen Entwicklung der Bundesrepublik Deutschland* (Bonn-Bad Godesberg: Verlag Neue Gesellschaft).
Hartmann, Heinz (1968) *Die Unternehmerin: Selbstverständnis und soziale Rolle* (Cologne and Opladen: Westdeutscher Verlag).
Hartmann, Heinz, Bock-Rosenthal, Erika and Helmer, Elvira (1973) *Leitende Angestellte: Selbstverständnis und kollektive Forderungen: Ergebnisse einer empirischen Untersuchung* (Neuwied and Berlin: Luchterhand Verlag).
Hartmann, Heinz and Wienold, Hanns (1967) *Universität und Unternehmer* (Gütersloh: C. Bertelsmann Verlag).
Held, Thomas and Levy, René (1974) *Die Stellung der Frau in Familie und Gesellschaft: Eine soziologische Analyse am Beispiel der Schweiz* (Frauenfeld and Stuttgart: Verlag Huber).
Helwig, Gisela (1975) *Frau '75: Bundesrepublik Deutschland – DDR* (Cologne: Verlag Wissenschaft und Politik).
Herber, Richard and Kung, Herbert (1968) *Kaderarbeit im System sozialistischer Führungstätigkeit* (East Berlin: Staatsverlag der Deutschen Demokratischen Republik).
Horvat, B. (1972) *Die jugoslawische Gesellschaft* (Frankfurt/M: Suhrkamp Verlag).
Losseff-Tillmanns, Gisela (1975) 'Frauenemanzipation und Gewerkschaften (1800–1975)', Diss. Bochum.
Pippke, Wolfgang (1975) *Karrieredeterminanten in der öffentlichen Verwaltung: Hierarchiebedingte Arbeitsanforderungen und Beförderungspraxis im höheren Dienst* (Baden-Baden: Nomos Verlagsgesellschaft).

Pross, Helge (1965) *Manager und Aktionäre in Deutschland: Untersuchungen zum Verhältnis von Eigentum und Verfügungsmacht* (Frankfurt/M: Europäische Verlagsanstalt).

Pross, Helge (1973) *Gleichberechtigung im Beruf? Eine Untersuchung mit 7,000 Arbeitnehmerinnen in der EWG* (Frankfurt/M: Athenäum Verlag).

Pross, Helge (1978) *Die Männer: Eine repräsentative Untrsuchung über die Selbstbilder von Männern und ihre Bilder von der Frau* (Reinbek: Rowohlt Verlag).

Pross, Helge and Boetticher, Karl W. (1971) *Manager des Kapitalismus: Untersuchung über leitende Angestellte in Großunternehmen* (Frankfurt/M: Suhrkamp Verlag).

Revesz, Laszlo (1969) *Die Frau im Sowjetreich: Reihe Tatsachen und Meinungen* (Bern: Schweizerisches Ost-Institut, Verlag SOI Bern).

Roesch, Hans (1970) *Das dritte Talent: Die Leistung der Frau als Unternehmerin–gestern heute, morgen* (Berlin, Frankfurt/M, and Vienna: Ullstein Verlag).

Roggemann, H. (1970)*Das Modell der Arbeiterselbstverwaltung in Jugoslawien* (Frankfurt/M: Suhrkamp Verlag).

Shell Italiana (1973) *La Donna Oggi in Italia: Inchiesta nazionale sui problemi della condizione femminile e sul ruolo della donna nella nostra societé*, Inchiesta Shell N. 10 (Copyright Shell Italiana, Genova).

Sokołowska, Magdalena (1973) *Frauenemanzipation und Sozialismus: Das Beispiel der Volksrepublic Polen* (Reinbek: Rowohlt Verlag).

Statistisches Bundesamt (1975) *Die Frau in Familie, Beruf und Gesellschaft* (Wiesbaden/ Mainz: Verlag W. Kohlhammer).

Witte, Eberhard and Bronner, Rolf (1974) *Die leitenden Angestellten: Eine empirische Untersuchung* (Munich: Verlag C. H. Beck).

Zapf, Wolfgang (ed.) (1965) *Beiträge zur Analyse der deutschen Oberschicht* (Munich: Verlag R. Piper).

Zwischenbericht der Enquête-Kommission 'Frau und Gesellschaft' des Deutschen Bundestags (1976) (Bonn-Bad Godesberg: Bonner Universitätsdruckerei, Bundestagsdrucksache No. 7/5866).

15

Public Bureaucracy and Private Enterprise in the USA and France:

Contexts for the Attainment of Executive Positions by Women*

CATHERINE BODARD SILVER

An important insight into the positions that are available to women derives from an analysis of the historical development of large scale organizations in both the public and the private sectors. In the Western world structures of employment, broadly speaking, take two forms: those located in public bureaucracies linked to government, and those located in firms and enterprises committed to profit-seeking in competitive or administered market contexts. This paper examines whether these two structures of employment in modern Western societies differ in the opportunity that they offer women for attaining leadership positions.

Historically, the public and private sectors have differed with respect to organizational principles, modes of recruitment and promotion, values, and objectives. Employment in public bureaucracies has been rooted in the merit system as expressed through competitive recruitment based on explicitly universalistic criteria, which has often taken the form of a national examination and competition for positions in the civil service. The public sector has also developed lifelong career structures with well-defined systems of rank, articulated seniority ladders, and distinctive pension arrangements. Market-based and profit-seeking enterprises, in contrast, have recruited and promoted employees according to criteria of productivity and risk-taking and have emphasized the career biography of the individual – including the type of college attended, the type of firm worked for, and previous training and experience – more than elaborate objectified structures of administration and promotion. Furthermore organizational expansion and career opportunities tend to reflect organizational performance (e.g. earnings) in the private sector but political decisions and the political climate in the public sector.

Differences between the public and private sectors have narrowed since the Second World War and will narrow increasingly in the future. This convergence of the two sectors is due to the emergence of mixed economies,

* I want to thank Paul Montagna and Lilly Hoffman for their critical reading of an earlier draft of this paper, and the MacDowell Colony for the precious gift of time with which this essay was written.

This research was made possible by a grant from the Research Foundation of the City University of New York and by a fellowship from the German Marshall Fund of the United States.

administered capitalism – as in France, where the state monitors a large part of the capitalist sector – and the growing similarity of organizational imperatives in large scale enterprises, whether profit oriented or governmental. These organizational imperatives have in both sectors led to the use of accounting and research departments and in general to executive planning and greater rationality and efficiency. Large corporations are increasingly concerned with goals that encompass collective interests and that cannot be understood only in terms of profit maximization. Within the public sector there are trends toward cost minimization; and nationalized industries are increasingly committed to profit-seeking, or at least to the avoidance of losses according to market criteria (e.g. the British Broadcasting Corporation in Britain, Renault in France, the Postal Service in the United States).

The features that distinguish the public and private sectors seem to be especially important for analyzing the situation of executives and high level administrators. Although it may be argued that the differences in earnings and job security for a secretary or a low level technician between the two sectors are rather small, such differences among managers and executives are much more significant. Decision-making involving financial risk, for example, tends to be characteristic of executives in the private sector but not of those in the public sector – a fact reflected in their earnings differentials. The quasi-absolute job security among executives in the public sector, for another example, has no equivalent in the private sector, where executives are under constant pressure to be successful in entrepreneurial, managerial, or financial endeavors.

My thesis is that women are most likely to attain managerial and executive positions in a context characterized by the use of universalistic employment criteria, a commitment to the pursuit of equality, and an organizational setting that emphasizes rationality and efficiency without an exclusive commitment to profit-making. A partial test of this thesis will be carried out through a comparison of women in managerial and executive positions in the private and public sectors in the United States and France.

In the terms outlined above these two countries have historically represented strong contrasts within the spectrum of Western industrialized nations. The United States, historically oriented toward private enterprise both in its institutions and in its values, was slow to develop notions of extensive public bureaucracy and slower still to express these notions in terms of high prestige and career rewards. The vast expansion of public bureaucracies since the New Deal and the Second World War has not yet been fully legitimized by corresponding notions of respect for public service. France, in contrast, has the oldest continuous system of public administration in the West – one that since the nineteenth century has ranked high in prestige and honor and has embodied key values of bourgeois society. Through a distinctive set of advanced educational institutions French bureaucracy has conspicuously recruited an intellectual elite with training in both substantive and administrative skills.

France and the United States reveal divergent trends with respect to the position of women in executive positions in the public and private sectors. Between 1950 and 1970 – the decades between the stabilization of the postwar world and the growing impact of the Women's Movement – there was in both France and the United States a stagnation or decline of female representation in executive positions in the public and private sectors, together with an increase in female professional, middle-management (*cadres moyens*), and technical personnel (i.e. in positions below the executive level). The stagnation or decrease in the proportion of women in executive ranks, however, was greater in the *private sector* in the United States but in the *public sector* in France.[1] In each country, that is, women during the postwar period failed to achieve gains within the sector that was historically the more dynamic and prestigious one. The situation has been changing somewhat since 1970, due to broad market and organizational trends as well as to political pressures and such legislative measures as affirmative action in the United States and administrative guidelines in France.[2] Limitations in available data, however, make broad assessments difficult for the very recent period.

This paper will focus on what Fogarty *et al.* have called the 'entrepreneurial bureaucrats' (i.e. women in executive or managerial positions working in private or public enterprises, excluding independent entrepreneurs or professionals).

THE CASE OF THE UNITED STATES

The rapid increase in the 1960s and 1970s in the number of women entering such male-dominated occupations as law, medicine, and engineering contrasts with the slow increase in the number of women executives and managers (Epstein, 1975, p. 9). The proportion of managers who were women dropped from 5·5 per cent in 1950 to 4·2 per cent in 1969 (Larwood and Wood, 1977, p. 16). This decline in the percentage of female managers, however, was not characteristic of all industries.[3] In manufacturing there was stagnation in the percentage of managers who were women, the proportion going from 5·9 per cent in 1950 to 6·7 per cent in 1960 and only 6·6 per cent in 1970. In banking and credit the proportion of managers who were women increased from 12·9 per cent in 1950 to 13·4 per cent in 1960 and 20·0 per cent in 1970. However, women managers still represented a small proportion of all female workers. An analysis by industry shows that in 1970 the ratio of female to male managers was the smallest in banking and manufacturing and the largest in professional and related services, as Table 15.1 shows.

This observation seems to corroborate a study that found that top jobs in 'women's industries' were more likely to go to women than were similar positions in durable goods industries (Shepherd and Levin, 1973). The lack of specification of census categorization, and of information on job characteristics, makes it imperative to consider additional information based on surveys and case studies, especially when studying women managers, who represent a very small group of the total population.

There are several studies of women in executive–management roles in banking and business in the United States that afford some clues to the stagnation of women at top levels of management. The case of banking is a good illustration of this state of affairs. In 1963 there were 168 women bank

Table 15.1 *Proportion of managers by industry and sex, 1970.*

Industry	(1) Female managers as % of all females in the industry	(2) Male managers as % of all males in the industry	Ratio (1)/(2)
Manufacturing	1·2	6·8	0·176
Banking and credit agencies	6·8	46·5	0·146
Personal services	2·5	12·7	0·196
Professional and related services	2·2	7·8	0·282

Source: US Department of Commerce, 1972.

presidents and 688 women vice presidents of banks, but ten years later there were only 40 and 400 women respectively in such positions (Archibald, 1973, p.28). A study of seven New York City banks in 1973 by the National Association of Bank Women found an increase during the previous decade in the number of women in junior positions but a decrease among senior women officers from 2 to 1 per cent of all bank officers (Steichen, 1973) – a small but meaningful reduction. This reduction of women in senior positions becomes especially striking in light of the fact that during the same time period the number of banks increased from 13,570 to 14,171 (Federal Reserve System, Inc., 1976a, 1976b).

In the United States the participation of women in very large firms did not increase at the executive level between 1966 and 1970. A study of the 200 largest industrial enterprises has shown that 1·5 per cent of officers and managers were women in 1966, compared to 1·4 per cent in 1970. The national average of executives who were women in the private sector in general was 9·2 per cent and 10 per cent respectively in 1966 and 1970 (Shepherd and Levin, 1973, p. 415). Until recently women have been more likely to achieve executive positions in smaller firms – a tendency that is true also in France. A study of 2,000 executives across the United States, half of them women, has shown that women executives are more likely by far than their male counterparts to work for small companies; 50 per cent of women executives but only 13 per cent of male executives were in firms with fewer than fifty workers. Among firms with up to 250 workers, still considered small by the authors of the study, the respective percentages were 76 and 30 (Bowman, Worthy, and Greyser, 1965).

The study by Fogarty *et al.* (1971) has also shown that women find it easier to reach management levels in small rather than large firms. However, another study of women managers in ninety-eight large and sixty-five small companies has shown that larger firms are more likely than smaller ones to have women managers. The study suggests that larger firms provide a more favorable climate to women's advancement to high managerial positions, without, however, specifying these conditions (Killiam, 1971, pp. 8–9).

These seemingly contradictory results reflect different definitions of what size of company is considered large or small.[4] A more elaborate distinction may clarify this picture. A study of women in management that divided the companies studied into small, medium, and large has shown that medium size companies offer the greatest opportunity to women managers and professionals (Johnston, 1974).[5] Another study of 174 women managers using the same breakdown among size of companies found that 36·2 per cent of the respondents were located in small enterprises, compared with 50 per cent in medium size ones and 6·3 per cent in large ones (Crawford, 1977, p. 42). Finally, another study, which included a variety of firms, 25 per cent of which were large (including multinational) corporations, has shown that women managers are more likely to be found in small to middle size firms (Burrow, 1976; see Table 15.2).

Table 15.2 *Distribution of women managers by size of organization.*

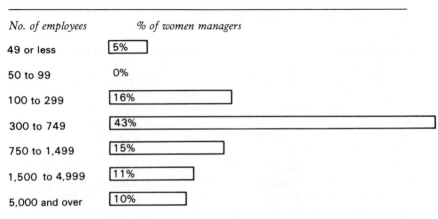

No. of employees	% of women managers
49 or less	5%
50 to 99	0%
100 to 299	16%
300 to 749	43%
750 to 1,499	15%
1,500 to 4,999	11%
5,000 and over	10%

Source: Burrow (1976), p. 11.

It may be difficult to evaluate the role of the size of firms in determining women's chances to attain high level positions, although it seems that 'medium' size firms exhibit organizational features that facilitate the integration of women into the organization and their ability to reach high management levels. 'Medium' size firms seem less particularistic, more amenable to legislative supervision, and less concerned with purely capitalist motives in the management of the firm than small firms or very large ones.

A trend toward greater female participation in larger firms would be consistent with what is known about organizations. Larger firms are in many respects more consistently administered than smaller ones and are more amenable to control by administrative agencies. Their greater managerial sophistication may enable them to respond to such pressures, willingly or not. Larger enterprises tend to have higher growth rates, creating a larger supply of new positions or requiring higher proportions of the newer types of technically trained business executives. At the same time employment in such firms usually means greater career stability and higher salaries. From the perspective of dual labor-market theory the position of women manager-executives seems to be analogous to that of lower level workers; that is, large organizations offer better and sometimes more egalitarian conditions for their workforce than smaller firms, which are more exposed to competitive pressures of the classical market type.[6] Only a study of women managers that took into account the size of the firm and the type of industry would specify the conditions under which women were more likely to reach top managerial levels. The emergence of women executives is not necessarily in response to a society-wide movement for increased egalitarianism; it may be a response to their growing presence in less discriminatory larger firms, although the larger social movement, especially in the Women's Movement, may unwittingly contribute to a change in this direction.

It appears that a major obstacle to the attainment of executive positions by women is the objection on the part of management to giving them responsibilities involving investment decisions or the power to make or influence decisions involving financial risk – choices that are at the heart of capitalist undertakings. Among bank managers, for example women are rarely found in departments dealing with loans and investments (i.e. with financial affairs that generate profits). They do have access to the administration of bank budgets, extending into banking the tradition of the feminine administration of family budgets.

The fact that women are seldom found in positions of decision-making involving high financial risks also illustrates a pattern in which women are more likely to obtain jobs that are defined in terms of 'replaceability' than jobs to which they are to be totally committed (Coser and Rokoff, 1971). The proportion of women in charge of actually preparing budgets is much higher in foundations and other non-profit organizations than in large businesses. Many more women sit on boards allocating funds for research and philanthropy than on corporate boards. 'There appears to be less reluctance to allowing female managers to be responsible for public or donated funds, than is found in private enterprises protecting profit-making' (Burrow, 1976, p. 15). It seems that the historic priority awarded to profit-based enterprises in the United States is clearly reflected in the low level of female executive participation in the private sector. Another possible reason for the stagnation of women in executive positions is the fact that male jobs are typically on a career ladder leading to management, whereas beginning female jobs are not (Robie, 1973, p. 10). Furthermore, women often become assistant executives rather than executives, even though they may have the qualifications and responsibilities of executives. Responsibilities may be increased without changing the job title (Rosenberg, 1976, p. 11).

Working in the other direction (i.e. toward greater inclusion of women in executive positions) is the professionalization of business. Several of the studies show an increase in the proportion of women *professionals* during the very period when women's presence among *executives* was decreasing or unchanging. Nationally, 13·0 per cent of professionals were women in 1960; this figure increased to 13·8 per cent in 1969 and 15·6 per cent in 1974 (US Department of Labor, 1975, p. 297). If the frequently described 'professionalization of business' is anything other than a metaphor, the increased demand for formal certification for business careers may well work in favor of women, particularly given the sharp rise in the proportion of women among those receiving degrees in business studies, which doubled between 1973 and 1975. Earlier patterns of women's presence at higher levels in business were quite different. Women on corporate boards were frequently relatives of company founders or presidents (Darling, 1975). Of the 202 women directors in 329 major corporations in 1968, more than two-thirds held the title only, without holding a position in the firm or elsewhere in the corporate world. Since 1972, however, there has been a considerable increase in the number of women on boards of directors who are functionally involved with the respective firms ('More women move into the boardroom,' 1976, p. 26). This 'professionalization' of business may thus work in favor of increased representation of women. As suggested earlier, the structure of corporate enterprise may be converging with that of public bureaucracy, in that technical and certified qualifications, as distinct from success in entrepreneurial activity, are becoming increasingly important for promotion to higher levels. If this is so, the striking increase of enrollment of women in schools of business may be the key to the future. At the Graduate School of Business of Columbia University, for example, the proportion of women students in 1968, 1973, and 1975 went from 5 per cent (32 women out of a class of 650) to 20 per cent (100 women out of a class of 500) to 33 per cent (206 women out of a class of 625) (from an interview with the school's director of admissions). The fuller implications of these developments, however, depend upon a detailed understanding of the interplay of technical qualifications and entrepreneurial–managerial factors in affecting business careers and the selection of executives at the very highest levels. Without such information we cannot judge whether the surge of women into the graduate schools of business indicates the emergence of a new class of executives or the development of new classes of skilled, but essentially routinized, functionaries in modern corporate enterprises that correspond to their counterparts in the public bureaucracies. Although it may be argued that in the latter case the entry of women may have few implications for decision-making power of a distinctively capitalist kind (i.e. influence over budgets and risk-taking), it must be added that their sheer visibility in middle management positions may create pressure for their further promotion and recruitment to higher levels.

The sharp increase in the number of women students in graduate business schools also converges with structural changes within business organizations. Although one may not agree with the argument that profit maximization has lost its importance in the conduct of large scale business, one can accept the notion that under complex technical and bureaucratic conditions the goal of profit no longer permeates the organization and the ethos of the private sector as thoroughly as in earlier periods. Furthermore, the sheer complexity of the modern business enterprise, combined with the emergence of social and collective goals not purely oriented toward short-term profit maximization and with new values among the young in the 1970s, may promote more collegial, collaborative, and even expressive non-instrumental forms of work and administration, creating greater receptivity for women (DiMarco and Whitsitt, 1975, p. 194; Giele, 1974).

Finally, an increased reliance on political pressure, legislative action, and government policy is more likely to be effective in promoting women to executive positions in contexts characterized by extensive planning, greater rationality, and efficiency in work organization, which have become permanent features of all large-scale enterprises. These features lend more visibility to the firm, creating the conditions that allow easier and more efficient control and scrutiny by public authorities.

The factors discussed above – an increase in the enrollment of women in business school; the 'professionalization' of business elites; structural changes, especially the growing importance of a bureaucratic sector in private enterprises, together with the emergence of a new work ethic and work styles; and finally, policies and legislative measures promoting sexual equality – have recently converged in facilitating the promotion of women to executive decision-making positions in private enterprises. This has happened especially in the largest and most bureaucratized enterprises, but at the same time it has strengthened women's traditional, more routinized, and less prestigious positions in middle management.

In the public sector – in what is referred to as public administration, including federal, state, and local governments – women managers and administrators have found greater opportunities in both the middle and the upper levels than in the private sector (Burrow, 1976, p. 10). The proportion of managers who were women was significantly higher in the public than in the private sector in 1970; in the former they made up 20·4 per cent. However, there had been little change between 1950 and 1970 (US Department of Commerce, 1973).

The proportions of female managers in the different sectors of public employment vary greatly, as Table 15.3 shows. In 1960 women managers and administrators in public employment seem to be at an advantage only at local levels, which are the least prestigious and visible positions in the public sector. By 1970 the picture had changed dramatically. While the proportion of male managers at all levels is at least twice as high as those of the female, women managers became equally distributed at all levels. The greatest gain had taken place in the Federal sector, among women professionals. All the other groups had experienced losses due either to transfers from the public to the private sectors, or reduction of public expenditure.[7]

Table 15.3   *Proportion of managers by public employment sector and by sex, 1960.*

Sector	(1) Female managers as % of total female employment in sector	(2) Male managers as % of total male employment in sector	Ratio (1)/(2)
Federal	2·26	11·47	0·197
State	3·82	18·15	9·210
Local	10·86	12·19	0·890

Source: US Department of Commerce (1972, 1973).

Among white-collar federal employees, excluding those in the military, there was a greater increase in women than in men in the upper grades (GS-13 and above) between 1967 and 1972; the increase in the upper grades was 40·5 per cent for women and 23·3 per cent for men (US Department of Labor, 1973, p. 115–8). Nevertheless, the overall proportion of women in the civil service in these grades remained small in this period, being 3·7 per cent in 1967 and 4·2 per cent in 1972 (US Civil Service Commission, 1973, pp. 4–6). It is important to note that there has been little change in government at the 'supergrade levels' (GS-17 and above), where salaries ranged from $36,000 to $40,000 in 1970. In 1959 there were eighteen women (1·2 per cent) and 1,500 men in the supergrades, and in 1972 there were sixty-five women (1·6 per cent) and 4,055 men there (US Civil Service Commission, 1972a, pp. 4–6). These levels in the federal civil service are highly influential in the administration of policy and in some instances in taking policy initiatives, but they are relatively invisible compared to appointments at the Cabinet, subcabinet, and judicial levels, at which there are even fewer women appointees.

Without going into detail, it is important to note that the same pattern of change is found among women managers and administrators in state and local governments, with the difference that these settings offer much greater opportunity to women in high grades. In 1972, at grade levels GS-13 to 16 or the equivalent, which corresponded to a salary between $16,000 and $24,000, 10 per cent of employees were women at the state and local levels, compared to 3 per cent at the federal level; for males the equivalent figures were 25 per cent and 36·2 per cent respectively. At these levels the pattern for males seems to be the reverse of the female pattern (US Civil Service Commission, 1972a, p. 4; Equal Employment Opportunity Commission, 1973 Vol. 1, p. 1). As in politics, the male arena is more likely to be national, whereas the female arena is more likely to be local.

The public sector has traditionally offered greater opportunity to women managers than the private sector and may continue to do so in the future. However, recent changes in the private sector may have started to reverse the situation. The Equal Pay Act of 1963, Title VII of the Civil Rights Act of 1964, Executive Order 11246, as amended by Executive Order 11375, Title IX of the Education Amendments of 1972, Title VIII of the Civil Rights Act of 1968, as amended, and the Equal Credit Opportunity Act of 1974 all converge toward promoting equal opportunity and equal promotion for women in all ranks.[9] The impact of these administrative and legislative measures certainly accounts in part for the changes in women's position in the economy, although no evaluation of the impact of affirmative action exists. It seems that in the future the impact of governmental guidelines and lawsuits in promoting greater equality between the sexes, combined with concerns for greater rationality and efficiency and new organizational imperatives in the private sector, may create a context that provides women managers with greater challenges and rewards than the public sector.

THE CASE OF FRANCE

There has been a near stagnation in France in the number of women executives in the public sector. In contrast, the private sector has shown a steady increase from a miniscule to a minute level: from 0·3 per cent of all female employees in 1954, to 0·4 per cent in 1962, 2·4 per cent in 1968, and 3·5 per cent in 1974. For men the comparable figures were 5·6 per cent and 7·3 per cent in 1968 and 1974 respectively (Ministère du Travail, Comité du Travail Féminin, 1975a, p. 1). The rate of increase of women in middle management has been much greater, going from 1·4 per cent in 1968 to 14·8 per cent in 1974 (*Le Monde*, April 2, 1976) – a pattern similar to that of the United States.

Women managers are not equally distributed among industries. They are more likely to be found in professional and administrative activities (21·2 per cent in 1972), commerce (21·9 per cent), banking and insurance (10·1 per cent), transport (4·0 per cent), and chemical industries (4·0 per cent). At the other extreme they are barely represented in such industries as textiles (1·6 per cent), leather (0·8 per cent), glass (0·2 per cent), paper (0·9 per cent), and, of course, heavy industries and manufacturing. These sectors represent the older and craftlike industries, which are characterized by older technologies and lack of administrative sophistication. They are usually smaller and often the least competitive. Women's access to management is more likely to occur in newer industries or in banking and insurance, which represent two dynamic and modern sectors of the economy.

Table 15.4   *Proportions of male and female managers in the private and public sectors, 1954 and 1962.*

| | Private sector | | Public sector | |
Year	Female managers as % of all females (%) (No.)	Male managers as % of all males (%) (No.)	Female managers as % of all females (%) (No.)	Male managers as % of all males (%) (No.)
1954	0·2 (11,829)	0·9 (111,830)	0·2 (11,986)	1·1 (141,545)
1962	0·4 (25,080)	1·5 (186,840)	0·3 (21,700)	1·4 (172,740)
Var (%)	+112·0	+67·1	+81·0	+22·0

Source: 'L'Emploi féminin en 1962 et son evolution depuis 1954' (1964), p. 14.

The role of the private sector as a context for women's promotion to managerial positions can only be understood by contrast with the public sector (Table 15.4). As the table shows, there was an increase in the number of managers (*cadres supérieures*) in the private and public sectors between 1954 and 1962. The greatest increase took place among female managers in the private sector. Although the increase in numbers of managers continued to be greater among men than among women in the next decade, in recent years the public sector has regained its past advantage in promoting women to top managerial positions.

A recent study has classified firms by the proportion of female managers. The firms with the highest proportion (between 20 and 12 per cent) were found in banking, chemical industries, and commerce, and among them 60 per cent belonged to public and semiprivate firms (*L'Expansion*, no. 84, April 1975).

Furthermore, the more traditional public industries (e.g. Air France (ground), electricity, the postal and telephone service, public transportation, and railroads) have a larger percentage of women managers than the other private industries. Private and public industries, characterized by greater economic growth, seem more likely to promote women to top positions. In recent years public and semipublic industries have seemed to offer the most favorable ground for women managers, whereas in the post-Second World War period characterized by economic recovery and expansion the private sector was a better context for the advancement of women to managerial positions. The recent increase of women managers in the public sector also reflects new legislative measures promoting greater equality between the sexes in the workplace combined with an increasing number of women choosing professional and scientific fields of training, their entry in *grandes écoles*, and the greater security and prestige offered to employees in public and semiprivate industries.

The stagnation in the growth of women executives in the highest ranks of the civil service is striking, because the civil service as a whole is becoming more 'feminized;' in 1956 women represented 38 per cent of employees, compared to 44 per cent in 1968 (Becane, 1974, p. 9). In an earlier paper I have suggested that this trend is due in part to the 'flight' of men from the middle levels of public service to the newly dynamic and rewarding business sector. In France men seem to be 'abandoning' middle positions in the civil service to women (Silver, 1973). At the highest level of the civil service in the various ministries (category A in the official records) there has been little increase in the proportion of women employees. In 1956 they made up 10 per cent of the total female population employed in the civil service, compared to 11·2 and 11·9 per cent in 1962 and 1968 respectively. Among males the figures for the same years were 20·2, 24·3 and 20·7 per cent respectively (Becane, 1974, p. 15). This stagnation among high level employees in the French civil service seems to have affected men and women equally and seems to reflect the lack of dynamism of this sector in France. Thus, despite the feminization of the civil service at all levels – but especially in category A, where the proportion of female employees went from 21 per cent in 1956 to 27·4 per cent in 1962 and fully a third in 1968 – women's participation in the highest and most prestigious positions is low. Furthermore, these figures are somewhat misleading, because a high percentage of women in category A are found in positions that do not require decision-making. For example, in 1970, 54 per cent of them were teaching in *lycées* and another 36 per cent were *attachés d'administration centrale*, with little decision-making power; only 10 per cent were *administrateurs civils*, having some discretionary power (Ministère du Travail, Comité du Travail Féminin, 1974). At the supergrade level, described as *hors catégorie*, the proportion of women executives between 1962 and 1968 increased more than in lower categories.

The attainment of women in the French civil service cannot be considered apart from the distinctive educational system that recruits, educates, and ranks candidates for such positions. In particular, the Ecole Nationale d'Administration (ENA), preparing for the highest civil service positions (e.g. *directeur de cabinet* and *secrétaire d'état*), was created in 1945 and opened formally to both sexes. Entry is through a highly selective competitive examination after completion of equivalent of a university education. The proportion of women candidates is small, and their rate of success is even smaller. Indeed, the proportion of women accepted at the ENA has not increased at any time since its creation, and in recent years it has decreased. In 1946 thirty-four women and 637 men competed, and three women were accepted, comprising 5·3 per cent of the female applicants, compared to 9·6 per cent of the men. In 1972, 108 women competed and five were accepted – a rate of 4·6 per cent (Becane, 1974, p. 27).

Recruitment to the highest civil-service posts can also be effected through the *grandes écoles*, the best known being L'Ecole Polytechnique, which prepares for the highest technical, as distinct from managerial, roles. It was opened to women only in 1970. All the *grandes écoles* are now formally open to women, although their number is still small. In 1970 women made up 3·9 per cent of students in these schools (Becane, 1974, p. 35).

The Grand Corps de l'Etat – Conseil d'Etat, Cours des Comptes, Inspecteurs des Finances – are the most prestigious non-elective institutions of the French government. In all they contained nineteen women, representing 3 per cent of their membership. There were two women *sous-préfets* – the second-highest position in the structure of delegated authority in local administration, opened to women only in 1974 (Comité du Travail Feminin, 1974, p. 7).

The civil service can be reached not only through the ENA and the *grandes écoles* but also by nomination, involving lateral transfers. In 1972 women were nominated in twenty-three out of a total of 351 such transfers. Their nominations were in the less prestigious departments (Becane, 1974, p. 28).

There exists for women an alternative to executive positions in the higher civil service in the non-executive, although prestigious, array of positions in elite teaching careers, particularly the *lycée* and university system. The qualifying examination for these teaching positions – the *aggrégation* – is as intellectually strenuous as the competition for the ENA but draws a far higher proportion of women, competing for a much larger number of opportunities. Apart from the more 'feminine' ethos of teaching, which is still, however, more equally shared between the sexes in France than in the United States, a consideration for women is that the outcome of an ENA education is more uncertain; they may be relegated to positions of little prestige and responsibility, whereas *lycée* and university teaching retain considerable prestige. Although comparable positions in the cultural sphere sponsored by the government do not exist for women in the United States (Silver, 1973), it remains true that these are not opportunities for decision-making; nor are they innovative.'

The distribution of women in executive positions in both countries and in both sectors follows a familiar pattern. In the private and public sectors of both the United States and France executive women are more likely to be found in the traditionally 'feminine' areas: education, social services health, retail trade, office management, personnel management, public relations, and accounting (Bowman, Worthy, and Greyser, 1965). The distribution of women executives in the US civil service follows the same trends as in the private sector, despite the fact that civil service workers received 'equal pay for equal work' protection in 1923 – forty years earlier than workers in the private sector. Women in the public sector are concentrated in such areas as general administration, personnel management, librarianship, supply, health, and accounting. In 1971 the proportion of women executives is highest in personnel management (28·9 per cent), but very low in medicine (1·4 per cent) (US Civil Service Commission, 1971, pp. 79–106).

In France similar patterns emerge. In both the private and the public sectors women executives are more likely to be found in the traditional feminine sectors. They are more frequent (more than 10 per cent) in the Ministries of Health, Education, Social and Cultural Affairs, Supply, and War Veterans; they are least frequent (less than 1 per cent) in the Ministries of the Interior, Justice, Transport, Economy, and Finance and in the Office of the Prime Minister (Comité du Travail Féminin, 1974, p. 11). Since 1974 women executives have appeared in all branches of the civil service, although in small numbers. Where there were previously almost none, their numbers rose to 42, 59, 66, and 42 respectively in 1974. These figures are, of course, not large; but given the exceptionally masculine character of the higher civil service in general, and of these ministries in particular, their significance cannot be dismissed (Comité du Travail Feminin, 1974).

CONCLUSION

In the post-Second World War era the first stage in the integration of women in administration has been through the expansion of middle management (*cadres moyen*), and in certain technical strata this has occurred in both the public and the private sectors in the United States and France. The representation of women in these positions has increased rapidly in response to organizational imperatives which cut across the public–private distinction. Whether or not such positions form a basis for advancement to executive positions depends not only on the outcome of the struggle for equal treatment of the sexes but also on the general question of whether such positions will form stages in careers that may culminate in executive roles. As suggested earlier, the rapid expansion of higher level administrative and technical positions, brought about by the professionalization of business – most advanced in the United States, but spreading now throughout western European countries – may represent a form of mass occupational upgrading in which women find some success without, however, the immediate availability of channels to positions of executive scope.

Although the strong increase in the number of women in middle management in the 1960s and 1970s, and to a lesser extent in professional and technical positions, may be due to organizational change and change in the demand for certain skills in an expanding economy, women's access to top positions in both the public and the private sectors is more likely to depend on a different set of factors. The promotion of women to top executive jobs is more likely to be a matter of political choice and political action, at the same time as it is being furthered through changes in legislation affecting women's position in the family and through changes in the modes of recruitment for training and employment. It depends, that is, more on deliberate policy than on the dynamics of organizational or competitive forces. The role of the Women's Movement in the United States and France has been instrumental in bringing about these changes. In the United States the Women's Movement seems to have had a more direct impact on policymakers and legislators. More generally, the greater efficiency and organizational scope of the Women's Movement in the United States may in part account for the difference between the two countries discussed in this paper.

In the case of each country the historically stronger and more prestigious sector – private in the United States, public in France – may in the past have strongly opposed the access of women to positions of leadership; however, it is precisely in these sectors that the major rewards of leadership are more likely to be allocated. In view of the different traditions regarding the prestige of state bureaucracies and private enterprises in France and the United States, my sense of the future is that in France the government is most likely to take the lead in promoting women to executive positions in the public sector, whereas in the United States the major impact of government is more likely to be indirect, acting on the private sector, particularly on its largest, least competitive, and most bureaucratized sections.

NOTES

(1) This change could be due to the greater increase among the civilian labor force employed in the public sector in the United States and in the private sector in France. In the United States the increase in total civilian employment between 1950 and 1970 was 38·5 per cent in the public sector (at the federal level) and 28·2 per cent in the private sector. Thus, the greater opportunities open to women in the public sector may in part be accounted for by this more general trend in employment. In France the increase in total employment between 1954 and 1968 was 41·7 per cent in the public sector and 4·75 per cent in the private sector (INSEE, 1976, pp. 71–2). The greater increase of women managers and executives in the private sector and their stagnation in the public sector cannot be accounted for by these general employment trends.

(2) In France there was a short-lived State Secretariat for Women's Affairs, created in 1974 to facilitate the integration of women into French society. With little power and no financial independence it was soon replaced by a lower level commission.

(3) The census categorization for managers and administrators is misleading in the study of high level managers and executives working in bureaucracies, because they include a variety of occupational groups (e.g. restaurant and bar managers and school administrators). One out of five women workers employed in this category was self-employed, inflating the figures for executives and managers (US Department of Labor, 1975, p. 96).

(4) The lack of a consistent definition of what is considered 'small' and 'large' makes the comparison of these studies difficult. Some, like that of Killiam (1971), have used these terms without specifying them.

(5) The studies of Johnston (1974) and of Crawford (1977) have used the following breaking points: small, under 500 employees; medium, between 500 and 20,000 employees; and large, over 20,000 employees.

(6) The concept of a dual labor market is an analytical tool used to analyze the distribution of working individuals between two major sectors of the economy. The primary sector is characterized by a highly stable labor force, with expectations of regular salary increases, seniority arrangements, and a movement up the job ladder. The secondary sector is characterized by a highly unstable labor force; there are no expectations of salary increases or seniority benefits, and in general employers do not invest in the development of skills among their workers. For further information see Piore (1975).

(7) The official definition of the category 'officers and administrators' is those with:

> ... occupation in which employees set broad policies, exercise overall responsibility for execution of the policies, or direct individual departments or special phases of the agency's operations, or specialized consultation in a regional district of area basis. It includes: department heads, bureau chiefs, division chiefs, directors, deputy directors, controllers, examiners, wardens, superintendents, unit supervisors, sheriffs, police and fire chiefs, and inspectors and kindred workers. (Equal Employment Opportunity Commission, 1973)

(8) These grades correspond to the various pay systems considered equivalent to specific General Schedule (GS) grades. As of October 31, 1970 the General Schedule represents the following pay system: *GS-1 to 6*, \$4,125–7,294; *GS-7 to 12*, \$8,098–14,192; *GS-13 to 16*, \$16,760–26,547; and *GS-17 and above*, \$36,000–40,000 (US Civil Service Commission, Bureau of Manpower Information Systems, Manpower Statistics Division, 1971, pp. 17 and 235).

(9) Good descriptions and analysis of these different legislative and administrative measures can be found among *Report of the National Commission on the Observance of International Women's Year, 1976* (1977), Meacham (1975, and Moskow (1973).

REFERENCES AND FURTHER READING

Archibald, Kathleen (1973) 'Sizing up the future of women in banking,' *Banking*, vol. 66, no. 1 (July), pp. 28–30.

'Banking,' *Le Monde* (April 2, 1976).

Bartol, Kathryn and Bartol, Robert (1975) 'Women in managerial and professional positions: the United States and the Soviet Union,' *Industrial and Labor Relations Review*, vol. 28, no. 4 (July), pp. 524–34.

Basil, Douglas (1971) *Women in Management: Performance, Prejudices, Promotion* (New York: Dunellen).

Becane-Pascaud, Geneviève (1974) 'Les femmes dans la fonction publique,' *Notes et Etudes Documentaires*, nos 4056–7, 25 January.

Black, Sheila (1974) 'Women at the top,' *The Director*, vol. 27, no. 2 (August), pp. 180–3.

Bowman, Garda W., Worthy, N. Beatrice, and Greyser, Stephen A. (1965) 'Problems in review. Are women executives people?,' *Harvard Business Review*, vol. 43, no. 4 (July–August), pp. 14–28 and 164–78.

Bureau of National Affairs, Inc. (1970) 'Few women in management,' *Bulletin to Management*, no. 1047 (March 5).

Bureau of National Affairs, Inc. (1971) 'Women and minorities in management and in personnel management,' *Personnel Policies Forum Survey*, no. 96 (December).

Burrow, Martha (1976) *Women: A Worldwide View of their Management Development Needs* (New York: Amacon, Division of American Management Association).

Business and Professional Women's Foundation (1970) *Women Executives: A Selected Annotated Bibliography* (Washington, DC: BPWF).

Calviac, M. (1976) 'La structure et la répartition des salaires dans les commerces, les banques et les assurances en 1974,' *Economie et statistique*, no. 76, pp. 66–75.

Chambers, Peter (1974) 'No easy path for women managers,' *International Management*, vol. 29, no. 5 (May), pp. 46–8.

Comité du Travail Féminin (1974) *Les femmes aux postes de la fonction publique* (Paris, Ministère du Travail, Comité du Travail Féminin).

Coser, Rose Laub and Rokoff, Gerald (1971) 'Women in the occupational world: social disruption and conflict,' *Social Problems*, vol. 18, no. 4, pp. 535–54.

Crawford, J. (1977) *Women in Middle Management* (Ridgewood, NY: Forkner Publishing).

Cussler, Margaret (1958) *The Woman Executive* (New York: Harcourt, Brace).

Darling, Martha (1975) *The Role of Women in the Economy: A Summary based on Ten National Reports* (Paris: Organization for Economic Co-operation and Development).

DiMarco, Nicholas and Whitsitt, Susan (1975) 'A comparison of female supervisors in business and government organisations,' *Journal of Vocational Behaviour*, vol. 6, pp. 185–96.

Epstein, Cynthia Fuchs (1974) 'Bringing women in: rewards, punishments and the structure of achievement,' in Rugh B. Kundsin (ed.) *Women and Success: The Anatomy of Achievement* (New York: William Morrow), pp. 13–21.

Epstein, Cynthia Fuchs (1975) 'Institutional barriers: what keeps women out of the executive suite?,' in Francine E. Gordon and Myra H. Strober (eds), *Bringing Women into Management* (New York: McGraw-Hill), pp. 7–21.

Equal Employment Opportunity Commission (1973) *EEO-4: 1973 Summary* (Washington, DC: US Government Printing Office).

Eurostat (1972) *Structure des salaires dans l'industrie: Résultats géneraux France*, Série Spécial 3A.

Federal Reserve System, Inc. (1976a) *Banking and Monetary Statistics, 1941–70* (Washington, DC: Board of Governors of the FRS).

Federal Reserve System, Inc. (1976b) *Annual Statistical Digest, 1971–75* (Washington, DC: Board of Governors of the FRS).

'Femmes: ce qui a changé,' *L'Express* (March 3–9, 1975).

Ferris, A. L. (1971) *Indicators of Trends in the Status of American Women* (New York: Russell Sage Foundation).

Fogarty, Michael, Allen, A. J., Allen, I., and Walters, P. (1971) *Women in Top Jobs: Four Studies in Achievement* (London: Allen & Unwin, in co-operation with Political and Economic Planning).

Fogarty, Michael, Rapoport, Rhona, and Rapoport, Robert (1971) *Sex, Career and Family* (London: Allen & Unwin, in co-operation with Political and Economic Planning).

'France: à la recherche des femmes cadres,' *Vie des cadres*, no. 3, 3ème trimestre (1972).

French Embassy (London), Service de Presse (1972) *French Women in 1972*, Notes d'Information (London, December).

Froning, Mary L. (1974) *Minorities and Women in State and Local Government* (Washington, DC: Equal Employment Opportunities Commission, US Government Printing Office).

Giele, Janet Zollinger (1974) 'Changes in the modern family: their impact on sex roles,' in Rose L. Coser (ed.), *The Family: Its Structures and Functions* (New York: St Martin's Press), pp. 460–70.

Given, John N. (1960) 'Women in executive posts,' *Office Executive*, vol. 35, no. 12 (December), pp. 32–3.

INSEE (1968) *Annuaire statistique de la France, 1968* (Paris: INSEE).

INSEE (1974a) *Enquête sur l'emploi de 1972*, série D, nos 33–4, (Paris: INSEE, June).

INSEE *Enquête sur l'emploi de 1974*, (1974b) série D, no. 37, (Paris: INSEE, December).

INSEE *Enquête sur l'emploi de 1975*, (1975) série D, no. 42, (Paris: INSEE, December).

INSEE (1976) *Annuaire Statistique de la France* (Paris: INSEE).

Institut National Etudes Démographiques (1975) *Structure de l'emploi* (Paris).

Johnston, J. J. (1974) 'A survey of women MBA graduates in management positions,' unpublished doctoral dissertation (Pittsburgh: University of Pittsburgh).

Kanter, Rosabeth Moss (1977) *Men and Women of the Corporation* (New York: Basic Books).

Killiam, Ray A. (1971) *The Working Woman* (New York: American Management Association).

King, Alice (1963) *Career Opportunities for Women in Business* (New York: E. P. Dutton).

Koff, Lois Ann (1973) 'Age, experience and success among women managers,' *Management Review*, vol. 62, no. 11 (November), pp. 65–6.

Kreps, Juanita (1973) 'The sources of inequality,' in Eli Ginzberg and Alice Yohalem (eds), *Corporate Lib: Women's Challenge to Management*, (Baltimore: Johns Hopkins University Press), pp. 85–96.

Larwood, Laurie and Wood, Marion M. (1977) *Women in Management* (Lexington: Lexington Books).

Le Monde (1976) (Paris), April 2.

'L'Employ féminin en 1962 et son evolution depuis 1954,' *Etudes et conjonctures*, 19 année, no. 12 (December 1964).

'Les femmes,' *L'Expansion*, no. 85 (April 1975).

L'Expansion, no. 84 (April 1975).

Loring, Rosalind and Wells, Theodora (1972) *Breakthrough: Women into Management* (New York: Van Nostrand Reinhold).

Manpower, vol. 4, no. 6 (June 1972); and vol. 4, no. 12 (December 1972).

Meacham, Colquitt (1975) 'The law: where it is and where it is going,' in Francine E. Gordon and Myra H. Strober (eds), *Bringing Women into Management* (New York: McGraw-Hill), pp. 59–76.

Michel, Andrée (1975) *Le Travail Féminin: Un Point de Vue* (Paris. La Documentation Française).

Ministère du Travail, Comité du Travail Féminin (1972) *Le Rôle des françaises dans l'economie* (Paris).

Ministère du Travail, Comité du Travail Féminin (1973), 'La formation professionelle des femmes,' *Revue française des affaires sociales*, vol. 27, no. 1 (January–March), pp. 11–38.

Ministère du Travail, Comité du Travail Féminin (1974) *Les Femmes aux postes de direction de la fonction publique* (Paris).

Ministère du Travail, Comité du Travail Féminin (1975a) *Eléments de réflexion sur les femmes cadres* (Paris: December).

Ministère du Travail, Comité du Travail Féminin (1975b) *L'Evolution des femmes dans la société française* (Paris).

Ministère du Travail, de l'Emploi et de la Population (1973) *Supplément au Bulletin mensuel de statistique du travail: Emploi et salaires* (Paris).

'More women move into the boardroom,' *Business Week*, no. 2421 (March 1, 1976), p. 26.

Moskow, Michael H. (1973) 'Government in the lead,' in Eli Ginzberg and Alice Yohalem (eds), *Corporate Lib: Women's Challenge to Management* (Baltimore: Johns Hopkins University Press), pp. 125–32.

Oppenheimer, Valerie (1970) *The Female Labor Force in the US: Demographic and Economic Factors Governing its Growth and Changing Composition* (Berkeley: University of California Press).

Orth, Charles and Jacobs, Frederic (1971) 'Women in management: pattern for change,' *Harvard Business Review*, vol. 49, no. 4 (July–August), pp. 139–47.

Piore, Michael J. (1975) 'Notes for a theory of labor market stratification,' in Richard C. Edwards, Michael Reich, and David M. Gordon (eds), *Labor Market Segmentation* (Lexington, Mass.: D. C. Heath), pp. 125–50.

'Près de la moitié des femmes gagnaient moins de 1,500 par mois dans le secteur privé,' *Le Monde* (February 7, 1975).

President's Commission on the Status of Women (1963) *Report of the Commission on the Status of Women, 1963* (Washington, DC: US Government Printing Office).

Report of the National Commission on the Observance of International Women's Year, 1976 (1977) (Washington, DC: US Government Printing Office).

'Resultats d'une enquête sur le travail des femmes à temps partiel,' *Revue française des affaires sociales*, 17e année, no. 14 (October–December 1973), pp. 101–37.

Robertson, Wyndham (1973) 'Ten highest ranking women in big business,' *Fortune Magazine*, vol. 87, no. 4 (April), pp. 80–9.

Robie, Edward A. (1973) 'Challenge to management,' in Eli Ginzberg and Alice Yohalem (eds), *Corporate Lib: Women's Challenge to Management* (Baltimore: Johns Hopkins University Press), pp. 9–29.

Rosen, Benson and Jerdee, Thomas H. (1973) 'The influence of sex-role stereotypes on evaluations of male and female supervisory behavior,' *Journal of Applied Psychology*, vol. 57, no. 1, pp. 44–8.

Rosenberg, DeAnne (1976) 'Clearing the way for the growth of women subordinates,' *Supervisory Management*, vol. 21, no. 1 (January), pp. 9–12.

Schein, Virginia Ellen (1973) 'The relationship between sex roles stereotypes and requisite management characteristics,' *Journal of Applied Psychology*, vol. 57, no. 2 (April), pp. 95–100.

Schwartz, Eleanor Brantley (1971) *The Sex Barrier in Business* (Atlanta: Georgia State University Press).

Shepherd, William and Levin, Sharon (1973) 'Managerial discrimination in large firms,' *Review of Economics and Statistics*, vol. 55, no. 4 (November), pp. 412–22.

'Shortchanged: minorities and women in banking,'*Economic Priorities Report*, no. 3 (September–October 1972), pp. 9–15.

Silver, Catherine (1975) 'Salon, foyer, bureau: women and the professions in France,' *American Journal of Sociology*, vol. 78, no. 4, pp. 836–51.

Sommers, Dixie (1974) 'Occupational ranking for men and women by earnings,' *Monthly Labor Review*, vol. 97, no. 8 (August), pp. 34–51.

Steichen, C. Everett (1973) 'Of women and banking,' *Burroughs Clearing House*, vol. 58, no. 3 (December), pp. 20–1.

Sullerot, Evelyn (1975) 'Report on the problems involved in the work and employment of women,' unpublished paper presented to the Conseil Economique et Social, France, October 15.

US Bureau of Labor Statistics (1977) *Handbook of Labor Statistics*, Bulletin, no. 1966 (Washington, DC: US Government Printing Office).

US Civil Service Commission, Bureau of Manpower Information Systems, Manpower Statistics Division (1971) *Study of Employment of Women in the Federal Government* (Washington, DC: US Government Printing Office).

US Civil Service Commission, Bureau of Manpower Information Systems, Manpower Statistics Division (1972a) *Federal Civilian Employment by Minority Group and Sex*, Federal Civilian Personal Statistics (Washington, DC: US Government Printing Office, November 30).

US Civil Service Commission, Bureau of Manpower Information Systems, Manpower Statistics Division (1972b) *Federal Civilian Employment: Women* (Washington, DC: US Government Printing Office).

US Civil Service Commission, Bureau of Manpower Information Systems, Manpower Statistics Division (1973) *Study of Employment of Women in the Federal Government, 1973* (Washington, DC: US Government Printing Office).

US Department of Commerce, Bureau of the Census (1951) *Statistical Abstract of the United States* (Washington, DC: US Government Printing Office).

US Department of Commerce, Bureau of the Census (1963) *Census of the Population, 1960*, subject report, *Government Workers* (Washington, DC: US Government Printing Office).

US Department of Commerce, Bureau of the Census (1972) *Census of the Population, 1970*, subject report, *Occupation by Industry* (Washington, DC: US Government Printing Office, October).

US Department of Commerce, Bureau of the Census (1973) *Census of the Population, 1970*, subject report, *Government Workers* (Washington, DC: US Government Printing Office, June).

US Department of Labor, Women's Bureau (1973) *Women Workers Today* (Washington, DC: US Government Printing Office).

US Department of Labor, Women's Bureau (1975) *Handbook on Women Workers*, Bulletin, no. 297 (Washington, DC: US Government Printing Office).

Vimond, Claude (1965) 'Une enquête sur les femmes fonctionnaires,' *Population*, vol. 20, no. 1 (January–February), pp. 22–5.

Waldman, Elizabeth and McEaddy, Beverly J. (1974) 'Where women work: an analysis by industry and occupation,' *Monthly Labor Review*, vol. 97, no. 5 (May), pp. 3–13.

Wallace, Phyllis (1973) 'Sex discrimination: some societal constraints on upward mobility for women executives,' in Eli Ginzberg and Alice Yohalem (eds), *Corporate Lib: Women's Challenge to Management* (Baltimore: Johns Hopkins University Press), pp. 69–84.

'Who are the women in the board rooms?,' *Business and Society Review*, no. 16 (Winter 1975–6), pp. 5–10.

'Women in the work force: where they stand, what they want,' *Management Review*, vol. 59, no. 11 (November 1970), pp. 20–3.

16

Women and Occupational Elites:

The Case of Newspaper Journalism in England

ROGER SMITH

Since the mid-1960s we have witnessed the rapid burgeoning of sociological interest in the 'social position of women.' One of the fastest-flowing research streams to have emanated from this general interest has been concerned with women's occupational roles and experiences. What has emerged from this research with distressing regularity is that a very high degree of job differentiation, both horizontal and vertical, is based on gender. Thus, in the labor market generally there is a 'balkanization' process that creates and maintains jobs that are almost exclusively female, and within the professions and other highly-ranked occupations there are 'female' areas of specialization (Phelps, 1968; Brager and Michael, 1969; Epstein, 1971; Fogarty et al., 1971). What is more directly relevant for a discussion of the participation of women in elites is that, in all fields studied so far, female participation has been found to decline radically as the upper echelons of power and prestige are approached (Mattfeld and Van Aken, 1965; White, 1967; Harris, 1970; Rossi, 1970; Epstein, 1971; Fogarty et al., 1971; Griffin, 1973; Currell, 1974). Explanations for this relative hierarchical distribution have generally concentrated on women themselves, rather than the structure, composition, recruitment patterns, market situation, and ideologies of occupations. As a result, either the presumed characteristics of women have been blamed for their low elite participation, or domestic and family roles have been held responsible. With regard to the first general explanation, although it would be foolish to maintain that there are *no* differences between the sexes, it is dangerous to work within such an explanatory framework, since differences discovered in unrepresentative samples tend to become generalized to whole populations. More seriously, characteristics of individuals, especially so-called 'sex differences,' are usually seen as fixed throughout the female life span, with the result that the contexts of development of characteristics are left unexplored. The rapid embracing of Matina Horner's (1969) idea of women's 'internalised desire to fail' very neatly fits in with the prevailing ideologies of those in controlling positions within occupations and thus can be used to divert attention from the occupations themselves. Similarly, the approach that links work and its demands with the female life cycle (i.e. domestic commitments at various phases) seems to perform the same function. It is unjustifiably assumed that the life cycle is the independent variable and work the dependent variable, when it is clear that occupational experiences and expectations can easily affect decisions relating to the life cycle of women, especially those engaged in relatively rewarding careers.[1]

the outcome of this theoretical focus is that the family is regarded as the prime determinant of participation and success, so that again the practices of particular occupations escape scrutiny.

My own research has focused on the structure and prevailing ideologies of one particular occupation, namely, journalism, to attempt to discover: first, the mechanisms whereby areas of female specialization are defined and maintained (for a more detailed discussion of my findings, see Smith, 1976); and second, the processes whereby women tend to be excluded from positions of power and decision-making. Journalism as practiced in the leading English newspapers[2] was chosen because it is one of the few prestigious career occupations where a university degree is not required for entry or success.[3] This occupation, with its emphasis on informal training and lack of formal qualifications, would provide valuable contrasts with occupations where higher education is expected.[4]

FLEET STREET AND JOURNALISTIC ELITES

A number of problems is involved in defining the composition of 'journalistic elites.' The senior editorial staff of several large provincial newspapers could be said to comprise part of that elite. The appointment of Harold Evans as editor of the *Sunday Times* directly from the editorship of the *Northern Echo* seems to confirm this. However, in terms of influence on knowledge and opinions the national Fleet Street papers, with their extensive circulations, are much more powerful than local papers, which tend to follow the lead of the national press and are frequently owned by the same groups. As Tunstall (1971) has observed:

> Dominance of London in British journalism is maintained by the dominance of London in other fields including the 'creation' of news; the great majority of newspapers sold each day in Britain are printed in London or one of its major satellite printing centres.

That Fleet Street is seen by journalists as the pinnacle of achievement in a career is testified by many autobiographies. It is perhaps best illustrated by a prominent Australian journalist's description of Fleet Street as the 'world headquarters of big league journalism' (Cannon, 1966).

WOMEN'S PLACE IN NEWSPAPER JOURNALISM

The participation of women in elites in journalism must be seen from the perspective of women in newspaper journalism as a whole. On the lower levels of journalism women tend to be relatively plentiful, constituting 40 per cent of probationary members (trainees) of the National Union of Journalists (NUJ) and almost 19 per cent of full members. Moreover, their participation rates on provincial newspaper staffs have increased considerably in the four years for which sex split figures are available: from 31 per cent in 1972 to 40 per cent at the end of 1975 for trainees; and from 15·6 per cent to 18·6 per cent for fully qualified journalists over the same period.[5]

However, on Fleet Street only some 10 per cent of journalists are women, and this proportion changed very little between 1973 and 1975. There are indications that in 1975 the proportion even *declined* somewhat,[6] although this was the year when the NUJ had its first woman president in the seventy years of its existence. Even 10 per cent in the higher echelons of newspaper journalism may seem a relatively sizable proportion; but if we focus on the elites within newspapers, the proportion drops radically.

One of the problems of using NUJ statistics, as presented in the union's *Annual Reports*, is that these give only the *overall* number of women employed in the national newspapers. This means that it is impossible to determine the number of women on individual newspapers or their hierarchical distribution. I therefore collected statistics of my own on the basis of questionnaires sent to each national newspaper. Even with official NUJ backing only seven out of seventeen questionnaires sent to the chief union official on each paper (the 'Father of Chapel') were returned. Further inquiries failed to produce more, I suspect because of concern about over-manning (and underwomanning?).[7] Approaches to the managing editors of the remaining papers produced another six returns, one of which was a duplication, so that altogether figures for twelve of the seventeen Fleet Street papers were obtained. As these twelve covered the full range of types of papers – popular, quality, daily, Sunday, and evening – it seems fair to generalise on the basis of these returns about the position of women on national papers as a whole.

Most women on Fleet Street are employed in relatively lowly positions as reporters, feature writers, and assistants. Although they act as gatekeepers in the information flow and thus can be said to have minor decision-making roles, the actual ethos of the paper dictates the treatment given to different issues, and this ethos, as Breed (1955) has shown, is handed down informally by those in higher positions.

Subeditors

At the lowest level of significant decision-making within the newspaper organization is the subeditor, or desk copy-editor in US terms. Essentially, the job of the subeditors is to select from the vast amount of material presented by reporters, stringers, and wire services the stories that will appear in a particular edition of the paper. They also determine by placement within the paper the relative prominence given to particular stories. They write headlines and captions, and trim, modify, and frequently construct stories. In media research subeditors have generally been regarded as important gatekeepers in the information flow. Later, I shall use the gatekeeper concept to examine a different aspect of their role.

Experience at subediting is almost mandatory for advancement to senior editorial and executive positions. Those who perform this role are 'on the verge' of power. Importantly, this is an area where the participation rates of women fall to a very low level. On the basis of my returned questionnaires they constituted only slightly over 2 per cent of news subeditors (1974) (six out of the 239 who worked on the papers that made returns). They were concentrated in four of the twelve papers, and the majority of papers had no women news subeditors at all. These figures support comments made by interviewees. A woman who had freelanced for many of the Fleet Street papers said that she could not remember having seen any woman subeditor on any of the papers for which she had worked. A male editorial writer commented: 'We've only ever had *one* woman sub in the twenty-two years I have been on the paper, and then she stayed only two or three weeks. She left hating the whole enterprise.' Charles Wintour (1972) – a Fleet Street editor – has stated that it is 'rare enough to see a woman sub-editor' (p. 199). It seems vital to discover why women do not find their way to the subeditors' desk and thus into an extremely important 'informal learning situation'[8] and on to a crucial rung of the ladder to editorial and executive positions.

Most men and some women whom I interviewed insisted that there are so few female news subeditors in Fleet Street because subediting did not appeal to women. This is belied by there being considerably more women employed as subeditors on house journals, specialist publications, and the women's magazines. Moreover, there is a considerably higher proportion of women *features* subeditors on Fleet Street (7·2 per cent in 1974, according to my returned questionnaires). However, these tend to be confined to the women's sections of the papers.

What does seem to contribute significantly toward explaining the low numbers of women in news subediting is that there is a reluctance to employ them even when they are available. A report in the *Guardian* of January 3, 1974 told of Margaret Hignett – a senior subeditor at the Press Association (a news agency) – and her confrontation with the management of the *Daily Express* – one of the larger popular daily national newspapers. Hignett was considering suing the paper for discrimination under the Sex Disqualification (Removal) Act, 1919. In late 1973 she applied for a subediting job at the *Express*, signing herself simply 'M. J. Hignett.' According to the *Guardian* report:

> When she arrived for the interview, she says, the managing editor's secretary was shocked to discover she was a woman, announced, according to Hignett, that it is against *Express* policy to employ women in these jobs. Much of the interview which followed, it seems, concerned the managing editor's insistence on the importance of applicants indicating whether they are a Mr., Miss or Mrs., and his actually filling an application form for her. She was eventually turned down for the job, for which, on the basis of past experience, she was admirably qualified.
>
> Ian McColl, the newspaper's editor, says, 'The *Daily Express* is not in the women's liberation business.'

Lest this be taken as an isolated example, other evidence indicates that this is not so and that there are in fact all kinds of informal pressures against employing women in subediting. Since the beginning of 1976 it has been illegal to specify the desired sex of applicants for jobs in the United Kingdom. However, it would be naive to assume that this legal change has done more than modify existing prejudices. The extent of preference for male subeditors can be seen in the job-advertising section of the *UK Press*

Gazette – a publication aimed at the newspaper world – where, until it was made illegal, notification of vacancies for subediting frequently specified that a man was required.

During one of my interviews an illuminating exchange took place between the interviewee and the assistant editor of the paper for which she worked, when at an opportune moment he walked into the office. I had just asked why, she thought, there were so few women subeditors on Fleet Street:

> *Journalist* (to assistant editor): One can't hire women subs, isn't that it?
>
> *Assistant editor*: Oh yes you can! There's no reluctance at all! The reason there are no women subs, in my view – it's not discrimination against women – but they know they're not suited to it. To use an old-fashioned term, I don't think it's a woman's job, actually.

The attitude of this assistant editor, who had much power, tended to be shared by other senior male journalists. It was ironically pointed out to me by two women who had subediting experience that, as many of the characteristics of subediting – represented as concern with detail, repetitiveness, and lack of necessity for any panoramic view of life – tended to fit in with woman's traditional stereotype, on those grounds it appeared to make a very suitable job for a woman. But it seems that, when one set of sexist assumptions ('female characteristics') is confronted with another ('women should not hold positions of power, especially over men'), the latter tends to win out.

Women in Fleet Street have been described as 'basically honoured guests in a masculine fortress' (Leslie, 1966). One of the most strongly defended turrets of that fortress appears to be that occupied by subeditors. Subediting tends to be a very masculine and self-protecting speciality, possibly because of its traditional links with printing.[9] This masculine orientation is cemented by a good deal of outside work participation in the Fleet Street pub culture. The importance of the exclusion of women from this occupational specialty becomes clear if it is realized that this keeps women away from situations where much of the informal learning that is crucial to journalists goes on. Only a very small number of the women interviewed had subediting experience, often gained for idiosyncratic reasons.

The older women had begun in journalism during or just after the Second World War, when informal restrictions had been relaxed as a result of the manpower shortage. One woman had gained knowledge of subediting in a way that was much disapproved of; she had taken a commercial course – a fact she had subsequently taken great pains to conceal. Since all these women now hold executive or editorial posts, it seems clear that subeditors are also important gatekeepers in women's occupational advance.

Editors and Executives
Returned questionnaires from twelve of the seventeen national papers showed that in 1974 nine women out of a total of 249 (3·6 per cent) held

executive rank. These were concentrated in the 'quality' papers. Many of the largest popular papers had no female executives at all.

The *Directory of British Journalism* which covered all the national papers, shows that in 1974 – the last year, unfortunately, that this publication was produced – there were altogether twenty-nine entries for women who held the title 'editor.' Since several women held more than one editorial position, 'fashion editor' and 'woman's page editor' being frequently combined, these entries referred to only twenty-three women:

Woman's editor	10
Fashion editor	7
Beauty editor	2
Home interests editor	2
Cookery editor	2
Travel editor	2
News editor	1
Assistant editor	1

Thus, twenty-three out of twenty-nine editorial posts held by females in 1974 were directly in women's fields and as such not directly in the power hierarchy (i.e. away from wider policy formation). Such areas are held in low regard by journalists generally and feared by many women as a ghetto into which they may be pushed.

The concentration of women in what may appear to be a totally disparate field, namely, travel, seems curious, until it is pointed out that 'women's pages' and 'travel' are departments that generally work closely together on newspapers. In one case this arrangement was institutionalized by the same woman serving as both women's editor and travel editor.

Since these are the areas where women 'controllers' are heavily concentrated, it is worth examining the function of the women's pages, fashion, and travel sections to see how much decision-making power these women actually have. Tunstall (1971) – a sociologist – has observed that the 'predominant goal of these fields is to attract advertising' (p. 94). Mary Stott (1973) – one of Britain's best-known women journalists and ex-editor of the women's sections on two Fleet Street papers – has made similar comments in her autobiography, adding as a specific example the fact that, when the *Guardian* moved its headquarters from Manchester to London, the women's page became more trendy and more oriented to fashion 'for our advertising department to offer as bait (p. 92). My own interviews confirmed not only that other journalists had a very low regard for those who worked in departments with an advertising goal, but also that the latter were often considered as little better than hacks. However, women within such departments readily admitted that in Fleet Street's current parlous financial state the advertising revenue gained from running these fields was a major reason for their existence.

An authoritative view has come from Fleet Street editor Charles Wintour (1972): 'No national newspaper would have the slightest hope of economic survival if all advertising revenue were withdrawn from it' (p. 35). Although this refers to all advertising, those areas employing a concentration of female editors and executives are where pressures are greatest. Ironically, the fashion correspondents in Tunstall's (1971) study of news specialists claimed to have the greatest autonomy in choosing stories; but as Tunstall has been quick to point out, 'more control is exercised by advertisers and news sources and hence less by executives' (p. 133). Wintour (1972) has elaborated on the public relations function that practitioners in this field are expected to fulfill:

> The task of fashion and shopping editors is complicated by the need to carry out certain ambassadorial functions at the ceaseless round of shows and launchings where the fashion editor or assistant is expected to appear, whether the event provides copy or not. Of course some of these launchings are fun ... but quite a few are strictly duty calls in the cause of good will (p. 39).

He has also been revealing about travel pages: 'Travel sections of newspapers are clearly influenced by the advertisers whose appeals surround the editorial content' (p. 35). Thus, there is a good deal of control by advertisers over such fields, both formal and informal – formal because potential advertisers tend also to be major news sources, and informal because they can provide many 'perks' (e.g. trips to fashion shows, holidays abroad, products for 'testing') as well as invoking the ultimate penalty of advertising withdrawal. Not only are many of the stories, features, and photographs furnished by potential advertisers, but in addition the content of published stories is likely to be highly constrained. Hence, the real decision-making elite within these fields appears to consist of major news sources, who are potential advertisers, and advertising managers, who operate through the fashion, travel, and women's pages.

Columnists

Women columnists are the most visible women on Fleet Street, most of them rating large bylines accompanied by inset photographs. The best known of them are in regular demand as participants in radio and television talk shows, panel games, and the like, and as such they are probably responsible for the illusion that 'Fleet Street might seem to be a citadel that has succumbed to marauding hordes of womanhood on the militant march to an emancipated dawn' (Leslie, 1966).

It is difficult to regard many of these women as comprising part of the journalistic elite. To be sure, several have had relatively long careers in journalism, culminating in jobs where writing a regular weekly column is shared with responsibility within the newspaper organization as woman's editor. But more frequently, female columnists have had considerably shorter careers and are employed specifically as column writers, having no other position within the newspaper and in several instances working from home rather than being office based. It was put to me by one woman, who had her own highly publicized column on a national daily at the age of 22, that the impetus to employ female 'personality' writers began in the late 1960s when Fleet Street finally recognized the youth boom. In order to exploit a new potential audience a youth page or column was added that was generally written by a young trendy photogenic female. Such individuals tend to be used for a short time and then replaced by a new 'personality girl.'

In general these women are held in low regard by other journalists. This is so partly because of the prominence that they receive in the papers and partly because they are consequently highly paid; some of the best known command very large salaries in Fleet Street terms. More often, the antagonism is due to their perceived lack of newspaper training and experience, many having entered Fleet Street at a young age, often directly from women's magazines and sometimes directly from university.[10] Most men, in contrast, have had to do things the 'hard way,' working their way up from the provincial papers in a highly competitive occupation.

One of Britain's best-known women columnists, Katherine Whitehorn, has suggested that females in her occupation can get away with scorching attacks on public figures and writing astringently about issues more easily than men in the same position, her explanation being that editors are less likely to check carefully the copy of women columnists, assuming that it contains references to nothing more noteworthy than 'lipsticks and nappies' (Whitehorn, 1976). This view seems naive, for although a woman might get away with this once, it seems highly likely that copy would be carefully checked in the future. How then is one to explain the predominance of female columnists and the fact that they tend to be outspoken – that they have an apparent mandate to criticize sacred cows? It seems that newspaper managements box cleverly by having women columnists of apparently outspoken views. If readers agree with their opinions, this is fine; if they disagree, they are unlikely to stop buying the paper, because, given the widespread sexism within society, these opinions will be dismissed as mere female hysteria and the writer as 'that silly bitch of a woman.' Like court jesters they can be used by the powerful as tools of ridicule and attack without the latter having to take responsibility.

ELITE WOMEN

The number of women who can be said to constitute part of the journalistic elite, in the broadest sense, is thus extremely tiny and falls broadly into two types.

There are those women who as non-graduates began in journalism during or just after the Second World War and who accumulated much relevant experience in news and subediting. These are the older ones, among whom several now approach retirement. Also, there are those women recruited to Fleet Street during the 1960s on to fashion or women's pages, often directly from magazines and sometimes straight from university. These are larger in number, and because of their specialties they tend to attract a good deal of hostility from newsmen. The strength of feeling against 'high-flying' women like these is likely to breed antagonism toward *all* women.

What is striking about many of the women who hold positions of power on newspapers is the extreme localism of their success. The pattern tends to be that they began on their present paper at a relatively low level and at an early stage in their careers. Their talents having been locally recognised, they climbed the ladder to executive or editorial position. Among Fleet Street males there tends to be a good deal of 'spiraling'[11] upward through jobs on several papers; women tend to stay in an environment that they find amenable and to 'drift' upward.

Also typical of these women is that they tend to have family ties with journalism – a parent, close family friend, or husband. In a previous paper (Smith, 1976) I have stressed the essentially informal occupational sociali-zation processes in journalism and explained that, for a variety of reasons, women tend not to gain access to certain key learning areas (e.g. hard news, subediting, the night shift, and the informal pub and club culture). As a result their technical and normative knowledge of journalism is less complete than that of males. Women have less access to job vacancy grape-vines; and this is important, because few jobs at Fleet Street level are openly advertised. Women have less access to behind-the-scenes power struggles. Such lack of knowledge puts most women at a disadvantage. However, as Oleson and Whittaker (1968) have pointed out, there is a multidimensionality in professional socialisation, and outside influences and sources of information are extremely important. These, then, seem to be the resources for the successful women journalists.

To return to a point made earlier, I do not wish to imply that marriage and family are irrelevant to the work experiences of women. All the top women whom I interviewed were married, and all laid great stress on the supportive role of their husbands. Moreover, most had children. What is significant is that these children were carefully planned, so that their impact on the career of the mother was minimised; in other words, basic-ally rewarding experiences in the work situation fed back to life cycle deci-sions.

CONCLUSIONS

In newspaper journalism it is very difficult for women to achieve positions that confer noteworthy decision-making power. Few specialize in 'hard news,' and only a tiny number manage to find their way into subediting, so that the usual routes to executive and editorial position remain relatively closed. Thus, female journalists can most easily succeed by entering the women's specialities or by transferring to women's magazines. It is hardly exaggerated to say that such specialties propagate and extend the sexist image of society that prevented them from entering other specialties in the first place.

Discussion of the importance of women in decision-making elites must be informed by an overall view of the role and maintenance of elites and by some idea of which elites in society are structurally more important. The increased participation of women in certain elites is no sure indicator of their changed position in society, for it may merely be that these elites are declining in overall importance (Holter, 1970). Increased female participa-tion in political elites, for example, as has taken place quite markedly in some countries (Currell, 1974; Haavio-Mannila, Chapter 4 above), may in reality only indicate that the locus of power has shifted elsewhere. Examination of what may be broadly termed 'ideological elites' shows that female participation is at a very low level. In Britain, apart from the relative exclusion of women from participation in decision-making elites in the national newspapers, such exclusion also takes place in broadcasting and television (Fogarty *et al.*, 1971). Moreover, women's absence from media elites is a phenomenon that appears in a wide range of countries for which information is available.[12] I suggest that the media are assuming greater importance in the political process and that this explains the position of women in these fields.

Not only is it necessary to ascertain the relative importance of various elites within society, but in addition it is necessary to ask how far increased female participation in any elite is likely to change the position of women in society generally. Although women who achieve high structural positions can have symbolic significance for other women, it is also possible that they can be manipulated as symbols by other elite members, thus deflecting attention from the position of women at lower structural levels.

Research on academics has demonstrated that there is an almost total inverse correlation between the number of women in a field and the number with professorial positions;[13] that is, the more women there are around, the fewer rewards they are likely to achieve. It therefore seems that it is in the interests of women already within these fields to keep other women out. Consequently, it is conceivable that increased elite participation may result in the retardation of women's progress generally. Moreover, although the connection between class structure and sex inequality is too complex to be examined here, it should also be pointed out that, where increased female participation in one particular elite, namely, the senior ranks of the British civil service, has been observed, it was accompanied by a reduction in the participation of those from lower socioeconomic classes (Kelsall, 1974). This consolidation of *class* control may in the end work against the general equalization of opportunity for women.

It is noteworthy in this regard that the feminist journalists of Women in Media, in line with a sizable minority of the NUJ membership, are more in favor of diversification of power and of participation in decision-making by all personnel in the media than they are in favor of legitimating authority structures that are in large part uninterested in the problems of women. Such a strategy seems far more likely to improve the position of women in the media.

NOTES

(1) Kreps (1971, pp. 82–4) has quoted material from an unpublished study by Matilda Riley, which on the basis of cohort analysis questioned the 'typical' work-life pattern of women. In fact few cohorts conformed to the pattern generally ascribed to women, and the major determinant of the variety in patterns appeared to be labor force needs in the .economy. The lack of regard for such a level of analysis by those who adhere to the idea of a typical female life cycle thus leads to a reification of the life cycle and the consequent ignoring of factors that may originate in the work situation of women.

(2) The offices of the leading English newspapers are located mainly on London's Fleet Street; hence comes the colloquial reference to 'Fleet Street' – the English newspaper 'establishment.'

(3) In fact, in British newspaper journalism there is a traditional antagonism toward university graduates by journalists who have 'done it the hard way' (i.e. worked their

way up from being junior reporters on local papers). The Acton Press Group (1975), in its report to the Royal Commission on the Press, has stated that 'the traditional prejudice of the industry has been against higher education for journalists. It has been said that journalists learn more about their society through their work than through formal education' (p. 72). The same document also points out that the proportion of graduates entering journalism in 1975 was around 10 per cent – a situation that contrasts vividly with that on American papers.

(4) Research on career women has tended to assume that all potential high achievers are university graduates. This ignores the many able and highly motivated women who may not have been able to go to university or indeed may have chosen not to. It is possible that the 'finishing school' role that universities have fulfilled for the daughters of the middle class in the production of cultivated wives may have dissuaded those least disposed to accept their traditional sex roles and prompted them to enter a career occupation straight from secondary ('high') school.

(5) These figures were calculated from the *Annual Reports* of the NUJ.

(6) Sex split statistics are unfortunately not available for Fleet Street for 1972. The proportion of women working on the national papers changed from 9·7 per cent in 1973 to 10·38 per cent in 1974 and 10·27 per cent at the end of 1975.

(7) Unfortunately for my purposes, journalism in general and Fleet Street in particular have been hostile to scholarly scrutiny during the 1970s. This hostility has been generated by a number of factors. First, there was the setting up of a Royal Commission on the Press in 1974, to which the industry was extremely antagonistic. Second, there was an independent inquiry into charges of political bias in press reporting during the campaign for the general election of October 1974, chaired by a professor of government from my own university. Finally, since 1970 there has been rising pressure from the feminist group Women in Media, composed largely of women journalists, to improve both the position of women working in media fields and the way in which women as a whole are treated by the media. Thus, varying degrees of suspicion and hostility greeted my requests for statistical information and, occasionally, interviews.

(8) I have discussed the significance of this concept and its application in journalism more fully in Smith (1976).

(9) Printers on Fleet Street form a very strong occupational community. They are part of the 'aristocracy of labor.' Strong union activity keeps wages high and firmly controls craft recruitment. Women, seen as potentially less likely to express union solidarity and more likely to accept lower remuneration levels, have been totally excluded.

(10) Formally, it is not now possible for graduates to go to Fleet Street without two years' training and experience in the provinces; however, there are still exceptions.

(11) The concept of 'spiraling,' meaning that people move *spatially* in order to rise *socially*, has been widely applied in other areas of sociology. The term was originally used by Watson (1964) in a study of managers.

(12) For Finland from Haavio-Mannila (see Chapter 4 above); for Yugoslavia from Bogdan Denitch (personal communication); and for Austria from Helga Nowotny (personal communication). International research on a more systematic basis is obviously needed, and I am collecting further statistics.

(13) Figures computed by Rose Coser from research carried out by Tessa Blackstone and Oliver Fulton (see Coser, Chapter 2 above).

REFERENCES

Acton Press Group (1975) *A Submission to the Royal Commission on the Press* (London: Acton Press Group, 9 Poland St, London WC1, mimeo.).

Brager, George and Michael, John A. (1969) 'The sex distribution in social work: causes and consequences,' *Social Casework*, vol. 50, no. 10, pp. 595–601.

Breed, Warren (1955) 'Social control in the newsroom: a functional analysis,' *Social Forces*, vol. 33, no. 4, pp. 326–35.

Cannon, Jack (1966) 'More London than the nightingale,' in V. Brodsky (ed.), *Fleet Street: The Inside Story of Journalism* (London: Macdonald), pp. 167–70.

Currell, Melville (1974) *Political Woman* (London: Croom Helm).

Epstein, Cynthia Fuchs (1971) *Woman's Place: Options and Limits in Professional Careers* (Berkeley: University of California Press).

Fogarty, Michael, Allen, A. J., Allen, I., and Walters, P. (1971) *Women in Top Jobs: Four Studies in Achievement* (London: Allen & Unwin, in co-operation with Political and Economic Planning).

Griffin, S. (1973) *Women in Top Financial Jobs* (Oxford: H. E. Griffin).

Harris, Ann. S. (1970) 'The second sex in academe,' *American Association of University Professors Bulletin*, vol. 56, no. 3 (Fall), pp. 283–95.

Holter, Harriet (1970) *Sex Roles and Social Structure* (Oslo: Universitetsforlaget).

Horner, Matina, S. (1969) 'Fail, bright woman,' *Psychology Today*, vol. 3, no. 6 (November), pp. 36–41.

Kelsall, R. K. (1974) 'Recruitment to the higher civil service,' in P. Stanworth and A. Giddens (eds), *Elites and Power in British Society* (Cambridge: Cambridge University Press), pp. 170–84.

Kreps, Juanita (1971) *Sex in the Market Place: American Women at Work* (Baltimore: Johns Hopkins Press).

Leslie, Ann (1966) 'Woman in Fleet Street,' in V. Brodzky (ed.), *Fleet Street: The Inside Story of Journalism* (London: Macdonald), pp. 81–6.

Mattfeld, J. A. and Van Aken, C. G. (1965) *Women and the Scientific Professions* (London: MIT Press).

Oleson, V. and Whittaker, E. W. (1968) *The Silent Dialogue* (San Francisco: Jossey-Bass).

Phelps, C. E. (1968) 'Women in American medicine,' *Journal of Medical Education*, vol. 43, no. 1.

Rossi, Alice (1970) 'Status of women in graduate departments of sociology,' *American Sociologist*, vol. 5, no. 1, pp. 1–12.

Smith, Roger (1976) 'Sex and occupational role in Fleet Street,' in Diana L. Barker and Sheila Allen (eds), *Dependence and Exploitation in Work and Marriage* (London: Longman), pp. 70–87.

Stott, Mary (1973) *Forgetting's No Excuse* (London: Faber & Faber).

Tunstall, Jeremy (1971) *Journalists at Work* (London: Constable).

Watson, W. (1964) 'Social mobility and social class in industrial communities,' in M. Gluckman (ed.), *Closed Systems and Open Minds: The Limits of Naivety in Social Anthropology* (Edinburgh: Oliver & Boyd).

White, J. J. (1967) 'Women in the law,' *Michigan Law Review*, vol. 65, no. 6.

Whitehorn, Katherine (1976) 'Deadlier than the male', BBC Radio 4 (November 10).

Wintour, Charles (1972) *Pressures on the Press: An Editor Looks at Fleet Street* (London: Andre Deutsch).

Biographical Notes on the Contributors

Erika Bock-Rosenthal is now with the Fachhochschule Munster, Fachbereich Sozialwesen. Her publications include *Leitende Angestellte: Selbstverständnis und kollektive Forderungen* (with Heinz Hartmann and Elvira Helmer) and *Mitbestimmung am Arbeitsplatz*.

Rose Laub Coser is Professor of Community Medicine and Professor of Sociology at the State University of New York at Stony Brook. She formerly taught at Wellesley College, Harvard Medical School, and Northeastern University. She has written on theories of social structure and on role theory and is the author of several books, among them *Life in the Ward*, and *Training in Ambiguity: Learning through Doing in a Mental Hospital*; she has also edited, with an introduction, *The Family: Its Structures and Functions*. She was a fellow of the Center for Advanced Study in Behavioral Sciences in Stanford, California, during 1979–80

Bogdan Denitch is Executive Officer of the Ph.D. Program in Sociology at the Graduate Center, CUNY, and is a Senior Fellow at the Research Institute on International Change at Columbia University. He is also a member of the faculty of Queens College, CUNY, and previously taught at Yale University. His research has focused on European politics and sociology, with particular reference to Yugoslavia. Recent publications include coauthorship of *Opinion-making Elites in Yugoslavia* and *Democratic Socialism*.

Cynthia Fuchs Epstein is Professor of Sociology at Queens College and the Graduate Center, CUNY, and Co-Director of the Program in Sex Roles and Social Change, Center for the Social Sciences, Columbia University, New York City. She was a fellow of the Center for Advanced Study in the Behavioral Sciences in Stanford, California, during 1977–8. She is the author of *Women's Place: Options and Limits in Professional Careers*, and is editor (with William J. Goode) of *The Other Half*, and has written a number of articles on black and white women in the professions and other occupations. She has been a presidential advisor on the economic roles of women and on issues of affirmative action. Her current research focuses on women lawyers and the changing context of the legal profession.

Carol Ann Finkelstein is a doctoral candidate in sociology at Columbia University, where she received her MA and M.Phil. Her dissertation is a comparative analysis of male and female stockbrokers, supported by a grant from the US Department of Labor. Her academic areas of specialization are the family, age and sex roles, professions and occupations, and education. She is a member of the faculty at Queens College, CUNY, and has also taught at the State University of New York at Purchase.

Christa Haase studied sociology, law, and social politics at Göttingen University. Since 1977 she has worked in the field of vocational counseling of high school students at an employment office in Nordhorn.

Elina Haavio-Mannila is Acting Professor of Sociology at the University of Helsinki and is a member of the Finnish Academy of Sciences. She was formerly a research fellow of the Social Science Research Council and Vice-President of the Westermarck Society. Her present research concerns Finnish women in cross-cultural perspective and current changes in sex roles. She has published *Suomalainen Nainen Ja Mies* (Finnish Woman and Man) and a number of sociological and political journal articles.

Helga Hernes is First Lecturer in Comparative Politics at the University of Bergen, Norway. She received her BA from Mount Holyoke College and her Ph.D. from Johns Hopkins University. As a member of the Norwegian Social Science Research Council, she is in charge of organizing a program of women's studies in Norway under the aegis of the council.

Helga Nowotny studied law at the University of Vienna and subsequently joined the Institute of Criminology. She later studied sociology at Columbia University; and since receiving her doctorate there, she has been head of the Sociology Department of the Institute of Advanced Studies in Vienna, has taught in Cambridge, and in 1974 became Director of the United Nations-sponsored European Centre for Social Welfare Training and Research. As chairperson of a working group, she took part in the Austrian government's inquiry into the situation of women in Austria.

Helge Pross is Professor of Sociology at the University of Siegen, West Germany. She previously taught at the University of Frankfurt (1954–65) and at the University of Giessen (1965–76). Her public and professional offices include positions on the Executive Committee, German Sociological Association, the Commission of the Federal Parliament on Women in Society, and the Executive Board of the Goethe Institute. Her publications include: *Educational Opportunities of Females in Germany; The Reality of Housewives;* and *Men: A Representative Survey of Self-images of Men and Perceptions of Women in Germany.*

Donna S. Sanzone is an editor in the reference division of G. K. Hall & Co., Publishers. Her background is in political science, international relations, and comparative politics. She spent a three-year period in Europe, during which she conducted research on the status of women in western Europe. More recently, she served on the editorial and research staff of the *International Encyclopedia of Higher Education* (Jossey-Bass, 1978).

Catherine Bodard Silver is an Associate Professor at Brooklyn College, CUNY. She is the author of *Black Teachers in Urban Schools: The Case of Washington, DC* as well as publications on women's roles in the United States and France. Her current research deals with equal rights legislation in these two countries; she is also studying the US Senate hearings on the abortion issue and the role of abortion in fertility and career patterns.

Torild Skard is a research worker at the Institute of Labor Research, Oslo, Norway, and is leader of the Norwegian National Commission for the UN Educational, Scientific and Cultural Organization. She has worked in municipal youth clubs and a children's psychiatric center and has lectured at the University of Tromsø. She has been active in politics for over twenty years and was a Member of Parliament from 1973 to 1977, representing the Left Socialist Party. She was the Norwegian delegate at the United Nations in 1974 and at the Women's Year Conference in Mexico City in 1975. Her several books include *Halve jorden* (Half of the World).

Roger Smith is a member of the Sociology Department at Essex University,

England. With a background in economics and sociology, he has taught widely in further, adult, prison, and higher education. He has also been involved in consultative work for the National Union of Journalists Committee on Equality and for the National Committee of Working Women's Organizations.

Magdalena Sokołowska is Professor of Sociology and Chairperson of the Medical Sociology Department of the Institute of Philosophy and Sociology of the Polish Academy of Sciences in Warsaw. She is also Professor of Medical Sociology at the Sociological Faculty, University of Warsaw, and is current Vice-President of the International Sociological Association. She is author or editor of twelve books and numerous articles on the sociological aspects of health, medicine, and health care as well as on the position of women in society and family policy.

Sylvia Streeck is at present at the International Institute of Management, Berlin. Her publications include *Parteiensystem und Status quo: Drei Studien zum innerparteilichen Konflikt* (with Wolfgang Streeck) and *Wenn Frauen Karriere machen* (with Erika Bock-Rosenthal and Christa Haase).

Betsy Thom is at present with the Social Research Unit, Bedford College, London. She formerly taught sociology in further education.

Richard Whitley is senior Lecturer in Sociology at the Manchester Business School. He has degrees from the Universities of Leeds and of Pennsylvania. He has published numerous articles on the sociology of science and the study of business elites. He is currently the director of a research project on the backgrounds and careers of business school graduates. He is also Managing Editor of the *Sociology of Science Yearbook*.

Index

Abortion 38, 40-1, 42, 44, 47-8, 84, 98; political affiliations and 162
Abortion Act (1967) (UK) 42
Abzug, Bella 136, 141
academia: and access to elites 21; male dominance of 5, 18, 20, 64; participation of women in 17-27; posts for women in 17, 18, 19, 20, 22-7, 64, 113n, 122, 160, 213 (salaries of 20, 21, 22)
access routes to elites 8-12, 13, 14, 69-71, 73, 119, 130-3, 136-7, 137-8, 140, 153-4, 169-70, 185-8, 189-91, 194, 195, 205-7, 215; see also higher education
accountancy, women in 160; and access to managerial elites 187
Albrektsen, Beatrice Halsaa 85
Allardt, Erik 55
American Council on Education, national survey (1975) of 199
architecture, women in 65, 66, 160
artists: female 65-6; male 65-6
Astor, Lady Nancy, (1879-64) 41
attitudinal changes to women's position in society: effected by women in political elites 40-50, 80, 87, 117; (and elites in general 166); legislation and 38-48 passim; in Norway 87; hostility to 79; (effects of 80, 87); ways of effecting 6, 87, 115, 120, 151, 155, 208; in W. Germany 216-17; in Yugoslavia 122; see also crisis situations
Austria: education in 149-50; equality within marriage in 150; labour force, percentage of women in 149; political elites, participation of women in 147, 150-1, 153-5; (access routes to 153-4; male attitudes to 152-3, 154-5; marital status of 154); position of sexes in society in 147; professional elites, percentage of women in 150; sex discrimination in 149, 151; working mothers in, attitudes to 156n

Baklid, Ingvild and Astrid Rangnes Bråten, quoted 86
Bandaranaike, Sirimavo (1916-   ) 137
Bank for International Settlements (BIS) 171
banking, participation of women in management elites of 221-2, 224
Barre, Raymond 40
barter economy, shift from, effect of 4
Bar-Yosef, Rivka 31
Basic Law (1949) (W. Germany) 38, 47-8
Bebel, August 32
Bellamy, Carol 136

Bird, Caroline 193, 195
birth control 38, 40, 42, 48, 84, 98, 117
BIS, see Bank for International Settlements
Blackstone, Tessa and Oliver Fulton 21-2
Bonfield, Margaret 41
Borton, Per 79
Boserup, Ester 4
Bourdieu, Pierre 147, 185, 186
Braten, Astrid Rangnes and Ingvild Baklid, quoted 86
British Broadcasting Corporation, access of women to 195
broadcasting and television, women in 64, 246
bureaucratic elites: access routes to 195, 229-30; executives/managers in, position of 220; and private enterprise 219-31 (convergence with 219-20, 225); proportion of lawyers in 10; recruitment policies of 73, 219; women in 59, 103, 105, 160, 188-9, 226-7, 228, 229, 230-2
business elites, see economic elites
business schools 9, 185, 186-8, 189-91, 197, 200; in UK 187-8; effect of, on women's potential in management 189-91; female enrolment at 200, 225; in France 187; and reproduction of business elites 186-8, 189-91
Business Week (USA) 195, 197, 200

Cambridge University 9, 187
Cannon, Jack, quoted 238
career success, of women: barriers to 3-4, 6, 8, 12, 13, 29-30, 67-9, 73, 84, 85, 112, 125, 149, 160, 169, 172; factors contributing to (in Finland, of both sexes) 69-70; political attitudes of attainers of 157-8, 161-7; social pressures resulting from 157-8; study of (in Germany), method used 159-60; ways of achieving 160-1; see also access routes; gatekeepers; informal structures; political elites, participation of women in
Castle, Barbara 42-3
Catholic Church: in Poland, and women's role in society 108; in Yugoslavia 117
children, day care facilities for 12, 13, 84, 107, 110
Chirac, Jacques 39
church leadership, exclusion of women from 65
civil service, see bureaucratic elites
class system: and access to elites 169, 246; movement away from 54; sex-role attitudes

class system: *cont.*
  within 67; women as an integrating force in 16-17
colonialism, effect of, on women 4
Columbia University Graduate School of Business, percentage of women at 200, 225
COMECON, *see* Council for Mutual Economic Assistance
Commission of the European Communities, poll conducted by (1975) 49
Common Market *see* European Economic Community (EEC)
computer science, women in and access to managerial elites 200-1
Cooney, Joan Ganz 194
'corporate bigamy' 196
corporate pluralism: (term), defined 80; representation of women in 81-3
Coser, Rose Laub 13; and Judith M. Tanur 21
Costantini, Edmond and Kenneth H. Craik 129, 136
Council of Europe 171
Council for Mutual Economic Assistance (COMECON) 171
Craik, Kenneth H. and Edmond Costantini 129, 136
crisis situations: and election of women to political office 117-18, 136; role change facilitated by 11, 117-18
cultural capital 185, 186, 187, 189

Daily Express (UK) 240
Declaration on the Elimination of Discrimination against Women, A (UN 1973) 172
Denmark: political behaviour of sexes in 61; salaries and wages in 55
Devereaux, George 17
Diensch, Marie-Madeleine 39
Directory of British Journalism 242
division of labour, sexual 10, 31, 85, 88; in Israel 30-1; in Norway 84, 85, 88; in Poland 97-8, 111; *see also* sex roles
divorce 47
Dorhlac, Dr Hélène 39

East Germany, *see* German Democratic Republic
École National d'Administration (ENA) (France) 230
École Normal (France) 187
École Polytechnique (France) 187, 230
economic and business elites 76; access routes to 8-11 *passim*, 69, 73, 185-8, 189-91, 194, 195, 199-201, 215; competition for jobs in 197-8; executives/managers in, position of 220; marital status of sexes in 72, 194, 196; 'professionalization' of 224-5; and bureaucracies, convergence

economic and business elites *cont.*
  with 219-20, 225; recruitment policies of 219; participation of women in 7, 55-9, 69, 119, 188-91, 193-208, 211, 212-16, 221-6; sexual equality in, absence of 214-15; structure of 211-12 (changes in, effects of 11, 225)
economic capital 148-9, 169, 185, 186, 188
economic resources, access of women to 8
education: and access to elites 185-6; and employment 54; and marriage, correlation between 73; segregated 13, 131; *see also* academia; higher education (university); teaching profession
EEC, *see* European Economic Community
Eiseman, Florence 201
elite (term), defined 53, 69
emotional capital 149, 153; (term) defined 148
ENA, *see* École National d'Administration
enfranchisement of women 38, 77, 88n
Engels, Friedrich (1820-95), and female emancipation 106
engineering profession: as access route to elites 200, 215; participation of women in 19, 37
entrepreneurs, female 195, 201, 212
Epstein, Cynthia Fuchs, *quoted* 198, 206, 207
Equal Employment Opportunity Commission (USA) 204
Equal Opportunities Commission (UK) 44-5
Equal Opportunities for Women (Ann-Marie Renger) 47
Equal Pay Act (1970) (UK) 42, 44, 45
equal pay for equal work: legislation to enact 42, 44, 45, 231; in Yugoslavia 120; absence of: in Finland 55; in Norway 84; in Poland 93, 94; in UK 45; in USA 20, 21-2; in USSR 27-9; in W. Germany 47, 214-15
equal rights, *see* women's rights
Equality of Status Act (1957) (W. Germany) 38
European Economic Community (EEC) 171, 212
Evans, Harold 238

Factory system, development of, and family life 4
family life: and career success 12-13, 70, 71, 73, 84, 85, 112, 125; in Germany, position of women in 211; legislation and 46-7; Marxist-Leninist ideology and 106; in Poland 107-8, 110-11, 112
FAO, *see* Food and Agricultural Organization
female behaviour: and leadership styles 170; used to manipulate men 194

female failure, and promotion 204
feminist movements and groups: effects of 7, 87-8, 140, 197, 201, 203, 224, 232; in Austria, attitudes to 154; in Norway 79, 83, 84; in UK 5, 246, 247n; in USA 201; in W. Germany, absence of 217; in Yugoslavia 121
Fenner, Peggy 42
Finland: education and marriage in, correlation between 73; elites (general), participation of women in 54-66, 69-74 (barriers against 67-9; success of 69-71); ideological and cultural elites, participation of women in 63-6; marital status of sexes in 71-2; political activity of sexes in 61; political elites, participation of women in 6, 7, 56, 57, 58, 59-63, 74, 75n; salaries and wages in 55, 75n; sex-role attitudes in 67-8, 74n; sex segregation at work in 68-9, 75n; university degrees, percentage of women with 73
First Act for Reform of Marriage and Family Law (W. Germany) 46-7
First National City Bank in New York, related employees in 199
Flora, Cornelia Butler and Naomi B. Lynn 126
Focke, Katharina 46
Fogarty, Michael and Rhona and Robert Rapoport 195
Food and Agricultural Organization (FAO), proportion of women on professional staff of 176
Fortune's Directory (US) 193
Fortune Magazine (US) 193, 195
France: abortion and birth control in 38, 40-1; bureaucracy and private enterprise in 220-1, 227-31 (participation of women in 220-1, 227-31); capitalist sector, state monitoring of 220; education system of, and entrance to elites 185, 186-7, 189-90, 220, 229-30; elite teaching careers, qualification for 230; elites (general), attitudes to participation of women in 170; higher education, participation of women in 38; legislation affecting women in 38, 40-1, 229, 232; political elites, participation of women in 37, 38, 39-41; voting behaviour in 133; women's rights, attainment of 38, 39-41
Fulton, Oliver and Tessa Blackstone 21-2
Funke, Lisolette 46, 47-8

Gandhi, Indira (1917-) 137
gatekeepers, and career success 6, 12, 21, 151, 208; (in journalism (UK) 239, 241)
General Agreement on Tariffs and Trade (GATT), proportion of women on professional staff of 177

Gerhardsen, Einar 79
German Democratic Republic (East Germany): economic elites, absence of women in leadership of 214; political elites, participation of women in leadership of 214
German Federal Republic (West Germany): abortion in 47-8, 162; academia, posts for women in 213; bureaucratic elites, participation of women in 212-13; democratic movements in, aims of 215; economic and managerial elites, participation of women in 211, 212-16; (access routes to 215; equality of sexes in 211, 214-15; structure of 211-12); education system of, and women 211; family life, women's position in 211; feminist movements in, absence of 217; higher education, participation of women in 38, 45, 211; labour force, women in 211; legislation affecting women's rights in 46-7, 48; political bias and voting behaviour in 157-9, 161-4, 166, 167n; political elites, participation of women in 7, 37, 45-8, 49, 213, 214; political parties of 167n; professional elites, participation of women in 213, 214; (study of 159-60); sex discrimination in and cultural attitudes 38, 45, 46, 48; trade unions, participation of women in 213; women's rights, attainment of 38, 46
German Federation of Trade Unions 213
Giddens, Anthony 53
Giroud, Françoise 39-40, 41
Giscard d'Estaing, Valéry (1926-) 39
Goddard, Mary 201
Goode, William J. 196
Goot, Murray and Elizabeth Reid 128
grandes écoles (France): and entrance to elites 186-7, 230; prestige of 9
Grasso, Ella 132, 141
Great Britain, *see* United Kingdom
Greenstein, Fred 125
Guardian (UK) 240, 242
Gymnasium (W. Germany) 211

Hamm-Brucher, Hildegarde 48
Harris, Patricia 194
Hart, Judith 42
Harvard Graduate School of Business, percentage of women at 200
Hennig, Margaret 194, 201
higher education (university): and access to elites 9, 13, 14, 69, 74, 169, 180n, 189, 197, 199, 215; female graduate students in 23, 24, 74 (degrees obtained by, figures for 18, 19, 64, 69, 74, 103); female undergraduate students in 9, 17, 37-8, 45, 64, 74, 91, 118-19, 150 (degrees obtained by, figures for 18, 66, 69, 73); *see also*

higher education *cont.*
    business schools; grandes écoles
Hignett, Margaret J. 240
Hodge, Robert W. and Patricia Hodge 31
Horner, Matina 237
Horsbrugh, Dame Florence 41
Huber, Antje 46
Hyman, Herbert 125

IAEA, *see* International Atomic Energy Agency
IBRD, *see* International Bank for Reconstruction and Development (World Bank)
ICAO, *see* International Civil Aviation Organization
ideas, cross fertilization of 4
identity crises, of women in elites 179
ideological and cultural elites 63; access routes to 73; participation of women in 63-6, 245-6
ideology 7; capitalist (conservative) 158; egalitarian 6, 8; of leftist political parties 7; Marxist-Leninist 90-1, 106; revolutionary, and women 6
ILO, *see* International Labour Organization
IMCO, *see* Intergovernmental Maritime Consultative Organization
IMF, *see* International Monetary Fund
infanticide, female 116
informal structures 11-12, 133, 205-7; isolation of women from 11-12, 206-7, 241, 245
ingroups: access to 8; participation of women in 5
Institut Européen d' Administration des Affaires (INSEAD) 9, 187, 189-90
Intergovernmental Maritime Consultative Organization, proportion of women on professional staff of 177
International Atomic Energy Agency (IAEA), proportion of women on professional staff of 177
International Bank for Reconstruction and Development (World Bank) (IBRD), proportion of women on professional staff of 176
International Civil Aviation Organization (ICAO), proportion of women on professional staff of 177
International Labour Organization (ILO), proportion of women on professional staff of 176
International Monetary Fund (IMF), proportion of women on professional staff of 176
international organizations: as 'dumping grounds' 171-2; elites in, composition of 171, 172; functions of 171; internal structures and policies of 171, 172; social fields covered by 171; women in 169-79;

international organizations *cont.*
    (aspirations of 170; attitudes to 172; discrimination against 173-5; identity crises of 179; position in hierarchies of 170, 171; problems encountered by 169, 172
International Telecommunications (ITU), proportion of women on the professional staff of 177
intervention: governmental, to change women's position in society 7, 13, 208, 226, 232; power of, and access of women to elite positions 6
Israel, role of women on Kibbutzim in 30-1
Italy, voting behaviour in 133
ITU, *see* International Telecommunications
Ivy League colleges (USA), status of 9

Jaros, Dean 125
Jennings, M. Kent 129, 130
Johnson, Marilyn 131
journalistic elites: access routes to 10-11, 170, 244-6; (isolation of women from 12, 241, 245); and advertising 242-3; composition of 238; and Fleet Street, status of 238; gatekeepers in 239, 241; graduates in, prejudice against 244, 246-7n; participation of women in: in Finland 64; in UK 7, 238-46; in Yugoslavia 122; (discrimination against 240-1; position of hierarchy of 239-40); printers in, status of 247

Kantner, Rosabeth Moss 203, 204
Kartovaara Leena 65-6
Kassebaum, Nancy Landon 132
Katherine Gibbs School (US) 197
Keller, Suzanne 17, 18
kibbutzim, division of labour, sex role associated in 30-1
Kirkpatrick, Jeane 132, 133

Labour force (in general), participation of women in 16; *see also under* individual countries
Landon, Alf 132
Lauder, Estee 201
Lawrence, Mary Wells 201
L'École Nationale d'Administration (France) 187
legal profession: law degrees, and access to elites 215; members of in elites 10, 130, 132-3, 138, 200; participation of women in 10, 37, 136, 160, 213; (effect of 140)
legislation, and women's rights 6, 31, 38, 40-5 *passim*, 46-8 *passim*, 90-1, 226, 227, 229, 232
Lenin, Vladimir Ilyich Ulyanov (1870-1924) 90; and position of women in society 106
Leslie, Ann, *quoted* 241, 243

Lesur, Dr Annie 39
life cycle patterns, of women: change during 5; in politics (Austria) 153; sexual inequality during, increase in 17; work/reproduction periods in 94-7, 215-16, 237, 246n
Life Peerage Act (1958) (UK) 41
Lipman-Blumen, Jean 11
Lipset, Seymour Martin, *quoted* 125, 126, 129, 133-4
London 238
London Business School 187, 189-90
Lynn, Naomi B. and Cornelia Butler Flora 126

McColl, Ian 240
McCormack, Thelma 128-9
McWhinney, Madeline H. 198
male behaviour styles and values, adopted by successful women 87, 166-7, 179, 194-5
managerial elites: access routes to 185-91, 194, 195, 199, 200, 215, 220, 229-30; competition for jobs in 197-8; husband and wife teams in 198-9; of multinational companies, problems of 185; participation of women in 7, 11, 99, 112, 122, 160, 188-91, 193-208, 211, 212-16, 220-32; (aspirations of 197; barriers against 208; conferences on (USA) 199-200; and interaction with subordinates 202-3; and job-hopping 205; marital status of 194, 196; problems encountered by 193, 196, 201-7; unity among 202); 'professionalization' of 224-5; structure of (in W. Germany) 211-12
Manchester Business School 187, 189-90
Mannheim, Karl 16
marriage and education, correlation between 73
married men, career success of 70, 71
married women: career success of 12, 71, 160 (factors against 73, 84, 85, 172) discrimination against 30, 196; in journalistic elites (UK) 245; in labour force (Poland) 94-5, 97; in UN secretariat, percentage of 179; *see also* family life; role conflict
Marxist-Leninist ideology, and position of women in society 106
maternity leave 40, 95
Means, Ingunn Norderval 87; *quoted* 85, 86
media elites, participation of women in 213, 246; *see also* broadcasting; journalistic elites
medical profession: participation of women in 5, 8, 18-19, 37, 101-6, 150, 160; status sequences of students in 8
Meir, Golda (1908-) 137
Merton, Robert K. (*Social Theory and Social Structure*) 8

Meyer, Pearl, *quoted* 198
Missoffe, Hélène 41
money economy, shift to, effect of 4
multinational companies, management problems of 185

National Health Services Act (1967) (UK) 42
National Union of Journalists (NUJ) (UK), participation of women in 238, 239
National Women's Political Caucus (NWPC) (USA) 140
NATO 171
nepotism 198-9
New York Times, The 194, 201
Nordic Council 171
North Atlantic Treaty Organization, *see* NATO
Northern Echo (UK) 238
Norton, Eleanor Holmes 141
Norway: corporate pluralism in 80-1; (female participation in 81-3); education in 84; female emancipation in, historical development of 84; labour force, women in 84; (discrimination against 84); patriarchal values in 76; population of 83; political behaviour of sexes in 61, 77; political elites, participation of women in 6, 7, 76-88; (effects of 80, 87-8; factors influencing 85-7; increase in 78-9, 80, 81, 82-3, 87; male domination of and reaction to 77, 79-80, 81, 86, 87); salaries and wages in 55
nursing profession 17
NWPC, *see* National Women's Political Caucus

OECD, *see* United Nations Organization for Economic Co-operation and Development
Office of Federal Contract Compliance (USA) 204
'old boy network' 206-7
Oppenheim, Sally 44
opportunity structures, *see* access routes
Orum, Anthony M. *et al.* 125
Oxford University 9, 180n, 187

Pace, Norma T. 194
participatory democracy, attitudes of women to 164-6
Pasquier, Nicole 41
patriarchal values 17, 119; effect of women in public life on 13-14, 71, 117-18, 179; in Germany 45; and Marxist-Leninist ideology 106; methods of changing 6, 14, 17, 31-2, 87-8, 115, 151, 155; in Norway 76, 86; and occupational roles 12, 30, 67, 99, 151-3, 179, 202-3, 240-1; perpetuated by colonialism 4; in Poland 108
Pelletier, Monique 40, 41

Perón, Eva 137
Perón, Isabel 137
Peterson, Martha 194
'pioneers', women as: difficulties of 203-5; political bias of (W. Germany) 163-4
Poinso-Chapuis, Germaine 39
Poland: academia, participation of women in 19, 103, 113n; bureaucratic elites, participation of women in 103, 105; birthrate in, decline of 98; (policies to increase 110); Catholic Church in, and women's role in society 108; division of labour (sexual) in 97-8, 99, 111-12; education in 91-2, 107, 112; (and occupations 92, 93, 95, 97); equal pay for equal work in 93, 94, 99; equality of opportunity in, attitudes to 99; family life in 107-8, 110-11, 112; history of 90; industrialization of 106-7; industry, percentage of women in 103; labour force of, percentage of women in 92-3, 94, 98; (work/reproduction patterns in life cycle of 94-5, 97); management elites, representation of women in 7, 99, 112, 214; Marxist-Leninist ideology, application of 90-1, 106-7; personality ideals (traditional) in 109, 111; political elites, participation of women in 8, 100, 101, 102; professional elites, participation of women in 18-19, 101-6, 112; salaries and wages in 94, 95, 96; sex-roles in, attitudes to 99, 108, 111-12; university degrees, percentage of women with 73, 101; women in society, position of, policy trends regarding 109-10; women's rights, attainment of 90-1, 99
Polish Society (Jan Szczepánski) 109
political bias and voting behaviour 6-7, 61, 77, 128-9, 133-6, 157-9, 161-4, 166, 167n
political elites: access routes to 7, 8, 10, 13, 73, 130-3, 136-7, 137-8, 140, 170; male dominance of 4, 77, 81, 86, 87, 124, 139; participation of women in 6, 7, 37, 39-52, 56, 57, 58, 59-63, 74, 76-88, 100, 117-18, 120-1, 124-41, 142-3n, 147, 150-1, 153, 166; (attitudes to 49-50, 79-80, 139, 152-3, 154-5, 245; personality myths about 129, 137; political bias of 134-6; resources required by 85, 139; role conflicts of 126, 130; and sexual liaisons 138; theories about 125; unity among 140-1); sex roles in 5; sexual equality in 214
Pompidou, Georges (1911-74) 39
Porter, John 65; *quoted* 53, 63, 69
Pross, Dr Helge 48
protest and reform movements, as access routes to political elites 136-7, 153
Public Schools (UK), prestige of 180n

Putnam, Robert 9, 10

'queen bee syndrome' 31, 202

Rapoport, Rhona and Robert and Michael Fogarty 195
Ray, Dixie Lee 132, 141
reform and protest movements, as access routes to political elites 136-7, 153
Reid, Elizabeth and Murray Goot 128
Renger, Anne-Marie 46, 47
role changes, effected by crisis situations 11, 118
role conflict, of women 12, 29-30, 160-1; (in international organizations 172; in managerial elites 193, 196; in politics 125-6, 154)
role models, lack of, for women in managerial elites 201-2
Rossi, Alice 17, *quoted* 20

Sacks, Michael Paul 19, 21, 27
salaries and wages: in Norway 55; in Poland 93, 95; in Scandinavia 55; in UK 44-5; in USA 20-1, 22; in USSR 27-9
Saunier-Seité, Alice 41
Scandinavia: political behaviour of sexes in 61; political elites, participation of women in 7, 88n; salaries and wages in 55; *see also* individual Nordic countries
Schlei, Marie 46, 48
school district politics, participation of women in 127
schools, *see* education
Schroeder, Patricia 136-7
Schumpeter, Joseph, *quoted* 115
Schwarzhaupt, Elisabeth 46
Scientific Manpower Commission (USA) 20
secretarial schools (USA), and management courses for women 197
self-employment/self-employed: attitudes of, to participatory democracy 165; and career success for women 160; political bias of 163
Seppänen, Paavo 74
Sex Discrimination Act (1975) (UK) 44, 45
Sex Discrimination (Removal) Act (1919) (UK) 38, 240
sex-role-appropriate activities (public sector), assignation of women to 5, 12, 39, 81-2, 107, 137, 152-3, 154, 156n, 171, 230-1, 237, 242
sex-role associated duties (home-centred), of women 12, 16, 29-31, 99, 108, 111, 147; (attitudes to 13, 99; limiting effect of 12-13, 30)
sex-roles (male and female): attitudes to 30-1, 67-8, 70, 99; changes in 99; Commission of the European Communities poll on 49; culture-associated 16,

sex-roles (male and female) *cont.*
  99, 111
sex segregation, in work places 67, 68-9
sex-typed occupations, of women 16, 17
sexual byplay, in work situations 194, 203
sexual liaisons, and women in political life
  138
sexual 'politics', in managerial elites 207
Shanley, Mary L. and Victoria Schuck 128
social capital 4, 149, 153, 155, 169, 185,
  188, 190; (term), defined 147-8
social change: effect of 4-5, 121; facilitated
  by World War II (in Yugoslavia) 116-17
social identity (male), realization of 17
social institutions, loss of power by, and
  women's position in society 13
Social Theory and Social Structure (Robert
  K. Merton) 8
socialism, position of women in society
  under 106 (and economic forces 121)
Somerville, John 204
Soviet Union, *see* Union of Soviet Socialist
  Republics
Stanford University Business School, percentage of women at 200
status judges 8
status sequence, concept of 8
stereotypes: female 6, 16, 86, 108-9, 151,
  195; male 16, 109, 111
Stiehm, Judith 139
Stott, Mary 242
Strobel, Kate 46
Sunday Times (UK) 238
Suolinna, Kirsti 65
support systems: husbands role in 154, 245;
  for male executives 206-7; for mothers 12,
  13, 87, 107, 110, 112; private sector of
  society as 147; women as 16-17, 107-8,
  198
Swafford, Michael 27
Sweden: political behaviour of sexes in 60;
  political elites, participation of women in
  60-1; salaries and wages in 55; university
  degrees, percentage of women with 73
Szczepański, Jan (*Polish Society*), *quoted* 109

Tanur, Judith M. and Rose Laub Coser 21
Tatkon, Carol 196
teaching profession: career changes of
  members of 199-200; men in hierarchy of
  5; numbers training for, fall in 199;
  women in hierarchy of 5, 19, 64, 150,
  230; *see also* academia
technology, effect of 11
Thatcher, Margaret 41, 43-4
'tokens' (female), consequences of being
  203-5
tracking systems 8-9; *see also* access routes
trade unions, participation of women in 7,
  59, 151, 213, 238, 239

Tunstall, Jeremy, *quoted* 238, 242, 243
Tweedsmuir, Priscilla Jean Fortescue,
  Baroness of Belhelvie 41-2

UK Press Gazette 240-1
UN, *see* United Nations
UNDP, *see* United Nations Development
  Programme
unemployment, and jobs for women 121
UNESCO, proportion of women on professional staff of 176
UNICEF, proportion of women on professional staff of 176, 178
Union of Soviet Socialist Republics (USSR):
  academia, posts for women in 18, 19-20;
  economic elites, participation of women
  in 19, 214; higher education, women in
  19; (degrees obtained by 73); industry,
  participation of women in 19-20; labour
  force, percentage of women in 16, 19;
  political elites, participation of women in
  19, 155n; professional elites, participation
  of women in 5, 18, 19; salaries and wages
  in 27-9; sex discrimination in 30
UNITAR, *see* United Nations Institute for
  Training and Research
United Kingdom: academia, participation of
  women in 18, 22, 24, 26, 38; birth control
  and abortion in 38, 42, 44; education
  system of, and entrance elites 187-8;
  journalistic elites, participation of women
  in 238-46; managerial elites, participation
  of women in 188-91; political elites,
  participation of women in 7, 37, 41-4, 49;
  women's rights in 38, 42-3, 44-5
United Nations: function of 171; functional
  agencies of 170-1; (proportion of women
  in 176-7); participation of women in 171,
  172-9; (discrimination against 172-3,
  attempts to end 173-5; identity crises of
  179)
United Nations Children's Fund, *see*
  UNICEF
United Nations Development Programme
  (UNDP), proportion of women on professional staff of 176
United Nations Educational, Scientific and
  Cultural Organization, *see* UNESCO
United Nations Institute for Training and
  Research (UNITAR), and discrimination
  against women in UN 172-3
United Nations Organization for Economic
  Co-operation and Development (OECD)
  171
United States of America: academia, posts
  for women in 17, 18, 23, 25, 27;
  bureaucratic elites: participation of women
  in 220-7, 230-1; and private enterprise
  220-7; engineering, percentage of women
  in 19, 221; equal pay for equal work in

United States of America *cont.*
231; higher education, percentage of women in 18; labour force, percentage of women in 16, 193; legislation, and women's rights 6, 227; managerial elites, participation of women in 193-208, 220-7, 231; political bias and voting behaviour in 128-9, 133-4; political elites, participation of women in 6-7, 19, 124-41, 138-9, 142-3n; (access routes to 130-3, 136-7, 137-8, 140; discrimination against 139; male dominance of 124, 139; marital status of 126; myths about 125-9; political bias of 134-6; and sexual liaisons 138; unity among 140-1); professional elites, participation of women in 5, 8, 10, 18, 199, 221, 230, 231; salaries and wages in 20, 21, 22; schools, segregated, in 131
Universal Postal Union (UPU), proportion of women on professional staff of 177

Veil, Dr Simone 39, 40-1
Vertical Mosaic, The (John Porter) 53
Voje, Kirsten 85
voluntary organizations, as access routes to political elites in the USA 132
voting behaviour, *see* political bias and voting behaviour

Wage and Hours Division (USA) 204
wages and salaries, *see* salaries and wages
Weber, Max (1864-1920) 130
Werner, Emmy E. 132
West Germany, *see* German Federal Republic
Wharton School of the University of Pennsylvania, percentage of women at 200
Whitehorn, Katherine 244
WHO, *see* World Health Organization
Who's Who (Finland): marital status of sexes in 71-2; percentage of women in 55-7, 64, 65, 74
'widows' succession', and access to elites 10, 132, 141
Williams, Shirley 42, 43, 44
Winter, Florence 17
Wintour, Charles, *quoted* 240, 242-3
WMO *see* World Meteorological Organization
Women and Low Incomes (Equal Opportunities Commission report) (UK) 45
Women in Media (UK feminist group) 246, 247n

Women's Movement, *see* feminist movements
women's rights 5, 39, 211; discussion of, effect of 14; and economic forces 121; intervention and 6, 7, 13, 208; legislation and 31, 38, 40-5 *passim*, 46-8 *passim*, 90-1, 226, 227, 229, 232; Marxist-Leninist ideology and 90-1, 106; role of women in politics and 40-8; and unemployment 121
women's suffrage movement 5, 38
Women's Who's Who (UK) 188
work hierarchy, women's position in (in general), 5, 16-32, 37-8, 237-8; ways of changing 6; *see also under* individual elites
World Health Organization (WHO), proportion of women on professional staff of 176
World Meteorological Organization (WMO), proportion of women on professional staff of 177
World War II: female heroism in 118; role change facilitated by 11, 117-18; and social change (in Yugoslavia) 116-17

Young, Janet Mary, Baroness of Farnworth 44
Yugoslavia: academia, representation of women in 122; birth control in 117; Churches in 117, 122n; economic and historical development of 115-17; education in: attitudes to 116, and job opportunities 123n; equal pay for equal work in 120; feminism in 121; higher education in, percentage of women in 118-19; (egalitarian career patterns of 120); Islamic traditions (legal and political) in 116; journalistic elites, participation of women in 122; labour force of, women in 122, 123n; (and unemployment 121); managerial elites, participation of women in 122; political elites, participation of women in 6, 7, 8, 117-18, 120-1; (and elites in general 119, attitudes to 122); reactionary attitudes in 119-21; religious traditions in 115; rural population of 117; World War II in: opportunities for women created by 11, 118, 121; resistance movements during 116; social revolution resulting from 116-17

Zycie Warszawy (Poland) 111